The BAD

Baby-Sitters

H A N D B O O K

BY SUSAN WHITE

ILLUSTRATIONS BY B.K. TAYLOR

Published by
Dell Publishing
a division of
Bantam Doubleday Dell Publishing Group, Inc.
666 Fifth Avenue
New York, New York 10103

Cover illustration by Richard Williams

ISBN: 0-440-40633-1

Printed in the United States of America

October 1991

10   9   8   7   6   5   4   3   2   1

CONTENTS

INTRODUCTION

Sure, baby-sitting is great. The sense of accomplishment. The money. The fun of being with young children and helping to mold and shape them. The money. The independence, the responsibility—and, of course, the money.

But tell the truth . . . Don't you get just a little bit tired, a little bit bored, a little bit annoyed about some of the not-so-great parts about being a baby-sitter?

WELL, JOIN THE CLUB!
The Bad Baby-sitters Club!

THE BAD BABY-SITTERS HANDBOOK is a funny book about all the things those other books never say about baby-sitting. It's about whiney kids and weird parents. It's about the secret things all baby-sitters do—and about the awful things baby-sitters sometimes wish they could do. It's about truth. It's about justice. It's about—let's not get carried away here—it's about 64 pages and it's about to begin!

TEN DANGER SIGNALS FOR BABY-SITTERS

1. When the parents are a little *too* glad to see you.

2. When every member of the family except the baby is in a cast.

3. When the baby's nickname is Rambo.

4. When the baby's *real* name is Rambo.

5. When you find tooth marks on the dog.

6. When it's a hot summer day, but every member of the family is wearing heavy earmuffs.

7. When you tell your friend who you are sitting for and she laughs so hard her macaroni and cheese goes up her nose.

8. When the mother asks you if you have health insurance.

9. When the baby's crib has bars on the top, too.

10. When the parents said they'd be back by ten and that was two weeks ago.

This is a test. Are you a good baby-sitter or a bad baby-sitter? Borrow a pencil——or steal a crayon from the kids——and get ready to see how you rate.

THE NATIONAL BABY-SITTERS TEST

INSTRUCTIONS: Choose the best answer for each question. If you can't decide which answer is best, choose the second-best answer. If you can't decide which is second-best, choose a different answer. If you can't choose a different answer, choose a different test.

Besides—shouldn't you be watching the kid instead of taking this test??

1. Your reason for wanting to baby-sit is:
  a. I like kids.
  b. I like kids about as much as a tuna-fish milkshake.
  c. I like sitting.
  d. I like taking stupid tests.

2. A piece of equipment not needed for carrying out your baby-sitting duties is:
  a. a backhoe.
  b. rubber gloves.
  c. rubber mittens.
  d. three gallons of whipped cream.
  e. whoopee cushion.
  f. all or none of the above.

3. A baby-sitter's most important job is:
  a. I don't know.
  b. Hard to say.
  c. I'll have to think about this one.
  d. Don't you have any easier questions?

4. The kid's parents offer to pay extra if you do a little cleaning. You should:
  a. clean out the refrigerator.
  b. clean out the silverware.
  c. clean out their checking account.

5. When the parents ask what would be a fair
price for an evening's baby-sitting, you should say:
   a. "Who said anything about being *fair*?"
   b. "How much have you got?"
   c. "I take credit cards, so you can pay in easy
   installments."

6. If the kids refuse to go to bed at bedtime, you
should:
   a. try child psychology.
   b. try hypnosis.
   c. try for another job.
   d. try prayer.

7. You are baby-sitting for a seven-year-old boy.
A storm knocks out the electricity. He cries that
he's afraid of the dark. You should tell him:
   a. "BOOOO!"
   b. "I am too! Let's get out of here!!"
   c. "Don't worry. The worst thing that could happen
   is that a hideous monster will come through the
   window and gobble you up in a single bite."

8. It's getting late and you're beginning to feel sleepy.
You should:
   a. ask the kids to wake you up when their parents
   get home.
   b. go home where you'll be much more
   comfortable in your own bed.
   c. invite several dozen friends over to help
   you stay awake.
   d. Sorry. I'm too tired to answer right now.

9. The two innocent-looking girls you're sitting for have locked you in the coat closet. You should:

a. pick yourself out a new jacket.

b. look through all the pockets for money.

c. ask them to slip a few slices of pizza under the door.

d. Sorry. I'm still thinking about the last question. Please don't go so fast.

10. True or False?

a. True.

b. False.

c. All of the above.

11. Although you were hired to baby-sit one kid, the kid claims to have 18 personalities. To entertain such a child, you should:

a. forget about playing Solitaire.

b. choose up sides for two baseball teams.

c. let him race himself across the yard.

d. have him sit in a circle and tell scary stories.

12. The children would like you to play a sport with them in the living room. The sporting activity most recommended for indoor play is:

a. hang gliding.

b. Roller Derby.

c. shooting clay pigeons.

d. Nerf Russian Roulette.

13. When giving a toddler a snack, it's good to remember that:

a. a whole, unsliced melon is a little difficult for a child to swallow.

b. small bugs and other items found in the carpet should be washed before being eaten.

c. they have small stomachs. One potato chip for them, the rest of the bag for you is perfectly fair.

d. grass is a good source of chlorophyll.

14. There were four kids in the house when you came on duty. Now there are only three. You should:

a. revise your rates in such a way as to make sure you don't lose any money.

b. divide one kid in two.

c. go next door and borrow a kid.

d. congratulate yourself—you are truly a *bad* baby-sitter!

BONUS ESSAY QUESTION

INSTRUCTIONS: Write twenty words or less.

_____

_____

_____

April's Diary

The Journal of a Very Bad Baby-sitter

Dear Diary,   **Monday, April 1**

Happy birthday to me, me, me! I'm 13 today, the first of April, the month my mom named me after. I just know things are going to go great for me, me, me all month. From the top of my shoulder-length, streaked, crimped, blond hair to my big brown eyes to the tips of my blue-polished toenails, I feel lucky!

I don't know about this new idea of Suey Beth's. Of course, seventh-graders aren't qualified to do that much else, and I could for sure use the extra cash to get my spring wardrobe going, but *baby-sitting*? Suey Beth and Laurette think it's the greatest idea since press-on nails, but personally, I have my doubts.

Sweet dreams,

April

Suey Beth got to meet me and Laurette at the mall today because she'd made such good progress with what her mother calls her "little eating disorder." (Suey Beth throws up a lot.) When we got there, she convinced us that we should all buy look-alike T-shirts and they could be our baby-sitting uniforms. The ones she picked out were purple, naturally, like every single item in Suey Beth's wardrobe, including her underpants and bras, and on the front there's this brown furry teddy bear with plastic blue eyes. Laurette, who is into the self-help movement in a big way, says the T-shirts are perfect because little kids will relate to the bear and not scream bloody murder when their moms leave them with us.

I bought the T-shirt, I mean, they were in the sale bin and only cost $2.50 each, but seriously, I have always gone out of my way to avoid little kids, and I'm not sure if I'll like being alone with one for very long. Okay, okay, I just have to keep my mind fastened on the $5 an hour, but as I told Suey Beth: no kids in diapers for moi.

Wondering,

April

Went over to Laurette's after school with Suey Beth to organize this sitting thing. Suey Beth said she should be president since this was all her idea, and then she said we should make some fliers to put up in places where mothers might hang out, like at the mall, in tanning parlors and nail salons. We wrote down Suey Beth's phone number and said to call between 4:00 and 5:00 week nights and we'd all be there.

On her flier, Laurette wrote down that we'd all passed this Red Cross baby-sitting course, which is a total lie, but she said that for sure we could have passed if we'd thought about taking it. She also wrote that we were "totally mature" and she was going to put down that we were responsible, but none of us knew how to spell it, so she changed it to "really together."

After we finished the fliers, we pigged out on chips and pretzels and popcorn and stuff and then Suey Beth went into the bathroom for so long that Laurette and me got bored and went home.

I've got to put up my fliers at the mall tomorrow. All my fingers are crossed that I'll run into Shawn!

Sleepy time,

April

Dear Diary,   **Friday, April 5**

Suey Beth is all bent out of shape because I got the first sitting job. I mean, if it weren't for the bucks, she could have it. It's just that Mrs. Crider knows Suey Beth and Laurette because their families have houses at the lake near where they go, and for some reason, Mrs. Crider said she'd rather "take a chance on April." I'm supposed to sit for her baby, Harry, who is about one or something, so I guess this blows my no-diaper approach, but, I mean, just 'cause a baby *wears* a diaper doesn't mean I have to change it.

With mixed feelings,

April

15

Dear Diary,   **Saturday, April 6**

I saw Shawn Rugger at the mall today. He looks so cool with his hair shaved off on one side that way and his skull earring dangling down. I know I'm only in seventh grade and he's doing ninth grade for the second time, so he is lots older than me, but he was standing right outside Sneaker Heaven and I could tell from the direction his sunglasses were pointing that he was looking right at me.

Totally in love,

April

Dear Diary,   **Sunday, April 7**

I swear, I'm never baby-sitting for the Criders again. I have never seen anyone get so totally red in the face as Mrs. Crider when she came home and walked into the dining room. I mean, how was I supposed to know that nail-polish remover would take the finish off her stupid table? She even admitted it was old—over two hundred years old!—so why doesn't she just go out and buy a new one? And besides, what did she want me to do after I accidentally spilled my polish, just leave this big puddle of Passion Purple?

Plus that baby of theirs is really gross. I swear, if little Harry puked once, he puked 17 times. Every time I turned around, there he was in his playpen with yellow slime running down his front. I couldn't even carry on a decent phone conversation. I don't know, that baby seemed so hungry, but maybe I shouldn't have let him eat six Twinkies.

Good night for now,

April

Dear Diary,　　　　　　　　　　**Wednesday, April 10**

I don't care if Suey Beth and Laurette think baby-sitting is the best idea since piña-colada lip gloss, I'm getting out of the business. That twerpy little Kevin I sat for last night only has two teeth on the bottom, but boy, can he bite! I wonder if I should get a rabies shot or something. Tomorrow I'm cutting English to go over to the mall and see if I can get some other kind of job where you don't have to come into contact with little kids.

With crossed fingers,

Dear Diary,   **Thursday, April 11**

I got a job! Okay, so it's only making cones at Yogurt
Palace and my boss, Mr. Gleech, says he can only pay
me half what the other workers are getting because
I'm underage, but at least it's a job, and even if the
whole place does smell like spoiled milk, I mean, it's
still better than baby puke, am I right?

Yogurt Palace Princess,

April

Laurette and Suey Beth came into Yogurt Palace after school and I snuck them free cones, okay? I mean, is this a federal offense, or what? You would have thought I'd robbed a bank the way Mr. Gleech carried on. So he *fired* me. I couldn't believe it. Right in front of my friends. And talk about wasteful, he didn't even let Laurette finish her cone! (Suey Beth had already devoured hers.) Laurette says he is a really sick person to care more about some globs of frozen cow juice than a young girl's self-esteem.

After the big blowup, I was walking around the mall with everybody, trying to calm down, and I saw this really outrageous pair of sunglasses in the window of Chic Chick that I have got to own. But they are soooo expensive, and me without a job, so tonight when Mrs. Kleindish called and asked me to sit for Noah way at the end of the month, I said FOR SURE!

Ex-Princess,

April

Dear Diary, **Friday, April 19**

I baby-sat for Mercedes Packer tonight. I mean, is the kid named after her father's car, or what? But sitting with Mercedes is what I call a great job. She's five years old, out of diapers, and her mother has got one fabulous wardrobe! Mercedes didn't even cry that much when I put her to bed at 5:30 and then I called Suey Beth and Laurette and there was plenty of time for them to come over and we had a ball trying on Mrs. Packer's things. She's got diamond necklaces and earrings and furs and slinky black silk nightgowns that seem totally weird for a married lady to have around, but the best was this silver spaghetti-strap dress made totally out of sequins. The only thing is that Mrs. Packer must like be allergic to food or something she's so skinny, and I told Laurette not to try to zip up the dress, but did she listen? Noooo. Luckily, the sequin number had been way in the back of the closet anyway, so we just stuffed it back there again, and probably it'll be years before she ever wants to wear it and discovers the rip.

Love that job!

April

Dear Diary,   **Saturday, April 20**

I really thought baby-sitting at the Wilsons' tonight went okay. Rachel is seven and Rhonda is eight, so when they told me their mom and dad always let them stay up till midnight and watch MTV, I thought, hey, no problem. But it turns out that not only are they forbidden to watch any TV except for *Mr. Rogers* and *Nature* and stuff, but they also aren't allowed to play games on their father's computer like they said. Boy, when Mr. Wilson came home and discovered that some big file of his had gotten accidentally erased, he started using language that would get you kicked out of Nancy Reagan Junior High for good. I mean, how was I supposed to know that both those snotty little Wilson girls are pathological liars? Sheesh! And the worst part is that Mr. Wilson got so capsized about this stupid computer data that he suddenly started getting pains in his chest and he got all wheezy and had trouble breathing, so Mrs. Wilson called 911 and this bunch of paramedics showed up and in all the confusion I didn't even get paid!

Broker than ever,

Dear Diary,   **Thursday, April 25**

When I got home from school, my mom was still at
Mr. Wilson's funeral, but she left me a note saying
that Mrs. Packer had called. Whoopee! I can't wait to
sit for her again. I tried to call her back, but her line
was busy all evening. I'll try again tomorrow.

Kiss, kiss!

April

Boy, was Mrs. Kleindish upset when I called at around 5:00 this afternoon and told her I couldn't baby-sit for Noah tonight. Okay, so she scheduled me two weeks ago for this date and she and her husband have some big-deal $200 opera tickets, but can I help it if Shawn Rugger called at 4:30 and finally asked me out? I mean, what are priorities for anyway?

Not that I couldn't have used the money now that Mrs. Packer claims that I owe her $150. She says that's what it cost to get her sequined gown repaired. What did they do, use solid gold thread? Give me a break.

But as Laurette says, I just have to wipe this incident out of my mind while I wash my hair and get ready for my date or I will carry negativity with me.

So excited!

April

I am still so steamed I can't see straight. Okay, when Shawn called me yesterday, I was too like over-whelmed to ask a lot of questions about our date and I was ready at seven, when he said he'd pick me up. I had put on my mom's best perfume and everything. I thought we'd probably go to the mall and hang out and maybe take in a movie or something, but we started heading for his house. So I still thought, okay, maybe Suey Beth and Laurette, who were waiting at the mall, wouldn't get to see me out on my date, but a night in front of the tube could be cool and maybe kind of romantic. But it turned out that Shawn's parents were out of town and that he was supposed to baby-sit his little sister, Ginger. Ginger is seven and is missing most of her teeth, so she covers you with spit when she talks. I still thought that if Ginger hit the sack early, maybe she wouldn't ruin the evening, but then the worst thing of all happened. The doorbell rang and there stood Denice Brisket, this totally overdeveloped girl in the ninth grade, and Shawn flipped me a wave and said he'd be back around midnight! And there I was, left behind baby-sitting with Ginger who was spraying me with spit and asking me if I want to play Candyland or Operation.

I swear, I thought I might have to call 911 for myself, I was so upset, but I called Laurette instead, and she completely couldn't believe the psychic damage this creepy boy had done to me, and she said I ought to call our friend Tara, who moved to Saskatchewan last year, so I did, and after about two hours on the phone with her, I felt a little bit better.

In agony,

April

Dear Diary,   **Tuesday, April 30**

Well, here it is, the last day of April. It seems like about a year since the beginning of the month, when I felt so lucky. But as Laurette says, I have experienced a lot of strong feelings during these past 30 days.

I experienced sadness about not making enough money to buy those sunglasses and now they're not even in the window of Chic Chick anymore.

I experienced happiness when I heard that Denice Brisket had given Shawn Rugger head lice and he had to get the other half of his hair shaved off.

I experienced anger when Laurette told me that even though it was her fat rear end that had caused Mrs. Packer's dress to rip in the first place, she thinks she would resent me as a friend if I asked her to chip in to pay Mrs. Packer back.

And finally, I experienced totally awesome bliss when Mrs. Kopel called and asked me to sit for little Amy. The reason I felt so good is that I said NO WAY.

I've decided to give up baby-sitting forever and ever because I've figured out a much easier way to make some cash: mugging grade-schoolers for their lunch money! The only down sides are that you can't make that much money and I still have to have some contact with little kids. But, hey, it beats baby-sitting!

Things are looking up, *April*

20 Things You Should Not Say When Reporting to a Baby-Sitting Job

1. I sure hope your neighbors like their rock 'n' roll really loud.

2. You don't have one of those devices on your phone that prevents long-distance calls, do you?

3. If you want my opinion, I really think you'd be more comfortable driving your old Chevy and leaving the Porsche here.

4. I think it's only fair to tell you that I am a member of the Kruds, the toughest teenage gang in the world, and if any members of the stinking Dregs show up around here looking for a rumble, it's part of the blood oath that I've got to whip them even if it means trashing your whole house.

5. Are you sure you won't pay me in advance? I mean, I can practically guarantee I'll still be here when you guys come home.

6. It's very nice of you to give me money to order a couple of pizzas, but what about food for your kids?

7. I want you to know it's a real privilege to baby-sit for Calvin, and I'm sure when it comes to paying me, you're nowhere as cheap as everyone says you are.

8. Sure, I'll be glad to help Sharnell with his algebra homework. I ought to know something about the subject, I'm taking the course over for the fifth time.

9. I can't tell you how much this baby-sitting job means to me, especially after what happened that time I baby-sat over at the Keenes'.

10. What do you mean you don't want any boyfriends over here? I only have seven of them.

11. Sure, I'll take down the phone messages. I'll just scratch them into the telephone table with my Lee press-on nails.

12. I can read Jessie a story at bedtime. But I think it might be a better idea if she practices reading on her own, so I'll toss her a book or something.

13. Oh, you don't really want to know how I got the nickname Butterfingers, do you?

14. I promise to keep an eye on things. How was I supposed to know at the last place I baby-sat that those guys in masks were burglars? I thought it was Halloween. Besides the TV, stereo, and the silverware, I gave each of them a candy bar.

15. I don't actually charge any particular amount for baby-sitting. I kind of leave it up to the people who are hiring me. But since you asked, I think a fair return for my services is the minimum wage plus 40% for each child, plus another 75% of that figure for additional requests such as tucking the kid into bed. And I expect a transportation allowance, social security, federal tax withholding, and a 20% gratuity.

16. That is a very nice outfit, Mrs. Baldridge. I assume you aren't going anyplace special.

17. I really like baby-sitting. It beats one of those jobs with real responsibility.

18. Actually I'm one half of a super baby-sitting team. I'll take care of Jeff, and my pit bull Sam here can play with your little dachshund.

19. This is a really nice house you've got here. I hope it still looks this good when you get home.

20. I may not be the smartest person in the world, but I'll tell you this: I know the difference between a good baby-sitter and a bad one, and when I grow up and have my own kids, I'll never hire someone like me.

THE BAD BABY-SITTERS RAP

We're the bad baby-sitters
And we get around.
You can leave your baby with us
And go out on the town!

We will feed your baby bottles
Filled with Coke to drink,
But we draw the line at diapers
'Specially if they stink!

If your baby starts to whimper
It won't have us goin' south!
We'll just take that little baby
Pop a Ding-Dong in his mouth!

If your baby starts to crying
It won't bother us at all!
We'll just take your baby with us
And go shopping at the mall!

If your baby starts to screaming
And the neighbors start to knock
We'll just teach 'em how to boogie
While the party starts to rock!

If your baby throws a tantrum,
Bangs his head, starts turning blue,
Hey, no problem for us sitters!
We'll just give him gum to chew!

Bring on any situation!
We will handle it with ease
'Cause we're bad baby-sitters,
And we're only here to please!

But remember while you're dining,
Or out dancing at some bash,
We don't take no checks or Visa,
So come home with lots of cash!

Here is where excellence in Bad Baby-sitting is rewarded.
Here are the best Bad Baby-sitters of the year.
You won't find these baby-sitters wasting valuable
personal time by playing Old Maid, giving piggyback
rides, or actually talking to the kids they take care of.
After all, these are this year's members of . . .

THE BAD BABY-SITTERS
HALL OF FAME

LINUS BIZZY
Ran up a phone bill of $2,650—all on local calls!

MAURA DEMERRIER

Baby-sat for a family of nine kids—and when the evening was over, seven kids were still there!

JOSH KIDDING

Heard loud cries all night, but never figured out that he was sitting on the kid!

LARS VAY GUS

Taught the kids how to cheat at Candyland!

ROBIN de NAYBORES

Earned $1,000 for a three-hour baby-sitting job by cleaning out the family's wall safe!

CARA WAYSEED

Gained 14 pounds during one three-hour baby-sitting job by cleverly moving the living-room armchair next to the fridge!

A baby-sitter who showed up for work on time?
A baby-sitter who brought carrot sticks to snack on?
A baby-sitter who helped the kids with their homework?

Disgraceful—right? Well, you haven't heard anything yet. Here are the Bad Baby-sitters of the Year—this year's inductees in . . .

THE BAD BABY-SITTERS HALL OF SHAME

CASS SETPLAYER
Failed to crank up her Walkman full volume, accidentally allowing herself to hear the baby crying.

APRIL PHULE
Played 32 consecutive games of Chutes 'n' Ladders, and allowed the kid to win once.

STU PIDJURK
Wasted the entire evening in the living room, completely forgetting to go through the parents' bedroom dresser drawers.

VAL E. GURL
Asked permission to invite her boyfriend over. When the parents said no, she actually didn't invite him.

DELLA KAY TESSEN

Although she ate continuously, using both hands,
failed to clean out the refrigerator, leaving two carrots
and a jar of sour pickles behind.

JOY STICKE
While playing Nintendo all night, slipped up and let the kid take a turn.

BOB FERAPPLES
After the kid's parents left, invited four friends over for a party, then failed to make enough noise to force the neighbors to call the police.

JUAN SAPPONATYME
Wasted valuable telephone time reading books to the kids.

AL WEYSLATE
Arrived half an hour late for his baby-sitting job and gave a good excuse, instead of saying, "Sorry—I got hung up."

BEA KWYAT
Ran up a pitiful phone bill of only $300—even though the baby-sitting job lasted for more than an hour.

You find yourself sitting for a new family.
You are hoping to chat with the parents for a while before
they go out for the evening. Unfortunately, as you step
into the house, the parents step out. "I've left you a note on
the kitchen counter!" the mother shouts over her shoulder.
"Bye!" Well, there are notes and there are notes. And here
are several originals from the collection in the Museum of
Baby-sitting. They are definitely . . .

NOTES YOU HOPE YOU'LL NEVER SEE

Dear Sitter:

The baby's still sleeping so when she wakes up, you'll want to change her. The diapers are in the bin next to the changing table. Just feed her the strained pork and beans, which I've left sitting out on the counter, and then you can give her the medication that's in the refrigerator. Oh, silly me! I forgot to ask—you have had chicken pox, haven't you?

Enjoy the evening,
Mrs. Thigpen

Dear Sitter:

Thank you for answering my urgent call at the last moment. I just can't believe how hard it is to find a repeat sitter for little Hugo, especially since his fifth birthday. I just can't figure it out. But anyway, no special instructions except that Hugo hates it when anyone touches his "Dr. Doom's Torture Set." It was his favorite birthday present and I guess he's just at that possessive stage right now. So, if you even pick up the key to the handcuffs or lay a finger on the little dental drill, he'll pitch a fit. Just try to humor him and do what he says and you probably won't have any trouble. And we do have 911 right on the dialer, so if he does manage to tie you up, like he did that last silly girl, you can always push the button with your nose or your elbow or something.

Enjoy your night with Hugo!

Best,
Mrs. Klavin

Dear Sitter:

Hope you could find this little note under all the clutter on the counter. Ha ha! Listen, could you pitch in and kind of clean up the dirty dishes? They are in the sink, at least all of them that would fit. The pots and the eggy skillet are stuffed under the sink, I think. Ha ha! The rest are kind of scattered around the house, so just gather them up as you walk around. (Don't miss the ice cream bowls by the TV in the den—look under the bicycle.)

Have fun with little Chip!

Sincerely,
Mrs. Gerber

P.S. And check Judy's room for dirty dishes too. I haven't even been in there since she left for reform school, but I bet that's where most of the silverware has disappeared to.

Dear Sitter:

At the last minute, my sister's sitter canceled on her, so she's brought her brood over and then my next-door neighbor called and asked if I could help her out, and how could I say no? I hope you don't mind. All eleven children are in the den watching *The Little Mermaid*, which should be about over by the time you arrive. They've been cooped up all day because of the rain, so they may be a little hyper. If things get out of hand, my advice is—count to ten. Or should I say eleven?

Have a good evening,
Mrs. Mister

GETTING THE KID TO BED

A Simple 30-Step Approach

It's nine o'clock. Little Roger's bedtime. As the baby-sitter, your job is quite simple: You must get Roger from in front of the living-room TV up to his bedroom, where he must be tucked into bed.

There's nothing to it, really. Especially if you follow this scientifically tested, 30-step approach.

1. Tell Roger it's bedtime. Ask him to go up to bed.

2. Show Roger the clock. Tell him again that it's bedtime. Ask him again to go up to bed.

3. Explain to Roger the many benefits of getting a good night's sleep.

4. Reason with Roger.

5. Argue with Roger.

6. Plead with Roger.

7. Beg Roger.

8. Bribe Roger.

9. Scream at Roger.

10. Scream at the top of your lungs at Roger.

11. Search for Roger.

12. Look everywhere for Roger.

13. Call the neighbors; ask if they've seen Roger.

14. Explain to Roger why it's not wise to hide in a dresser drawer.

15. Unfold Roger.

16. Take Roger to the kitchen for a bowl of cereal and a glass of juice.

17. Give Roger another glass of juice.

18. One more glass of juice—and that's it!

19. Hurry Roger to the bathroom. Too much juice!

20. Chase Roger.

21. Catch Roger.

22. Pick up Roger.

23. Apologize to Roger for dropping him on the floor.

24. Plead. Beg. Cry.

25. Threaten Roger.

26. Search for Roger.

27. Take a short, well-deserved rest from all the begging and searching and chasing.

28. Wake up. Find Roger in dresser drawer.

29. Unfold Roger.

30. Start at Number 1 again.

Bette Yurlife has been giving advice to baby-sitters for several years. Bette was a former baby-sitter herself, until forced to retire because of charges that were never proven.

Her advice is simple, easy-to-follow, and always fun. Now, Bette answers some letters and offers suggestions just for you . . .

THE BAD BABY-SITTERS ADVICE COLUMN

DEAR BETTE:

I baby-sit for a six-year-old named Eddie once or twice a week. He's a nice little boy and I like him, but sometimes he gives me problems. Maybe you can help with some advice.

Sometimes Eddie calls my name. Sometimes he shouts. Sometimes he whispers. And sometimes he sneezes or coughs or laughs really loud. Sometimes he runs around the house. And sometimes he giggles a lot.

I've complained to Eddie's parents, but they just pretend that it's all perfectly normal.

What can I do? Any suggestions?

WORRIED SICK

DEAR WORRIED SICK:

I've had that very same experience with kids Eddie's age. Strangely enough, their parents also pretended their kid was perfectly normal.

But don't give up hope. There are things you can do. Have you tried painting his room with honey and covering the walls with feathers? Sometimes the simple solutions are the best. Good luck!

BETTE

DEAR BETTE:

I baby-sit for the sweetest little eight-year-old. She has long golden braids and big blue eyes, and she's loads and loads of fun.

The only problem is, when I baby-sit, my boyfriend and I want to be left alone. We don't want to be bothered by an adorable little girl.

What should we do? I've tried everything!

TROUBLED

DEAR TROUBLED:

The most important thing to remember is that you are not alone. There are caring people who sympathize with your problem and will listen to you and be there for you. Never lose heart.

Perhaps you should tell her to try dipping her braids in a mixture of peanut butter, grape jelly, and tomato paste.

I haven't tried it myself, but it sounds like good common sense to me.

BETTE

DEAR BETTE:

The little girl I baby-sit for always wants to hug and kiss me. What should I do?

DESPERATE

DEAR DESPERATE:

Of course, this outrageous behavior must be stopped at all costs. You poor thing, this has been such a trial for you! If all else fails, notify the authorities at once.

BETTE

DEAR BETTE:

Your advice to baby-sitters is sick!

The people who write to you are sick too. The kids they baby-sit for are perfectly normal, healthy kids. And you always tell them to do horrible, sick things to the kids.

I baby-sit for three kids down the block, and I'd never think of doing any of the sick things you suggest. Sometimes I tickle them till they throw up. But that's all.

I think you and your advice are wrong, wrong, wrong!

HORRIBLY UPSET

DEAR HORRIBLY UPSET:

Sometimes we all get the feeling that things are going wrong. Just remember that you are not the only one who feels this way. Your mixed-up feelings are perfectly normal.

The next time you baby-sit for these children, simply tie yourself to the cat.

You may not think it's helping—but just wait.

BETTE

BREAKING THE CODE

A Public Service Message from
The Bad Baby-sitters Handbook

WHEN PARENTS SAY:
"He's very active."

THEY REALLY MEAN:
"He bites."

WHEN PARENTS SAY:
"He's full of curiosity!"

THEY REALLY MEAN:
"He walks in on you when you're
in the bathroom."

WHEN PARENTS SAY:
"It's simply shocking how inventive she is!"

THEY REALLY MEAN:
"The kid gnaws on electrical cords."

PRAISE FOR OUR GODS WEAR SPANDEX

"Magnificent layers of information have been sifted through so we can find the real background of our superheroes."
 —Ron Turner, Publisher, *Last Gasp*

"Amazons and avatars abound in Knowles' excellent history of the myth and magic behind comics."
 —Trina Robbins, author of *Eternally Bad* and *From Girls*

"A lively and compelling history of mankind's eternal need for heroes and gods and the superhuman figures who answer the call."
 —Clint Marsh, *Wonderella.org* and author of *The Mentalist's Handbook*

"*Our Gods Wear Spandex* has convinced me that magic, mysticism, and esoteric knowledge shaped superhero comics from the beginning. As much as any interpreter of the comics, Knowles helps us understand superhero tales as theologies for today's young people."
 —John Shelton Lawrence, author of *The Myth of the American Superhero*

"Joseph Campbell, world-renowned mythologist, challenged the people of the twentieth century to create new myths. Christopher Knowles eloquently demonstrates that these new myths were already there, hiding in the humble pages of the comic book. Amazing, insightful, and timely stuff!"
 —Michelle Belanger, author of *The Psychic Vampire Codex*

"Christopher Knowles' *Our Gods Wear Spandex* is absolutely delicious—as fun and colorful as its title would suggest. It is not, however, just another litany of comic book trivia served to quell the adolescent appetites of basement-dwelling bachelors. It is a profound examination of what is in essence modern mythology—the archetypal characters, fears, hopes, and dreams that battle for truth, justice, and enlightenment in each of us. Our Gods *do* where spandex, and Knowles has positioned himself as the Joseph Campbell of comic books!"
 —Lon Milo DuQuette, author of *The Magick of Aleister Crowley*

"From the ghettos of Prague to the Halls of Valhalla to the Fortress of Solitude and the aisles of Comic-Con, *Our Gods Wear Spandex* is the first book to fully explain this meta-history of comics. And, finally, Hawkgirl, Black Canary, Phantom Lady, Scarlet Witch, and She-Hulk get well-deserved attention. A MUST READ!"
> —Varla Ventura, author of *Sheroes: Bold, Brash (and Absolutely Unabashed) Superwomen*

"I cannot imagine my own childhood without the comforting presence of comic book superheroes. And Christopher Knowles explains why. Carefully probing the genre's mythological, literary, and spiritual origins, Knowles helps us understand what these colorful characters mean and why they have assumed such an essential place in the lives of so many. *Our Gods Wear Spandex* is more than just a fan's appreciation of superheroes. The "secret history" presented here is a reflection on the eternal human compulsion to transcend the limits of body, mind, and mundane existence. This is an important contribution to the growing scholarship on comic book heroes and their rightful place in cultural history."
> —Bradford W. Wright, author of *Comic Book Nation: The Transformation of Youth Culture in America.*

"*Our Gods Wear Spandex* belongs on every college student's bookshelf, right next to the copy of the Joseph Campbell book he or she bought and pretended to read. The comic book protagonist has long been overlooked as the contemporary American hero figure. Knowles has written the anthropological companion to Scott McCloud's *Understanding Comics.*"
> —Bucky Sinister, author of *All Blacked Out and Nowhere to Go* and *King of the Roadkills*

OUR GODS WEAR SPANDEX

THE SECRET HISTORY OF COMIC BOOK HEROES

CHRISTOPHER KNOWLES

WITH ILLUSTRATIONS BY
JOSEPH MICHAEL LINSNER

WEISERBOOKS
San Francisco, CA / Newburyport, MA

First published in 2007 by
Red Wheel/Weiser, LLC
With offices at:
500 Third Street, Suite 230
San Francisco, CA 94107
www.redwheelweiser.com

ISBN-10: 1-57863-406-7
ISBN-13: 978-1-57863-406-4
Library of Congress Cataloging-in-Publication Data

Knowles, Christopher, 1966-
    Our gods wear Spandex : the secret history of comic book heroes / Christopher
Knowles.
        p. cm.
    Includes bibliographical references.
        ISBN 1-57863-406-7 (alk. paper)
            1. Comic books, strips, etc.--History and criticism. 2. Heroes in literature.
        3. Myth in literature. 4. Heroes. I. Title.
    PN6714.K56 2007
    741.5'352--dc22   2007020350

Cover and text design by Roland "Pete" Friedrich, Charette Communication Design.
Typeset in Scala, Meanwhile, and Helvetica.
Cover illustration © 2007 Joseph Michael Linsner.

Printed in Canada
TCP
10 9 8 7 6 5 4 3 2 1

ACKNOWLEDGMENTS

First and foremost, I need to acknowledge the wisdom and genius of my personal Bodhisattva, Joseph Michael Linsner. This project took shape in a series of free-wheeling phone chats while we were both scribbling our lives away, and it was Joe's mystical listening powers that allowed these ideas and concepts to come to fruition.

Next, I need to acknowledge the vision, hard work, and nurturing of Brenda Knight, whose rare intuitive gifts helped bring this project to life. A special thanks to everyone at Red Wheel/Weiser for their hard work and forbearance: Jan Johnson, Bonni Hamilton, Jordan Overby, Caroline Pincus, Amber Guetebier, Donna Linden, Rachel Leach, Meg Dunkerley, and Amy Grzybinski.

Then I'd like to thank the men who help keep me out of the poorhouse: my mentor Chris Fondacaro, the man who taught me that "good enough" is never good enough. The IF was working overtime on this one, sir! And to Tom Marvelli, a consummate professional, who lives up to his name in more ways than one. If Chris and Tom ran the world, we wouldn't need superheroes.

Then a round and a bag of crisps to my main man Scott Rowley, an editor most writers would swim the Atlantic to work for. A hearty cheers to Ian Fortnam as well. Eternal gratitude to Jon B. Cooke, the most talented man I've ever known, and to John Morrow, who ultimately is to blame for me getting started in the writing racket. Special thanks to Jim McLauchlin and especially Stan the Man, who first taught me the love of language. Excelsior!

And eternal love and gratitude to my wife, Vicky, for saving my life more times than I can count. And extra love and hugs to the Rooster, Jibbles, and Extra Ponies.

CONTENTS

I WANT TO BELIEVE

One of the great American innovations of the twentieth century—besides comic books and superheroes—is the sanctity of childhood. Countless billions are spent making modern childhood a 24/7 Disneyland of indulgence and delight. One could argue that this myth of childhood is the only thing still held sacred in our dehumanized, commercialized society.

Me, I didn't have much of a childhood. Even by 70s standards, it was pretty awful. America's child worship was going through a particularly Calvinist phase in those days of *Rosemary's Baby* and *The Exorcist,* and there were times when my world seemed like a live-action adaptation of *Lord of the Flies.* And almost from the moment of my birth I was in and out of the hospital with chronic pneumonia and bronchitis.

Back then, there wasn't much on TV, no video games to speak of, and the less said about 70s toys the better. What did I have to pass the long hours spent convalescing alone? Well, I had comic books. Comics then were cheap and disposable. If your mom gave you a quarter for the afternoon you could either buy a can of soda or a comic book. I usually opted for the latter. I actually taught myself to read at the tender age of three, finally getting the hang of it with an old *Superboy* comic. In my first few years of elementary school I read *The Children's Bible, The Children's Dictionary* and the *World Book Encyclopedia* in their entirety. But it was the lowly comic book that really taught me the love of reading.

Another constant in my life was religion. On any given weekend, I could be found attending the Jewish temple where my mother worked as an organist on Friday night, Catholic mass with my friends on Saturday night, and sitting through Methodist marathons with my family on Sundays. But as much as I loved the sacred ambience of these holy places, it was the heroes of the comics and not the Bible where I learned morality and fair play and compassion and decency. It was mythic heroes like The Mighty Thor, Doctor Strange, and Captain America that most inspired me and instilled in me that vital sense of wonder.

I believe that our lives are a rich and complex tapestry, woven together by a web of coincidence. I even believe that trauma can sometimes be beneficial if we use it to our advantage. For instance, a particularly horrible stint in the hospital shortly before I turned five effectively ended my childhood and put me into a perpetual state of hyper-awareness and agitation thereafter. But it was at this time that I saw something in one of my uncle's comic books (*Witching Hour* #12, to be precise) that changed my life forever.

That something was a full-page ad announcing the arrival of comics genius Jack Kirby to DC Comics in 1971. Kirby had created a trinity of titles based on a race of super-beings that he called "The New Gods." Under a banner screaming "THE MAGIC OF KIRBY!" were the covers of the three new comics: *The New Gods, The Forever People* , and *Mister Miracle*. My five-year-old brain was entranced by the unabashedly religious character of these new heroes. I wouldn't read any of these books until years later, but that one page in that one comic began a lifelong obsession with the man who is largely responsible for dreaming up the gods and demons that made Marvel Comics the powerhouse it is today.

I still proudly remember buying my first Jack Kirby comic book (*Kamandi* #30, "UFO: The Wildest Trip Ever!"), and I am constantly amazed at how many occult, mythological, and esoteric ideas he introduced to young readers like myself. Today, it seems like these new gods came into my life just when I needed them most.

This book will explain how superheroes have come to fill the role in our modern society that the gods and demigods provided to the ancients. It will catalog the movements and magicians who played a crucial part in the development of social phenomena like the *Batman* or *X-Men* films, or of TV shows like *Heroes* or *Smallville*. But I want to dedicate this book to the man who more than any other believed in our new gods and has inspired generations of other creators and fans to reach beyond the limitations and pitfalls of human existence. If we as a race ever do achieve our apotheosis, it will be in no small part thanks to the vision and inspiration of Mr. Kirby.

This one's for you, Jack.

SUPERHEROES, REBORN

CHAPTER 1

LOOK, UP IN THE SKY

INVOCATION

Suddenly, superheroes are everywhere. Superman, Batman, and the X-Men rule
the box office, with the Spider Man movies alone earning almost $2.5 *billion*
dollars worldwide. Superhero-themed shows like *Heroes*, *The 4400*, *Smallville*, and
Kyle XY are major cult hits on TV. All across the world, superheroes can be seen
on t-shirts, lunch boxes, backpacks, and bedclothes. The superhero industry is
very big business indeed, in many ways bigger than ever.

The modern superhero came to life in the midst of the Great Depression and at
the dawn of the Second World War. Americans were afraid, and superheroes
provided a means of comfort and escape. Superman, the first of the great superheroes, didn't fight robots or space aliens in his early adventures; he fought the

villains that people were really worried about at the time: gangsters, corrupt politicians, fascists, and war profiteers. After Pearl Harbor, superheroes became the mascots of the war effort. Comic books enjoyed circulations in the millions during the war, and were essential reading material for G.I.s overseas.

The story is as old as time; we only call on our gods when we need them. When life is easy, we ignore them. The prophetic books of the Bible are full of wild-eyed visionaries wandering in from the desert and shouting down the people for neglecting Jehovah when the granaries were full. Likewise, we can chart the fortunes of comic-book heroes in American culture by the rise and fall of public confidence and sense of well-being.

The comics boom brought on by Batmania in the late 1980s, for instance, reflected a feeling of genuine terror in urban America fueled by the crack epidemic and the explosion of gang violence that accompanied it. Comic-book creators responded to headlines in the *New York Post* and other crime-driven tabloids and set their four-color vigilantes to work against drug gangs, smugglers, and assorted other street thugs. In the happy-go-lucky Clinton years, however, the popularity of superheroes dropped to its lowest ebb. That would all change on September 11, 2001.

There was a brief moment in time after the World Trade Center towers came crashing down when the world seemed as clear and unambiguous as a super-hero comic. Once again, there were good guys and bad guys, villains and victims. The events of 9/11 tapped into a deep-seated need for something or someone to save the civilized world from a faceless, nameless evil that had the power to wreak instant havoc—a kind of destruction previously seen only in comic books or comic-book inspired movies. To fight these invisible demons, we needed *gods*. And indeed, once again, the comic-book industry rebounded—supplying a confused and terror-driven nation with superheroes who would put things to right.

DECLINE AND FALL

But just two years before 9/11, the superhero industry was on its knees. Thousands of comic-book specialty stores evaporated in a slow but inexorable decline that began in 1994, caused by rampant profiteering and a glut of the most poorly written and drawn comics in the history of the medium. Shell-shocked

fans now refer to those dark times as the "Chromium Age"—a time when tacky gimmicks like covers printed on chromium plastic enticed hobbyists to buy multiple copies of unreadable comics in hopes that their resale value would triple or quadruple. Some fans actually believed that they would get rich on "hot" books, even though tens of thousands of other speculators had also bought dozens of copies. It was a shameless pyramid scheme, one in which only publishers and retailers profited. In the end, it only discredited the medium and hastened the industry's decline. The rise of hi-res video games, home video, and the Internet also threatened the future of the poor, humble comic book.

Comics had been to the brink before, when plummeting sales had threatened the future of the industry in the 1970s. They were saved by the introduction of the "direct market" system, a distribution model in which publishers were guaranteed sales from specialty retailers who bought the books outright, rather than on consignment. In return, the retailers kept the books they didn't sell as back issues and were offered a greater discount for their trouble.

Freed from the crushing financial weight of unsold product and the restrictions of the censorious Comics Code Authority (see chapter 15), creators began to experiment with more mature and challenging storylines. In fact, many of the themes that attract millions of moviegoers today have their roots in the ground-breaking stories of the 1980s. Sales began to climb as the content became more sophisticated. These mature works drew in new fans while retaining the interest of older readers who, in the past, usually abandoned comics as they left their teens. Publishers retained the services of talented artists and writers, who might otherwise have left the field for more lucrative work. And royalty and profit-sharing programs allowed top creators to actually get rich. As a result, the 1980s saw a renaissance in American comics.

All this money, however, became the root cause of comics' near-death experience in the 1990s. Titles like *Batman: The Dark Knight Returns* and *Watchmen* not only earned big sales, but they also attracted the interest of the mainstream media. A new breed of creator arose, motivated almost entirely by the money. Many of them were talented and sincere; many were not. But too many of the talentless quickly learned the art of making a sale. At the same time, publishers abandoned long-held standards intended to prevent comic characters from being overexposed or misrepresented. Combine these trends with the artificially inflated sale of back issues, and the floodgates were open.

By the early 1990s, publishers like Image, Acclaim, and Malibu were pushing a sort of crack-cocaine version of superheroes. The model was created by former Marvel artist Rob Liefeld, who developed a garish vocabulary of visual gimmicks calculated to excite gullible fans. Instead of sleek, idealized athletes with colorful-yet-tasteful outfits, superheroes became a riot of bulging veins and ballooned muscles, absurd punk-influenced costumes, cybernetic limbs, and grotesque automatic weapons. Their faces were invariably frozen in grimacing expressions of hate, and they all seemed bent on death and mayhem for its own sake. Stories became nothing but incomprehensible jumbles of action poses, poorly choreographed fight scenes, and explosions. The trend spread, until even the august heroes of Marvel and DC Comics were being done Liefeld style, and the entire market became saturated with promotional gimmicks—variant covers, chromium covers, diecut covers—whose only purpose was to move product.

The turning point came in 1993 with DC Comics' "Death of Superman" stunt in *Superman #75*, which sold millions and brought thousands of new customers into comic stores. The ill-fated marketing ploy left a sour aftertaste, however. True fans knew DC would never leave their signature character dead, and finally realized they were being ripped off. By the middle of the decade, thousands of retailers found themselves buried under piles of unsold product; many stores simply went under. Yet, publishers simply continued spewing out more of the same garbage.

Things went from bad to worse. *Batman and Robin,* the nearly unwatchable 1997 film directed by Joel Schumacher, brought the Batman franchise to its knees and nearly took the Warner Brothers empire down with it. This was followed by a string of superhero flops like *Judge Dredd, Tank Girl,* and *The Phantom* that threatened the future of the entire "comic-book movie" genre. There is an ironic symmetry to this, for it was the success of the first *Batman* film in 1989 that launched one of the most feverish booms in the comic-book industry's fifty-year history, just as the success of the *Batman* TV series had done in 1966.

CHAPTER 2

KINGDOM COME

In 1996, two creators decided they had had enough. One was Alex Ross, an astonishingly talented painter and preacher's son from Texas. Ross grew up obsessing over the work of classic illustrators like Andrew Loomis and Norman Rockwell, and the music of the classically trained rock band Queen. His great passion, however, was for the noble, self-sacrificing superheroes of the so-called Silver Age of comic books (1957–1970). Ross burst onto the comic-book scene in 1994 with a series entitled *Marvels*, in which he presented Marvel Comics' most popular heroes in his graceful and impressionistic, yet photorealistic, style. Ross' noble characters had an immediate effect, making all the other superhero comics look ugly and cynical by comparison.

With the help of another ornery Southerner (dialogue writer Mark Waid), Ross declared war on the Chromium Age. His 1996 epic mini-series *Kingdom Come* is nothing less than an apocalyptic tract, awash in fiery Biblical wrath. The story presents a world in which the old-school superheroes (Superman, Batman, Flash, Wonder Woman, and others) are either in forced retirement or operating underground. In their place, a new generation of heroes arises—violent maniacs who spend most of their time engaging in pointless battles with each other. Foremost among these is Magog, a none-too-subtle parody of Rob Liefeld's most successful creation, Cable. During one of their meleés, this new breed of heroes causes a nuclear accident that irradiates the Midwestern farm belt and reduces it to a wasteland. Savvy readers recognized this as a metaphor for what the new breed of superhero comic was doing to the medium and the market.

Alarmed by this, Superman emerges from retirement and reassembles DC's Justice League. In an eye-grabbing series of battles, Superman and the League descend from the heavens like archangels and smash the new breed of superpowered lunatics, finally placing them in an enormous gulag in the radioactive wasteland of Kansas. Superman's arch-foe, Lex Luthor, has other plans, however. Luthor assembles his own band of heroes (led by a mind-controlled Captain Marvel) to fight the League. The climax comes when Superman and the more-powerful Captain engage in battle, while nuclear missiles meant to destroy all super-powered beings rain down from the heavens. At the very last moment, Captain Marvel tears himself free from the influence of the mind control and summons lightning from the heavens to destroy the missiles in mid-flight. He dies in the act. The story ends with peace on Earth and Wonder Woman pregnant with Superman's child. *Kingdom Come* marked the end of the Chromium Age, even though it would be several years before the comics market recovered from the damage it had wrought. The book is remarkable, however, for another reason. *Kingdom Come*—perhaps more than any other comic book in history—delineates what superheroes are to their most devoted fans. They are nothing less than gods.

THE HERO AS MESSIAH

Ross and Waid clearly depict the Captain—a discorporate entity incarnated by occult magic—as the new Christ. Though Superman is the book's star, Marvel is the linchpin of the series, and his death is the salvation of mankind. In *Kingdom Come*, Captain Marvel is endowed with an invulnerable, almost totemic, power.

In many ways, Captain Marvel is the ultimate icon of wish-fulfillment. A young orphan, Billy Batson, accidentally stumbles on a great wizard in an underground chamber. The wizard then teaches him a magical incantation that gives the boy the powers of a god. Captain Marvel isn't stained by the faults and foibles of ordinary heroes. His costume, with its royal, militaristic flourishes, is more dignified than Superman's longjohns. Nor is he saddled with the psychological baggage that figures like Batman and Spider-Man carry. It's no surprise, then, that he was the favorite character of the most important creator in the history of superhero comics, Jack Kirby. Two of Kirby's most iconic characters, the Mighty Thor and OMAC, borrow heavily from Captain Marvel, as does Kirby's signature character, Captain America. And it is probably no coincidence that two other pivotal creators, Alan Moore and Neil Gaiman, began their careers writing for Captain Marvel's British counterpart, Marvelman.

Kingdom Come summoned the spirit of Captain Marvel because its creators felt that his absence—or rather, the absence of what he represented—was destroying something they loved. The grim and gritty superheroes of Rob Liefeld and his mob of coconspirators—dark, violent vigilantes like Wolverine and The Punisher—were no longer even *likable*, never mind admirable or worth emulating. The catalyst for this trend was Frank Miller's 1986 graphic novel, *Batman: The Dark Knight Returns* (or simply *Dark Knight*).

Dark Knight was a relentlessly brutal look at urban violence, seasoned with heavy doses of crypto-fascist propagandizing and sexually transgressive imagery. The book's apocalyptic fury (complete with nuclear warfare) had the emotional impact of a bludgeon, and soon all of comicdom was following suit. Superheroes began to shed their naive, kid-friendly aura, and soon became up-to-the-minute urban warriors. This appealed to inner-city youths, many black and Hispanic, who were living through similar mayhem in their own neighborhoods. Indeed, the bulk of new readers who came into the comic-book market in the late 1980s were urban. American cities were in the midst of an existential crisis, and it is in times like these that gods appear. Likewise, it is probably no accident that the comics boom began to wane as the crack epidemic and the horrific gun violence that accompanied it began to ease in the mid 90s.

The landscape changed, however, when the tragedy of 9/11 struck. Politicans and pundits alike responded to the event with a calculated series of statements and actions that seem lifted straight from the pages of *Superman* or *The X-Men*. And the comic-book industry wasted no time rising to the occasion. A series of commemorative magazines and comics quickly flooded the racks, featuring Marvel's top characters reacting to the tragedy.

The following summer, a big-screen adaptation of *Spider-Man* hit the screen. The damage done to Manhattan by the Green Goblin in that film tapped into the primal fear unleashed on that beautiful September morning, and Spider-Man's eventual victory guaranteed that the movie would become a box-office juggernaut. The trauma of 9/11 explains why the film packed the visceral punch it did. As we watch Spider-Man triumph over the forces of chaos and evil, in some sense the psychic damage done on that day is repaired. And those primal fears still linger. Witness the success of the 2005 *Batman Begins*, which also featured similar acts of apocalyptic mayhem wreaked on Gotham City.

HOLLYWOOD HOMEGROWN HEROES

The box office success of superheroes has led many movie studios and animation firms to attempt to build their own superhero properties from scratch. *Space Ghost, Birdman and the Galaxy Trio, The Mighty Isis, The Greatest American Hero, Thundarr the Barbarian, The Thundercats, Darkman, Dark Angel, Meteor Man,* and *M.A.N.T.I.S.* are all examples of this. Most of these attempts, however, have been short-lived. There have also been movie characters that are superheroes in all but name—Terminator and Rambo, for instance. But there is something about the medium of the comic book that seems to be the best incubator for our substitute gods. People seem to sniff out the insincerity of these prefab Hollywood properties. And insincerity is instant death for a superhero—or a god, for that matter.

The two films that have successfully created superheroes from the ground up have drawn heavily on comic books to do so. In 1999, *The Matrix* was created by two comic-book-fans-turned-movie-directors, Andy and Larry Wachowski. The brothers enlisted two flashy comic-book artists, Geoff Darrow and Steve Skroce, to help them develop their concepts. In fact, Darrow and Skroce essentially created a comic book out of the script. The directors then used the comic book to pitch the film. *The Matrix* also drew heavily on religious mysticism and cyberpunk science fiction, effectively creating the first Gnostic, computer-hacking, Zen Buddhist superhero in Neo, played by Keanu Reeves. After writing and producing another big-budget movie based on a comic book (*V for Vendetta*) in 2006, the Wachowskis took the plunge and started their own comic-book line, Burlyman Entertainment.

A more family-oriented band of heroes, *The Incredibles*, was created by animator Brad Bird for the computer-animation studio Pixar. This heroic family was either a tribute to or a blatant knockoff of Marvel's *Fantastic Four,* depending on your outlook.

Efforts have also been made to present superheroes in film and on television without all of the iconic trappings (i.e., Spandex). M. Night Shamalayan's film *Unbreakable* (2000) posited the existence of real-life superheroes who are unaware of their powers. More recently, the cable series *The 4400* has presented a new race of humans, who are given superpowers by scientists from the future in order to prevent a projected disaster. The series, however, draws heavily on *The X-Men*, in that the 4400 are endowed with individualized powers and are perceived by the government and the society at large as an existential threat. Following in this tradition, NBC's smash-hit series *Heroes* (co-produced by top comics writer Jeph Loeb) has made these everyday superheroes sexy.

Yet the printed comic book remains, as it has for 70 years, the primary incubator for superheroes, even for film and television. The reason for this is two-fold. Comic books use a highly effective form of storytelling that resonates directly with the reader's unconscious mind. Comics are also very cheap to produce and print. A talented cartoonist can break your heart with nothing but a #2 pencil and a few sheets of paper.

While the technology that supports comic-book creation has improved significantly—computerized coloring lets artists render scenes in near-photographic detail—it all still starts and ends with the most basic of tools. While very popular comics have been printed inexpensively in black-and-white, most readers today generally expect comics to be very finely rendered by high-priced talent and printed in full color on high-grade paper. But compared to a feature film or even a video game, the cost is negligible. With lower production costs and less upfront financial risk, creators and publishers are, at least theoretically, able to experiment and pursue very idiosyncratic visions, which can result in truly groundbreaking material.

CHAPTER 3

THE CULT OF THE SUPERHERO

The diehard passion of comic-book creators gives their work a visceral conviction unlike that of any other storytelling medium. Comics fans are often aspiring creators and comics creators are usually avid fans themselves. For better or worse, most casual comic-book readers drift off into other pastimes; those that remain are a highly specialized, highly sophisticated audience. They know what they like and what they don't, and they take their favorite characters very, very seriously. In fact, artists and writers who don't hold their heroes in the same esteem, or portray them in a way seen to be insufficiently worshipful, often find themselves unofficially blacklisted. Since *Kingdom Come*, comic-book artists are expected to render their superheroes with a similar reverence.

Moreover, the accessibility of direct-market distribution makes competition among comic creators fierce. This has resulted in a constant evolution of the medium, particularly when it comes to the way stories are told. Today's comic-book artists are not cartoonists; they are illustrators, and most are expected to adhere to the highest standards of draftsmanship. Rob Liefeld's own work, and work of its caliber, is rarely seen on the stands today. He and others like him are seen as infidels in the new Church of the Superhero.

It may be that the general level of anxiety invoked by 9/11 and the Iraq War has encouraged the amped-up level of devotion among fans. In the recent past, super-hero parodies were particularly popular, as were self-mocking, comedic takes on favorite characters. For instance, the 80s incarnation of *The Justice League* was a wildly popular superhero comedy title. When the writers and artists of that book were recently reunited for a mini-series entitled *Formerly Known as the Justice League,* they dealt only with the peripheral, D-list characters from the series, as if third-rate characters like Blue Beetle and Booster Gold were fair pickings for parody, but stars like Superman and Batman must be treated with the utmost solemnity.

It is exactly this level of seriousness that has fueled movie adaptations of comic books and is probably most responsible for their incredible success. Tim Burton's Batman was an eccentric, but essentially faithful, rendering of the character. The film reinvigorated Batman and kicked off the era of the modern superhero film. In contrast, Joel Schumacher's Batman was a campy self-parody that nearly destroyed the franchise and the genre of superhero films with it. Christopher Nolan's *Batman Begins* (2005) drew heavily on the tone and context of contempo-rary comics and restored the character to his former glory.

It is precisely the reverential treatment of these characters—the essentially *reli-gious* portrayal of them—that resonates with the mass audience today. We have, in fact, witnessed the emergence of a strange kind of religion here. Indeed, super-heroes now play for us the role once played by the gods in ancient societies. Fans today don't pray to Superman or Batman—or at least most won't admit to doing so. But when you see fans dressed as their favorite heroes at comic conventions, you are seeing the same type of worship that once played out in the ancient pagan world, where celebrants dressed up as the objects of their worship and enacted their dramas in festivals and ceremonies.

In a few short years, comic conventions have stopped being sad, dingy assem-blies of marginalized wallflowers and have become mass celebrations of the

new gods and popular culture in general. "Cosplay," or costumed play, has become a major draw at conventions, as men, women, boys, and girls have found a safe space to live out their fantasies dressed as their favorite superheroes or fictional characters. Shows like Dragon*Con in Atlanta have become notorious for the throngs of beautiful young women who swarm there to show off their painstakingly constructed costumes, as well as their Pilates-sculpted figures. An ancient Egyptian or Roman might not recognize the characters, but they surely would understand the basic impulse behind it all. And though some costumes may be taken from other media, it all basically emanates from roots deep in comic-book culture.

This culture is far more influential (and insidious) than most realize. Most contemporary action movies take their visual language from comic books. The rhythm of constant hyper-violence of today's action movies comes straight from Jack Kirby. Likewise, rock 'n' roll has always fed off of comic-book imagery. Many of rock's most influential figures have been strongly influenced by comics. Elvis Presley idolized Captain Marvel Jr., to the point of adopting his hairstyle. Donovan giddily boasted that "Superman and Green Lantern" had nothing on him. Black Sabbath crooned odes to Iron Man and Mister Miracle. Pink Floyd name-checked Doctor Strange, and the Kinks sang about Captain America. Shock-rockers David Bowie, Kiss, Alice Cooper, Marilyn Manson, and Glen Danzig are all serious comic-book fans, and nicked many of their visual ideas straight from the pages of Marvel Comics. Marvel even returned the favor and published comics featuring Cooper and Kiss in the 1970s. It's no accident that most of these artists are well known either for their religious devotion or for their interest in mysticism and the occult.

Although most of us don't realize it, there's simply nothing new about devotion to superheroes. Their powers, their costumes, and sometimes even their names are plucked straight from the pre-Christian religions of antiquity. When you go back and look at these heroes in their original incarnations, you can't help but be struck by how blatant their symbolism is and how strongly they reflect the belief systems of the pagan age. What even fewer people realize is that this didn't occur by chance, but came directly out of the spiritual and mystical secret societies and cults of the late 19th century—groups like the Theosophists, the Rosicrucians, and the Golden Dawn. These groups turned their backs on the state cult of Christianity and reached back in time to the elemental deities of the ancient traditions. Inspired by the same cultural and spiritual ferment that afflicts us in our post-9/11 world, artists and architects of this Neoclassical movement portrayed the gods and beliefs of the ancient world in works that survive today in the major cities of the West.

In Manhattan alone, we find Mercury, messenger of the gods, at Grand Central Station. We see Isis, Queen of Heaven and Star of the Sea, at the Statue of Liberty[1] and a whole host of images and symbols of ancient gods at Rockefeller Center. The young artists who created the great superheroes grew up immersed in this atmosphere. All over the finest neighborhoods in Manhattan, you find gods lurking everywhere—in lobbies, over doorways, in elevators, and on rooftops. These young artists—city kids, really—looted the treasures of the ancient world from art schools and museums to create our new gods.

Comics superstar Frank Miller noted that those kids learned their lessons well, pointing out that in the early comics, "the superhero was an unusual often *mystical* element that focused and defined real-world situations and issues in a way that was clearer and more direct than a simple recitation of the facts could."[2]

In the ancient world, culture was inseparable from religion. So it is perhaps fitting that gods like Mercury, Hercules, and Horus found themselves plucked out of the pages of history and put to work on the pages of comic books. These gods shook off the dust of centuries and have emerged when and where they were most needed—at the forefront of our popular culture at a time of personal alienation, economic uncertainty, and endless war.

---

1   See Graham Hancock and Robert Bauval, *Talisman: Sacred Cities, Secret Faith* (London: Element, 2004), p. 440.

2   Interview, *The Comics Journal* # 101, Aug. 1985 (italics mine).

PART II

ANCIENT MYSTERIES

CHAPTER 4

DAWN OF THE GODS

Every culture has had its superheroes. In early times, when strength and courage meant the difference between life and death, the strongest and bravest were held in the highest esteem. It's only natural, therefore, that they would encourage the telling of stories to extoll their prowess and record their exploits. The most exciting and creative of these stories were passed down from generation to generation, and carried to other cultures through migration. With each retelling, these stories became more fantastical. From these original tales of superheroes came the first stories of the gods.

SUMER AND EGYPT

One of the earliest texts known tells the story of the Sumerian hero Gilgamesh. Other Sumerian texts and tablets detail the exploits of a pantheon of suspiciously human-acting gods. These myths are told in such detail that some observers, like linguist Zechariah Sitchin, claim they are not myths at all, but garbled accounts of a race of extraterrestrials that colonized the Earth and created humanity as its slave race.[3] Whatever the case, it's certain that these stories of gods and heroes traveled with Sumerian goods and technologies (like writing) to other parts of the ancient world. Ancient Egypt was one of Sumer's foremost trading partners, exchanging not only goods and services, but also ideas and culture.

Ancient Egypt was a society almost as saturated in media as our own. Thanks in part to the dry climate and the ever-shifting desert sands, an astonishing number of artifacts have survived from the glory days of that great empire, including statues, reliefs, papyri, figurines, amulets, totems, and jewelry. All of these cultural artifacts were inseparable from their religious context. In many ways, the heiroglyphs and picture-stories of the ancient Egyptians can be seen as a precursor to modern comic strips.

The Egyptians worshiped a vast array of colorful and exotic gods, whom they called the *Netjer*. Their gods controlled all aspects of creation and existence, leading some to believe that the word "nature" is a Latin adaptation of *netjer*. Since their exoteric religion focused primarily on the "next world"—that is, death, judgment, and the afterlife—the Egyptians raised the god Osiris, lord of the underworld, above all others. Osiris sat in judgment of the dead and determined whether they went to paradise, or whether their souls were destroyed. Later, Osiris was overshadowed by his sister and wife, Isis, a goddess who served many functions and over time absorbed those of earlier goddesses.

Isis was the mother of Horus, the hawk-headed god of kings. Horus was the god of the Sun, of the sky, and of the horizons ("Horus-zones"). Some scholars believe that the very word "hero" derives from his Egyptian name, *Heru* (Horus is the Greek rendering of the name).[4] Horus was also the star of one of the first great action-adventure dramas, *The Contendings of Horus and Set*. In these dramas, Horus and his evil uncle, Set (who was responsible for sending Osiris to the afterworld), contend for the throne of Egypt in a series of battles that would do any comic-book writer proud. The two gods shape-shift; they race boats of stone; they maim each other; their body parts become lotus flowers. In the end, Horus wins

---

3   See Zechariah Sitchin, *The 12th Planet* (New York: Harper, 1999).

4   Marvel is currently using the Eye of Horus as the logo for its Icon imprint.

the throne and Set is granted dominion over the western desert. Thus in life, every king of Egypt is an incarnation of Horus and, in death, becomes the new Osiris.

Egyptians were extremely syncretic in their religion. They absorbed gods and goddesses from other tribes and cities, even from other nations. It is now believed that Horus was actually imported into Egypt by tribes of chariot-driving warriors who came down from Mesopotamia.[5] Horus then absorbed the roles of earlier gods and came to be closely identified with Ra, the primeval god of the Sun.

Today, Egypt's power over the popular imagination is undiminished. Since the discovery of the Rosetta Stone in 1799, an astonishing number of texts left from ancient Egypt have been translated. We see Egyptian iconography everywhere, not just on the back of our dollar bill. The greater legacy of Egypt, however, is in its role as birthplace of the mystery religions. The pyramids and tombs of Egypt were places of initiation for scholars all across the ancient world. Isis eventually became the supreme goddess of Rome. The trinity of Osiris, Isis, and Horus became central to the Hellenistic mystery cults, and some would say to Rosicrucianism and Freemasonry as well. For thousands of years, esotericists have sought to resurrect the Egyptian mysteries so that the power that built those inexplicable monuments can be harnessed once again.

GREECE AND ROME

The early Greeks and the Romans worshipped roughly the same pantheon as the Egyptians, albeit under different names. Gods like Zeus/Jupiter, Hera/Juno, Hermes/Mercury, and Helios/Apollo starred in fanciful dramas that were depicted in murals, friezes, pottery, poems, and statues. The gods fought epic battles against their predecessors, the Titans, and later interacted with humans in allegorical parables. Each god was assigned mastery over a specific art or science, or facet of nature. Their icons and images persist to this day, especially in our modern superheroes.

The epic myths of the Greeks all centered around godlike superheroes. The outcome of the Trojan War hinged, not on the armies of Greece and Troy, but on the mighty warriors Hector and Achilles. Odysseus lent his name to the title of

---

5   W. M. Flinders Petrie, *The Making of Egypt* (London: Macmillan, 1939), p. 77.

Homer's epic poem, *The Odyssey,* which is still used as a synonym for high adventure. Hercules and his Twelve Labors were a favorite in the classical world, as were the stories of the great sea captain, Jason, and his brotherhood of warriors, the Argonauts. To the Greeks, these heroes were essentially demigods. Reverence for Hercules as a hero developed later into cult-like worship.

The same is true of real-life heroes. Alexander (356–323 B.C.E.), the Macedonian prince who had conquered most of the known world before dying at the tender age of thirty-three, became a superhero in the ancient world. Every would-be conqueror in antiquity measured himself against Alexander. Julius Caesar (100–44 B.C.E.) came on the scene when historians were far less likely to deify their subjects, but he still set a standard to which alpha males have aspired ever since.

The question is raised: were the ancient myths that developed around these superheroes ever meant to be read the way Christians read their Scripture? Were these stories all considered sacred, or were some meant simply as entertainment? The people of the Hellenistic world were not naïve. Their culture produced great thinkers on whom we have built our modern society. It's unlikely that educated Greeks took the gods and their myths at face value. It's far more probable that these stories simply supplied a cultural context that allowed the Hellenes to metaphorically interpret the meaning of life and the world around them, much as Aesop's or Jesus' parables did.

Gradually, the Greeks and the Romans turned away from these imperfect gods in favor of more idealized deities, particularly the great mother goddesses like Cybele and Isis, and dying/resurrecting solar gods like Mithras and Adonis. The merging of these pagan cults with Platonic philosophy and Hebrew morality resulted in the emergence of Christianity, a cult that eventually dominated most of the Western world. In retrospect, it all seems inevitable. The old gods were too fanciful and the mystery cults too abstract. Yet, Hellenes like Luke and Paul simply drew upon this same blend of myth and morality to spin their own tales. And the history of religion always comes down to who tells the best stories, doesn't it?

PEOPLE OF THE BOOK

The Hebrews were always great storytellers, expertly embroidering myth and parable into their tribal history. In many ways, the great prophets of the Old Testament are the small "g" gods of their monotheistic culture. They were supermen who had a sort of bat-phone to the divine. Unlike the Greek heroes, however, their power was not their own. It was granted to them by Yahweh, and their feats were meant to bear witness to his wrath.

The contribution the Jews made to Western mythology was to present heroes worth emulating for their morality, not merely their strength or courage. Heroes like Moses, David, and Saul were warriors, liberators, and kings, but they carried the added burden of having to adhere to the incredibly complex Mosaic laws of the Old Testament.

Many theologians have pointed out the essentially solar nature of heroes like Elijah and Samson, both of whom are thought to derive from stories of Hercules. Like Hercules, Samson (whose name means "Of the Sun") was betrayed by a woman. Hercules created the two pillars named for him by smashing through a mountain that sealed the Mediterranean at Gibraltar. Samson destroyed the Temple of Dagon by knocking down two pillars. Like Hercules, Elijah wore animal skins. Hercules was often identified with the Sun, and Elijah ascended to heaven in a flaming chariot identical to that of Helios, god of the Sun.

Following the Babylonian captivity, later prophets were portrayed as seers, which some scholars believe shows a Zoroastrian influence on Judaism.[6] They also express an increased messianic expectation. Zechariah 9:9 prophesies that the Messiah would ride into Jerusalem on two asses, a colt and a foal, which Christians cite as a prophecy of Jesus. The "manger" (*Praesepe*) and "the two asses" (*Assellus Borealis* and *Assellus Australis*) are stars in the constellation of Cancer, which the Sun enters on the Summer Solstice.[7] This may show that Asian solar traditions had a definite impact on Hebrew iconology. Many alternative historians believe that the solar traditions had an especially strong influence on the Jesus stories as well.

---

6   See Paul Kriwaczek, *In Search of Zarathustra: The First Prophet and the Ideas that Changed the World* (New York: Knopf, 2002).

7   See Alice A. Bailey, *The Labours of Hercules: An Astrological Interpretation* (New York: Lucis Pub, 2000). Labor IV - Part 2. Also Storm, Dunlop, *Collins Atlas of the Night* (New York: Harper Collins, 2005), p. 66.

THE NORSE SAGAS

The Norse had a pantheon that included a father deity (Odin), a mother goddess (Frigga), a goddess of love and sex (Freya), a dying/resurrecting Sun god (Balder), and a warrior god (Thor). Like the Greeks, the great gods and heroes of the North were warlike, and their greatness was proven in battle. Mortal men earned their way into the Nordic heaven, *Valhalla,* by proving their courage as warriors.

The Norse myths deal with the gods and their battles against demons, giants, witches, and mythical monsters. In addition to their gods, however, the Norse revered human heroes like the dragon slayers Sigurd and Siegfried, the martyred king Volsung, and the great warrior-maiden Brunhilde. The Norse hero Beowulf was celebrated in an epic poem that is acknowledged as the first great literary work in the English language. Later, English author J.R.R. Tolkien drew heavily upon the Norse sagas when creating his epic story-cycle, *The Lord of The Rings.*

Like Judaism, the Norse religion is apocalyptic and linear. All of history is a progression toward *Ragnarok* or the "Twilight of the Gods." Ragnarok is the final battle between the forces of order (led by Odin) and the forces of chaos (led by Loki), followed by the end of creation. Like the Hebrew prophecies, which promise a new heaven and a new Earth, *Ragnarok* is to be followed by a golden age in which all men and gods will live in peace.

The Norse legends had a major influence on modern comic-book superheroes. In many ways, the ancient Norse heroes are the closest in spirit to the superheroes in their noble and self-sacrificing warrior ethos. Two of comics' most important creators, writer Stan Lee and writer/artist Jack Kirby, drew heavily on the old Norse epics and legends for their hero, the Mighty Thor. Many of the gods—Balder, Sif, Odin, Loki, and Heimdall—became regular characters in the Marvel Universe, where they play the same kind of role that the Greco-Roman gods played in Fawcett's *Captain Marvel* stories.

All of these ancient gods and heroes took a long and circuitous route back to cultural prominence in the modern world, when the social upheavals of the Industrial Revolution finally summoned them from their long and fitful slumber.

CHAPTER 5

AN EMPIRE OF THE MIND

In the 19th century, the Industrial Revolution powered a rapid expansion of the British Empire under Queen Victoria, as indigenous spears and swords were overcome by mechanized firepower. England's imperial reach was such that their motto became "The Sun never sets on the British Empire." The common British citizen didn't benefit greatly from this imperial expansion, however. Conquered nations were difficult to keep conquered, and the spilling of British blood was needed to hold faraway protectorates. Military recruiters enticed men with the promise of exotic delights in balmy lands. This had a particular appeal for the working classes trapped in the cold, rainy, dirty, and repressed British Isles.

THE FRUITS OF EMPIRE

Even if it didn't always benefit its citizens financially, Western imperialism bore fruit in the looted cultural treasures brought home to museums and universities. For along with colonialism came a relentless, worldwide campaign of archaeological exploration. Discoveries in Egypt rekindled an interest in Egyptian mysticism, particularly in Britain and France. One of the most important Egyptologists, Sir William Matthew Flinders Petrie (1853–1942), was responsible for excavations at sites like Abydos and Amarna. Petrie discovered the "Merneptah Stele," an account of the military conquests of Pharaoh Amenhotep III, who ruled in the 14th century B.C.E. This stele is called the "Israel Stele" because it is the earliest known text to mention the kingdom of Israel.[8] Another famous Egyptologist was Sir Ernest Alfred Thompson Wallis Budge (1857–1934), who is responsible for many of the translations of ancient Egyptian texts still in print today, including *The Papyrus of Ani*, better known as *The Egyptian Book of the Dead*. Budge also wrote extensively on Egyptian religion, influencing writers like William Butler Yeats and James Joyce, as well as occult groups seeking to revive the Egyptian mystery religions. Sir James Frazer drew extensively on Budge's work in his landmark work on mythology, *The Golden Bough*.

The most important event in modern Egyptology is the discovery of the tomb of the young King Tutankhamun (better known as "King Tut") in the Valley of the Kings in November 1922. Led by British Egyptologist Howard Carter, the excavation of Tut's untouched burial chamber produced an amazing wealth of artifacts. The discovery of the tomb reignited the Egyptology craze, just in time for the rise of the pulp magazines. The early deaths of Carter's patron, Lord Carnarvon, and others involved in the Tut excavation had a powerful influence on pulp fiction, since it was widely believed to be the result of "the Curse of King Tut's Tomb." Cursed tombs soon became a staple in pulp and comic-book stories, and figured in the origins of Golden Age superheroes like Hawkman and Doctor Fate.

The Victorian Era also saw a craze for all things "Oriental." At the forefront of this movement was Sir Richard Francis Burton (1821–1890), a soldier, mercenary, explorer, writer, translator (he reportedly spoke twenty-nine languages), and diplomat. Not surprisingly, he was also a Freemason. Burton was best known for

---

8   Michael G. Hasel, "Israel in the Merneptah Stela," *Bulletin of the American Schools of Oriental Research*, No. 296, Nov., 1994, pp. 45–61.

extensive travels in Asia and Africa, traveling to Mecca in Arab dress and leading an expedition to find the source of the Nile in 1856. He also became famous for his translation of *The Arabian Nights*. Burton made the Orient seem alluring and intoxicating, and by doing so helped loosen the stranglehold that Puritanism still had on British society. Burton's promise (or implied promise) of high adventure in foreign lands became a major influence on the globe-trotting heroes of popular fiction.

THE RADICALS

Adding to the social ferment in late 19th-century America were a number of radical political movements. The Woman's Suffrage movement, led by activists like Susan B. Anthony and Elizabeth Cady Stanton, and the Civil Rights movement, led by men like Frederick Douglass and Booker T. Washington, came to prominence at the same time that political movements like anarchism and socialism arrived on the East Coast with waves of immigrants from Europe.

Horrified by widespread poverty and economic inequality in Europe, socialists called for the redistribution of wealth and the abolition of private property. From this movement came "Scientific Socialism," better known as communism, which regarded socialism as a transitional phase—a mere prelude to communism, which would scientifically reorder society and abolish poverty, oligarchy, and wealth. This new order, established by a revolutionary vanguard, would eventually give way to a dictatorship of the proletariat (the working classes). Needless to say, it never worked quite that way in practice.

Anarchism, a system calling for the abolition of all central government, is not taken seriously today. In its time, however, it posed a threat to the established order, particularly in Europe. One of the earliest anarchist thinkers was English philosopher William Godwin (1756–1836), father of Mary Shelley (*Frankenstein*), who preached a brand of anarchism he called utilitarianism. Other important 19th-century anarchist thinkers include the Frenchman Pierre-Joseph Proudhon, and the Russians Mikhail Bakunin and Prince Peter Kropotkin, who advocated a strange admixture of communism and anarchism.

In the early 20th century, a group of Italian immigrants called the Galleanists (named after anarchist leader Luigi Galleani) spearheaded a bombing campaign in cities across America. One Galleanist, Mario Buda, bombed Wall Street on September 16, 1920 to protest the indictment of Nicola Sacco and Bartolomeo Vanzetti, two anarchists blamed for a deadly robbery in Braintree, Massachusetts. The Galleanists provoked a massive crackdown against a host of radical groups in the early 1920s that came to be known as the Palmer Raids.

Along with this political activism, came movements promoting sexual freedom. The Oneida Community, founded in 1848 by John Humphrey Noyes, practiced an early form of communism called Communalism. The Oneidans included among their teachings the doctrine of "Complex Marriage," under which every man was essentially married to every woman and monogamy actually forbidden. A less religiously based notion of sexual freedom was advocated by Victoria Woodhull (1838–1927), who also fought for women's suffrage and became the first woman to run for president in 1872. Woodhull also worked as a traveling faith-healer and later allied herself with the Spiritualist movement.

Another pioneer in spirtuality and personal freedoms was Pascal Beverly Randolph (1825–1875), who founded the first established Rosicrucian Temple in Boston in 1858, and another in San Francisco in 1861. Randolph advocated the practice of sex magic and may have had an influence on Theodor Reuss, who founded the Ordo Templi Orientalis, and Aleister Crowley, who succeeded Reuss as the OTO's leader.[9] Clearly, by the middle of the 19th century, America was ready for a new revolution, though not necessarily one of a political nature.

SPIRITUALISM

When Spiritualism burst on the Western world, it shook the Christian worldview to its core. The movement had an inauspicious start, however. In 1848, a trio of sisters—Kate, Leah, and Margaret Fox—reported a series of "spirit rappings" in their home in New York. The sounds seemed to have no earthly cause, and soon they were said to respond to questions posed to these "spirits." Later, two of the sisters admitted they faked the rappings by cracking their knee

---

9   See Catherine Yronwode, "Paschal Beverly Randolph and the Anseiratic Mysteries," *Sacred Sex* (*luckymojo.com*).

joints. Still later, at least one of the sisters recanted this confession.[10] Whatever the case, the Fox sisters sparked a wildfire that burned across the dry spiritual kindling of America. Already prone to cyclical religious revivals known as "Great Awakenings," the country responded enthusiastically to the sisters' claims, with seemingly little concern for their authenticity.

As soon as the story of the Fox sisters hit the press, both sides of the Atlantic were flooded with mediums, clairvoyants, and other assorted spiritualists. If you wanted to speak to your dear, departed Aunt Matilda, you had only to make a small "donation" to a medium, who would be more than willing to put you two in touch. The Spiritualist movement became even more widespread after the grief and carnage of the Civil War made widows and orphans desperate to contact their lost husbands and fathers.

The success of Spiritualism depended on more than the credulity of a grieving public, however. It tapped into the greater discontent aroused by industrialization and its attendant social woes. If spirits could now speak to us without the aid of priestcraft, a whole host of cultural, political, and religious assumptions could also be brought into question. By piercing the eternal veil, Spiritualism opened minds to a whole host of Bohemian, radical, and freethinking movements that changed traditional society forever. At the same time Charles Darwin had kicked lose assumptions that dated to the Book of Genesis with his treatise on evolution *The Origin of Species*. Darwin's theories had unwittingly planted the question in inquiring minds: After humanity, what next?

Spiritualism also sparked a renewed interest in stage magic. Using the latest in technology, magicians wowed audiences with their illusions, convincing many that their elaborate tricks were evidence of true supernatural powers. And stage magic, in turn, provided Spiritualist mediums with a whole new bag of tricks and gimmicks with which to convince their clients that they really could contact the etheric realms. As if all that were not enough, colonial expansion brought with it Eastern occultism and mysticism, particularly the varieties developed in India and China. All of these factors worked together to prepare the public for the explosion of occultism and alternative spirituality in the Victorian Era.

---

10   See Ann Braude, *Radical Spirits: Spiritualism and Women's Rights in Nineteenth-Century America* (Bloomington: Indiana University Press, 2001).

CHAPTER 6

SECRET SECTS

Victorian occultism synthesized Spiritualism, stage magic, Eastern mysticism, and Freemasonry. In the ferment of the moment, when science and technology were blossoming at unparalleled rates, London became the nexus of a host of secret societies and cults. The goal of these new occultists was to transform the human mind, body, and soul, just as steam engines and mechanical inventions were transforming industry and agriculture. Surrounded by super-powerful machines that threatened to overwhelm Humanity, these occultists conjured up a race of super-powerful humans to meet the challenge. They found ample precedent in ancient mythology and religion to justify and inspire their yearnings for a "New Man." The occultists turned to Renaissance individualism, alchemy, and the Hermetics to imagine a new race of god-men that could transcend the weaknesses, sins, and corruption of the society they saw around them.

This intellectual and spiritual ferment provided fertile ground for the growth of new religious and philosophical movements. These newborn occult and secret societies all found their ritual roots in the ancient mysteries and hermetic traditions of the past.

THE ROSICRUCIANS

One of the most obscure and least understood of these occult movements is Rosicrucianism. No one is exactly sure how the Rosicrucian Order started, who belonged to it, or exactly what they believed. For a group so shrouded in mystery, however, the Rosicrucians have had an incalculable influence. The professed aim of this enlightened mystical brotherhood was, as Michael Howard writes in his landmark work, *The Occult Conspiracy*, "the evolution of humanity from materialism to spiritual perfection."[11]

The earliest mention of a Brotherhood of the Rosy Cross occurs in 1604 in a manuscript called *The Restoration of the Decayed Temple of Pallas*. In 1614, the *Fama Fraternitatis* appeared, which purported to be a history of the order. This was followed by the *Confessio Fraternitatis* in 1615 and *The Chymical Wedding of Christian Rosenkreutz* in 1616. The *Chymical Wedding* referred to the work of the alchemists, who sought to marry the masculine and feminine properties of creation and produce the Royal Hermaphrodite, which some historians have linked to Harpocrates, or "Horus the Child," in the ancient mysteries. In fact, one of the first texts that can be called a comic book was the *Mutus Liber*, a 17th-century wordless alchemical text that told the story of the *Chemical Wedding of Sun and Moon* in sequential picture form.

The Rosicrucian order allegedly traced its origins to a German pilgrim named Christian Rosenkreuz who traveled to the Middle East to study the occult arts. He returned to Germany and founded the Order, whose goal was to bring about a "universal reformation of mankind." Shortly after the publication of the texts mentioned above, several Rosicrucian Orders arose, all claiming to be the true inheritors of Rosenkreuz's mantle.

---

11   Michael Howard, *The Occult Conspiracy* (Rochester, VT: Destiny, 1989), p. 49.

It is significant that, at the time of Rosenkreuz's reported founding of the Order, Germany was in the midst of a religious war between the Established Church and the Protestant Princes of the Empire, whom the Rosicrucians were said to favor. Martin Luther's personal seal was, in fact, a cross placed in a rose, leading some to speculate that the Reformation itself grew out of Rosicrucianism. Whatever the case, the combination of ancient occultism and alchemy that found its expression in Rosicrucianism had a powerful influence on the development of Freemasonry, a largely Protestant movement coming to prominence at the time in Great Britain.

Some historians who believe that Rosicrucianism predates 1604 claim that the Order was active in the court of Queen Elizabeth I, and that occultists like John Dee, Francis Bacon, and Edward Kelley had extensive contact with them. Many speculate that the Rosicrucians were, in fact, an outgrowth of the Knights Templar.[12] It is true, nonetheless, that, as the Masons became more powerful and militant, the Rosicrucians diminished in prominence, and may even have been absorbed by Freemasonry.

The advent of Theosophy in the 19th century brought on attempts to resurrect Rosicrucianism. Theosophists Annie Besant, Marie Russak, and James Wedgwood established an Order of the Temple of the Rosy Cross in 1912 that, predictably, fell into disarray. Russak then joined forces with H. Spencer Lewis, who had established the Ancient and Mystical Order Rosae Crucis (AMORC) in New York in 1915, but then moved the Order to San Francisco. AMORC enjoyed some prominence in the early 20th century, and Lewis eventually built a Rosicrucian temple in San Jose, California. The Order advertised extensively in newspapers and magazines, especially the pulp magazines. They offered correspondence courses in the mystical arts to readers with come-ons like: "Have You Lived Before This Life?"

FREEMASONRY

Shortly after the emergence of Rosicrucianism, another secret society arose that exerted a monumental impact on Europe's social and political landscape. Many people now believe that this group, the Order of Free and Accepted Masons, is the direct descendant of the medieval Knights Templar, a monastic order ostensibly

---

12   Howard, *Occult Conspiracy*, p. 49.

founded to ensure safe passage to Christians traveling to Jerusalem during the Crusades. The Templars instituted a complex banking system while safeguarding the treasure of European pilgrims, and are responsible for the invention of the credit system and branch banking. King Philip IV of France coveted the Templars' vast wealth to finance his dreams of conquest and used his puppet, Pope Clement V, to declare them heretics. Clement ordered their arrest and the confiscation of their vast holdings throughout Christendom. Legend has it that, although Templar Grand Master Jacques De Molay died at the stake, several knights escaped with the bulk of the Order's treasure. It is commonly believed that Scottish King Robert the Bruce offered them safe haven.[13]

The origins of Freemasonry are murky. Masons claim their order evolved from the stonemason guilds of the Middle Ages. These master craftsmen often traveled far from home to build cathedrals, taking the closely guarded secrets of their trade with them. These trade secrets developed into an elaborate system of rituals and secret codes protected by the Masons as they traveled a network of lodges frequented by other craftsmen. Eventually, the guild itself evolved into "Speculative Masonry," which focused on the symbolic and spiritual aspects of the craft. This new brotherhood attracted aristocrats and intellectuals from across Europe and ultimately became a force to be reckoned with.

Masonry was especially powerful in Britain and its colonies. The first established Masonic body was the Grand Lodge of England, which announced itself to the world in 1717. Masonic ritual traveled with colonists to the New World—several of America's Founding Fathers, including George Washington, were Masons. The famous Boston Tea Party was the work of a Masonic lodge, and the Great Seal of the United States is replete with Masonic imagery and numerology.[14] Freemasonry helped break the power of the Vatican by supporting the political fervor that sparked both the French and American Revolutions. It became so powerful in America, in fact, that in the early 1800s, an Anti-Mason political party was formed.

The backlash against Masonic power in the early 1800s sent the movement underground, only to emerge even more powerful in the late Victorian Age. In America, Masons became prominent in business, sports, and politics, and exerted

---

13   Bauval Hancock, *Talisman*, p. 318.

14   Howard, *Occult Conspiracy*, pp 82–86.

a strong influence on popular culture. Media moguls like Louis B. Mayer (MGM), Darryl Zanuck (20th Century Fox), and Jack Warner (Warner Bros.) were all high-level Masons.[15]

Many believe that Freemasonry is nothing but a modern incarnation of the old mystery religions, particularly the Mithraic and Osirian/Dionysian cults. Masonic symbols like the pyramid and the All-Seeing Eye, both of which are identified with Horus, come from ancient sources. Masons, in fact, refer to themselves as the "Widow's Sons," a reference to Horus, son of the widow Isis.[16] The iconic Masonic emblem of the square and compass represents the masculine and feminine aspects of creation. Although the Masonic community is generally thought to be in decline today, it's hard to overestimate its influence on American culture. Masonic ideals are part and parcel of our national creed, as well as our national mythology. When Superman stands for "truth, justice, and the American way," he is also standing for the Masonic way. It's almost impossible to separate the two in a definitive way.

OTHER CHRISTS

The 19th century also saw the rise of major alternative religious movements, particularly in America, and more particularly in New England. Three of the most important of these movements—Christian Science, Transcendentalism, and Mormonism—had important links to Freemasonry.

CHRISTIAN SCIENCE

Christian Science is based on the doctrines presented by Mary Baker Eddy in 1875 in *Science and Health with Key to the Scriptures*. Eddy (1821–1919) taught the virtues of healing through faith, preaching that illness is an illusion. For many, this led to the disavowal of medical science—admittedly a science in name only at the time. Christian Science was essentially a mystical faith that resonated with the rituals of

---

15   Louis B. Mayer was initiated at St. Cecile Lodge #568 in New York City and Jack Warner at Mount Olive Lodge #506 in Los Angeles. See "Famous Freemasons," Ellensburg Masonic Lodge #30, F&AM. *http://www.ellensburg.com/~masons39/index.html*. See also Marlys J. Harris, *The Zanucks of Hollywood : The Dark Legacy of an American Dynasty* (New York: Crown, 1989), p. 233.

16   Howard, *Occult Conspiracy*, pp. 15, 24.

the Masons, who paid tribute to Eddy by erecting an 11-foot pyramid at her New Hampshire birthsite, which the Church's embarrassed directors had destroyed.[17]

Christian Science attracted the literary and artistic elite, through whose support an enormous Mother Church was erected in Boston. The faithful also founded the influential newspaper *The Christian Science Monitor,* as well as several other long-running periodicals. Like Scientology in more recent times, Christian Science was popular in Hollywood, attracting a wide range of adherents active in the media.[18]

MORMONISM

The Church of Latter-Day Saints, more commonly known as the Mormon Church, traces its origins to hidden scriptures known as *The Golden Plates*, allegedly revealed by an angel named Moroni to Joseph Smith. *The Golden Plates* claim that Jewish tribes emigrated to America following the fall of Jerusalem and that Jesus reappeared to them. Mormonism is considered a pseudo-Christian cult by most Christian denominations. It preaches a cosmology more akin to Gnosticism than mainstream Christianity, teaching that God was once a mortal and that men have the potential to become gods themselves.

The Mormons were extremely unpopular in their early days and traveled west to flee persecution for, among other things, encouraging polygamy. The Mormons eventually settled on the shores of the Great Salt Lake in Utah. Many believe that Mormon rituals are based in Freemasonry. Founder Joseph Smith was initiated a Master Mason in 1842, and some claim that he was schooled in the rites of ceremonial magic and alchemy by Dr. Lumna Walter.[19] Indeed, Egyptian symbols are common in Salt Lake City, including a statue of the Great Sphinx bearing Joseph Smith's likeness. *The Golden Plates* were recently adapted into comic form by Mormon comic artist Mike Allred *(Madman, X-Factor)*.

---

17   "Directors Order Diabolical Destruction of Grand Pyramid Marker at Bow," *Mary Baker Eddy Letter,* No. 7, December 25, 1997.

18   Adherents include Frank Capra, Howard Hawks, Henry Fonda, Joan Crawford, Elizabeth Taylor, and Doris Day. Monkee Michael Nesmith and former Batman Val Kilmer are both active and practicing Christian Scientists. See "Famous Christian Scientists (Members of the Church of Christ, Scientist)," *adherents.com.*

19   See Lance S. Owens, "Joseph Smith: America's Hermetic Prophet," *Gnosis,* Spring 1995.

TRANSCENDENTALISM

Transcendentalism is a blend of Christianity and Eastern thought that had a strong influence on Theosophy. The movement began in September 1836, when poet and essayist Ralph Waldo Emerson founded the Transcendental Club. In January 1842, the Club announced itself to the world with a lecture read by Emerson at the Masonic Temple in Boston. Emerson read texts like *The Bhagavad Gita* and Buddhist scripture, as well as the writings of Christian mystic Emanuel Swedenborg. From these readings, Emerson developed a philosophy that taught the unity of creation and the virtues of mysticism over rationality and logic. Emerson's circle included novelist Nathaniel Hawthorne and philosopher Henry David Thoreau. There was even a Transcendental commune, but it was short-lived (as communes filled with intellectuals usually are).

CHAPTER 7

THE VICTORIAN OCCULT EXPLOSION

The rise of secret societies in the 18th century and the proliferation of alternative religious movements in the 19th prepared the way for an explosion of new religious thinking at the turn of the 20th century. In many ways, it all starts with the English politician, novelist, and occultist Lord Edward Bulwer-Lytton (1803–1873).

THE COMING RACE: EDWARD BULWER-LYTTON AND VRIL

A hereditary peer and a reformist member of Parliament, Bulwer was an ally of legendary Prime Minister Benjamin D'Israeli. He represented Hertfordshire, former British headquarters of the Knights Templar. A lifelong student of the occult, Bulwer was also an active Freemason and a high-ranking member of the Rosicrucian Order. He also formed a group with legendary French occultist Éliphas Lévi for the advanced study of magic. Bulwer channeled his interests into the writing of occult fiction, claiming that he created his novels to battle against what he called the "absorbing tyranny of every-day life."

One of his most popular and influential novels, *Zanoni,* concerned a high-ranking Rosicrucian who takes a young woman's place at the guillotine during the Reign of Terror in France. The novel deals extensively with Rosicrucian philosophy, to the point that it could act as a primer for the Brotherhood. Bulwer would write that "the supernatural is only something in the laws of nature of which we have been hereto ignorant."[20]

The Stephen King of his era, Bulwer wrote best-sellers like *Paul Clifford* and *The Last Days of Pompeii* that were popular worldwide. *The Last Days of Pompeii* delved into ancient magic and the cult of Isis, as well as the mystical ferment of first-century Rome. Two mystic characters—a Witch of Vesuvius and an Egyptian magician who claims descent from the line of Rameses—are prominent. Bulwer's 1857 short story "The Haunted and the Haunters," anticipates writers like H. P. Lovecraft, exploring metaphysics in the context of Gothic fiction. In addition to these stories, Bulwer wrote a number of historical novels like *Harald, Last King of the Saxons.* None of these, however, had nearly the influence of his 1871 work, *Vril: The Power of the Coming Race.*

For all its influence, *Vril* is hardly a page-turner. The book has no plot to speak of and consists mainly of an unnamed American narrator's observations of the history and customs of the *Vril-ya* (meaning "the civilized nations"). The Vril-ya are a race of superhumans driven underground in the distant past, where they form a new society lit by an interior Sun. The Vril-ya are far more advanced than surface dwellers, having discovered an all-powerful liquid called *vril* that seems to be roughly analogous to some form of atomic energy and is extracted from the interior Sun.

The Vril-ya are ruled by a benevolent dictator. They disdain conflict and debate, and equate philosophy with "wrangling." Their social creed is: "No happiness without order, no order without authority, no authority without unity." Women are

---

20 Quotes taken from "Introduction," Edward Bulwer-Lytton, *The Coming Race* (Middletown, CT: Wesleyan, 2006), pp. xxiv and xiv.

larger (some seven feet high) and more formidable than the men, yet make "the most amiable, conciliatory, and submissive wives." Robots seem to do most of the work. The Vril-ya are vegetarians; they disdain "carnivores"; they are convinced of their superiority over all other people. Bulwer describes them as beautiful and exotic, having "blue eyes, and hair of a deep golden auburn" and "complexions warmer or richer in tone than persons in the north of Europe." Like New Agers, they:

> …dwell in an atmosphere of music and fragrance. Every room has its mechanical contrivances for melodious sounds, usually tuned down to soft-murmured notes, which seem like sweet whispers from invisible spirits…they have a notion that to breathe an air filled with continuous melody and perfume has necessarily an effect at once soothing and elevating upon the formation of character and the habits of thought.[21]

The nameless narrator laments the Vril-ya's state of apparent perfection, however, claiming it has a stultifying effect on the arts and the creative spirit: "Without its ancient food of strong passions, vast crimes, heroic excellences, poetry therefore is, if not actually starved to death, reduced to a very meagre diet." He laments their lack of passion and notes that, without crisis and strife, there is no opportunity for heroism: "Where there are no wars there can be no Hannibal, no Washington, no Jackson, no Sheridan."[22]

Beneath their placid exterior, however, the Vril-ya nurse a dark agenda. They describe themselves as exiles, "driven…to perfect [their] condition and…destined to return to the upper world, and supplant all the inferior races now existing therein." Nor will the "supplanting" be a peaceful process. The Vril-ya openly predict that they will exterminate the inhabitants of the upper world upon their return. The Vril-ya's calm assumption of eventual return and conquest leads the narrator to hope that "ages may yet elapse before they emerge into sunlight our inevitable destroyers."[23]

---

21 Bulwer-Lytton, *The Coming Race*, chapters 9, 10, 15.

22 Bulwer-Lytton, *The Coming Race*, chapters 17, 26.

23 Bulwer-Lytton, *The Coming Race*, chapters 25, 29.

To the Victorians, the combination of Utopianism, genetic superiority, and irresistible technological force made for an intoxicating brew. The social displacement caused by the Industrial Revolution and demographic anxieties provoked by imperialism made Bulwer's vision of an all-powerful, highly evolved race a comforting vision of the future. This new type of Utopianism influenced untold legions of science-fiction writers and inspired the "World of Tomorrow" propaganda that helped many people weather the Great Depression.

H. G. Wells presented a more sympathetic version of the Vril-ya in his Utopian novel *The Shape of Things To Come*. Conversely, Aldous Huxley held up the Vril-ya as a warning against excessive government control in his novel *Brave New World*. In fact, with *Vril*, Bulwer began an evolution in fiction writing that led ultimately to present-day tales of super-races like *The X-Men* and *The 4400*.

Vril had a huge impact on the nascent occultism of the late 19th century. Theosophy founder Madame Blavatsky quoted extensively from it and presented a more palatable form of the Vril-ya in her "Ascended Masters." Blavatsky was so impressed by *Vril* that she argued that Bulwer must have gotten his ideas from an initiate of an Eastern tradition.[24] Aleister Crowley was also a noted fan of Bulwer and recommended Bulwer's fiction to his acolytes.[25] Masonic Grand Poobah Albert Pike may also have been influenced by Bulwer when he wrote, a year after *Vril*, in his landmark text *Morals and Dogma* of a potent force "by means whereof a single man, who could possess himself of it, and should know how to direct it, could revolutionize and change the face of the world." He described the force as "a ray detached from the glory of the Sun."[26]

On the other hand, Bulwer's novel is seen by many as a criticism of the corrosive effects of a scientific society and socialist Utopianism. The novel's narrator certainly doesn't seem overly fond of the Vril-ya, and Bulwer's opposition to Marxism and Darwinism, and to what he saw as science run amok, is clear throughout the book. In their landmark 1960 work, *The Morning of the Magicians*, Louis Pauwells and Jacques Bergier warn that Bulwer's fiction contains "the conviction that there

---

24   H. P. Blavatsky, *Collected Writings of H.P. Blavatsky*, vol.12 (Wheaton, IL: Theosophical Publishing, 1890), p. 636.

25   Crowley, Aleister, *Magick in Theory and Practice, Part III of Book Four* (New York: Castle Books, 1929), 1991 Appendix I "Bibliography and Curriculum of the A∴ A∴."

26   Albert Pike, *Morals and Dogma of the Ancient and Accepted Scottish Rite of Freemasonry* (Supreme Council of the 33rd Degree, Southern Jurisdiction of the US, 1871), p. 734.

are beings endowed with superhuman powers." They note the potential danger of this belief, pointing to Bulwer's popularity in *fin de siècle* Germany. Some scholars trace the roots of the infamous Vril Society, which allegedly counted among its members Adolf Hitler, Alfred Rosenberg, Heinrich Himmler, and Hermann Göering, back to a secret society originally called The All-German Society for Metaphysics that some say was grounded in Bulwer's work.[27]

Regardless of whether you accept this argument, it is difficult to overstate Bulwer's influence on his time. Using the conceit of science fiction, he pioneered the concept of a super-race whose powers far exceed those of ordinary men. In the turmoil of the Victorian Age, when scientific and technological breakthroughs held out the promise of improving or even perfecting the human machine, this was heady stuff. Moreover, it's no accident that this concept came from a practicing occultist. The promise of a new race had a powerful impact—positive and negative—in the century to come. But first a strange band of eccentrics, led by a corpulent, pipe-smoking Russian emigré would expand Bulwer's fanciful ideas into a worldwide movement.

MADAME BLAVATSKY AND THEOSOPHY

Perhaps the most important alternative religious movement in the 19th century was the Theosophical Society, founded by Helena Petrovna Blavatsky. A peculiar woman with a puzzling biography, Blavatsky revolutionized the counterculture of her time and founded a movement that became truly international in scope. She was one of the first to bring Eastern mysticism to the West. Among her core teachings are the fundamental unity of all existence, the regularity of universal law, and the progress of consciousness toward an ever-increasing realization of unity.

---

27   Willy Ley, an exiled German rocket scientist and member of the Los Angeles Science Fantasy Society, wrote about the Vril Society in his 1947 essay "Pseudoscience in Naziland," which first appeared in the pulp magazine *Astounding Science Fiction*. Later Pauwels and Bergier expanded upon Ley's assertions. Louis Pauwells and Jacques Bergier, Le Matin des Magiciens, quoted in *Grey Lodge Occult Review* #1, October 2002.

Blavatsky was a stout and homely woman with a restless intellect. She was also charismatic, domineering, and strong-willed. Born Helena von Hahn in 1831, she married a bureaucrat named Nikifor Blavatsky at 18, but soon left him. After a curious odyssey that allegedly took her to Turkey, Greece, Egypt, France, New Orleans, Mexico, South America, the West Indies, England, and Canada in search of spiritual enlightenment, she arrived in Tibet in 1868, where she encountered a band of immortal spiritual masters—the Secret Chiefs, among whom she counted Jesus, Muhammad, and Buddha—who tutored her in the spiritual arts and sciences. Her restless nature eventually led her to America, where she met Henry Steele Olcott, who played a decisive role in her life.

Olcott, a wealthy Manhattan lawyer, first met Blavatsky while investigating the Eddy brothers, two Vermont yokels trying to cash in on the Spiritualism craze. Olcott was impressed by what he believed were Blavatsky's great psychic powers; Blavatsky was impressed by Olcott's bank account. Together, in 1875, the two founded the Theosophical Society in New York.

In 1877, Blavatsky published her two-volume *magnum opus, Isis Unveiled.* She and Olcott then pulled up stakes and moved to India, where they launched *The Theosophist* magazine in 1879. The Society began to establish branches throughout America and Europe, as well as in the European colonies. They recruited other lieutenants, including Annie Besant (a socialist, feminist, and Irish nationalist from London), and the scandalous C. W. Leadbetter (a former Anglican priest). In 1887, the Society launched its official magazine, *Lucifer,* in London. In 1888, Blavatsky published another seminal work, *The Secret Doctrine.* After her death, Besant and Leadbetter took control of the Theosophical Society, which continued to grow, counting among its members baseball's founder Abner Doubleday and legendary inventor Thomas Edison.[28] After a series of scandals, the movement fell on hard times and its influence diminished rapidly as the century progressed.[29]

Ultimately, Theosophy would provide an umbrella under which a whole host of religious, spiritual, psychic, and paranormal trends could come together as a relatively coherent philosophy. It syncretized Eastern and Western teachings, setting the stage for many of the cult movements of the 20th century. The motto of the

---

28   Sylvia Cranston, *H. P. B.: The Extraordinary Life and Influence of Helena Blavatsky* (New York: Putnam, 1993), p. 333. See also Peter Washington, *Madame Blavatsky's Baboon* (New York: Schocken, 1995), pp. 59, 68.

29   James Webb, *The Occult Underground* (Chicago: Open Court,1988), p. 95.

Theosophical Society is: "There is no religion higher than Truth." As with the later New Age movement, Theosophy taught that there was an eternal truth—the *Sanatana Dharma*—at the core of all religious teachings. Among these core teachings are reincarnation, karma, nonphysical planes of existence, pantheism (the presence of God in all matter), humanity's conscious participation in evolution, mind over matter, and apotheosis (the process of achieving ultimate perfection).

Blavatsky was a prolific writer in her lifetime, although critics have noted that her books are rife with plagiarism, most taken from Masonic, Kabbalistic, Gnostic, Eastern, and other esoteric sources. One critic who exhaustively cataloged Blavatsky's writings concluded that "There is not a single dogma or tenet in Theosophy...the source of which cannot be pointed out in the world's literature."[30] At the time of her writing, however, most readers were completely unfamiliar with her source material. Despite her plagiaristic bent, or perhaps because of it, she was, therefore, responsible for bringing an important body of occult traditions to the public.

Other critics have criticized Blavatsky for being overly influenced by Bulwer-Lytton.[31] Although it may be true that her fascination with Isis originated in her reading of *The Last Days of Pompeii*, biographer Peter Washington claims that "it would not be unjust to say that her new religion was virtually manufactured from his pages."[32] And in Blavatsky's second major work, *The Secret Doctrine*, Bulwer-Lytton's fictional supermen begin to morph into objects of religion.

The Secret Doctrine explored the deeper mysteries of science, religion, and psychic power, claiming that the ancient civilizations of Lemuria and Atlantis fell because of their inferior state of spiritual evolution. Theosophy, of course, would lead humanity to its next stage of enlightenment. Blavatsky posited a seven-step progression of human evolution that led to apotheosis. She divided the ages of man according to a series of "root races," describing the present race as fifth in line, following the self-destruction of Atlantis. The sixth race would be superior in every way to our own, and would usher in a New Age of peace and enlightenment.

---

30 From William Emmette Coleman, "The Sources of Madame Blavatsky's Writings," quoted in Vsevolod Sergyeevich Solovyoff, *A Modern Priestess of Isis* (London: Longmans, 1895), pp. 353–366.

31 Michael Howard wrote in his landmark work *The Occult Conspiracy* that "Blavatsky had read Bulwer-Lytton's novels and was very impressed by their Occult content, especially *Zanoni* and *The Last Days of Pompeii*," p. 108.

32 Washington, *Madame Blavatsky*, p. 36.

Theosophy's influence has been incalculable. It created ripples of esoteric thought that eventually blossomed in Victorian occult movements, the work of Freud and Jung, the reemergence of the Freemasons and other secret societies, and finally the Age of Aquarius and the New Age movement. It provided a spiritual venue for the increasingly emancipated women of the West. It had a particularly strong following among artists, writers, and intellectuals, including Gauguin, Mondrian, Kandinsky, Klee, and Pollock. Composers Gustav Mahler and Jean Sibelius were also disciples.[33]

Some of Blavatsky's disciples would form their own influential groups. Rudolph Steiner, a German Theosophist with a strong interest in Christian mysticism, founded the School of Spiritual Science, which soon branched into a number of so-called "Steiner Schools" in Europe and America. The Lucis Trust, founded by Alice Bailey, propounded a globalist philosophy of "World Goodwill." Bailey's group is still affiliated with the United Nations and active in its causes.

Despite Blavatsky's eccentric nature, her impact has been undeniable. Theosophy and its offshoots ultimately created an expectation of greater human potential. And because Blavatsky's teachings of super-humans and Secret Chiefs were far more optimistic than Bulwer-Lytton's prophesied Vril-ya, the ideas expounded in *The Secret Doctrine* gives us a significant precedent for a religious movement based on fictional super-powered beings. In many ways, the conjunction of popular occultism and popular art brought to prominence by Theosophy and related movements has rearranged the very foundation of Western Culture. The first flowering on this conjunction would emerge with a group whose very name has become synonymous with the occult.

THE GOLDEN DAWN

The Hermetic Order of the Golden Dawn was a legendary, but short-lived, occult group founded in 1886, at the height of the spiritual ferment of Victorian England, by a London coroner named William Wynn Westcott. Westcott allegedly obtained hidden writings called the *Cipher Manuscripts* that described rituals

---

33   Silvia Cranston, *H.P.B.: The Extraordinary Life and Influence of Helena Blavatsky* (New York: Putnam, 1993).

and teachings drawn from Kabbalah, astrology, Tarot, geomancy, and alchemy. Westcott "decoded" the manuscripts and showed them to an eccentric Freemason named S.L. McGregor Mathers. Soon after, he and Mathers established the "Isis-Urania Temple of the Hermetic Order of the Golden Dawn" to disseminate the teachings of the manuscripts to occult adepts. Lodges dedicated to Osiris, Horus, Amen-Ra, and Hathor quickly sprung up in England, Scotland, and France. In 1892, Mathers claimed to have come into personal contact with Blavatsky's Secret Chiefs themselves.

It is difficult to ascertain exactly what the Golden Dawn was actually all about. Nonethless, it became very fashionable among the smart set of Victorian London. Freemasonry, ascendant at the time, didn't admit women and exuded a stodgy, establishment aura. But Spiritualism and Theosophy had set the table, and those hungry for a deeper occult experience flocked to the Golden Dawn to dine. Poet William Butler Yeats, actress Florence Farr, theater producer Annie Horniman, pioneering cinematographer Charles Rosher, Irish revolutionary Maud Gonne, famed occultists Israel Regardie and A. E. Waite, and authors Arthur Machen, Arnold Bennett, and Algernon Blackwood were all initiates. Aleister Crowley and Dion Fortune soon joined them.[34] Although most of these names are not familiar to us today, they were all important figures in their own time.

The Golden Dawn had a brief and troubled history. Despite its immediate appeal to spiritual aspirants—or perhaps because of it—dissension soon grew in the ranks. Mathers, a major player in the movement, was considered to be pompous and aloof. Initiates soon determined to bypass him and contact the Secret Chiefs on their own. The arrival on the scene of the controversial Aleister Crowley in 1898 further fractured the Order. The original group split, with Mathers establishing the Alpha and Omega Temple, and A. E. Waite taking command of the remnants of the original charter. Mathers' friendship with Crowley, whom many initiates found so objectionable, soon came to grief, and that duo and Yeats found themselves locked in a three-way battle of occult will that consumed the energies of the movement.

Although the Golden Dawn as a spiritual movement was short-lived, its impact was long-lasting. As with the Rosicrucians, the simple idea of a mystical Order harking back to ancient traditions proved more important and lasting than the

---

34 See Gary Lachman, *Turn Off Your Mind: The Mystic Sixties and the Dark Side of Aquarius* (New York: Disinfo, 2001), pp. 11–12.

organization itself. A secret society comprised of the cognoscenti of the time, reviving what they believed to be the genuine mysteries of the occult past, in one of the world's most powerful imperial cities projects a glamour and appeal to this day.

CHAPTER 8

OCCULT SUPERSTARS

The superhuman characters that populate comic books may have their roots deep in mythology, but their more immediate antecedents can be found in the thoughts and actions of a group of personalities that appeared on the world stage at a crucial point in the development of Western occultism. Larger than life figures like Friedrich Nietzsche, Aleister Crowley, Edgar Cayce, and Harry Houdini all helped set the stage for superheroes to capture the popular imagination.

FRIEDRICH NIETZSCHE

In his legendary work, *Thus Spake Zarathustra*, Friedrich Nietzsche spoke of the *übermensch*, a new post-Christian "overman" who would restore the old values of the Classical world. Übermensch translates into English as "superman." It is here that Jerry Siegel most probably encountered the term.

Nietzsche was born in 1844 in Prussia. After his clergyman father died, he was raised by a grandmother and aunts whose overbearing pomposity appears to have innoculated him against German religiosity, nationalism, and middle-class respectability. Nietzsche became a close friend of the myth-obsessed composer Richard Wagner (1813–1883), whose resurrected heroic myths greatly influenced his writing—although he eventually rejected Wagner's anti-Semitism and affinity for German nationalism.

Nietzsche wrote philosophical tracts against conventional morality, among them his three seminal works *Thus Spoke Zarathustra, The Gay Science,* and *Beyond Good and Evil.* He dismisses the Christian ideal, saying, "there was only one Christian, and he died on the cross." [35] He rejects the Platonic Ideal as an illusion and proclaims that man must elevate himself toward his destiny as the *übermensch.* He argues against absolute morality and advises men to choose their own morals. He prophesies the Superman more as a super-individual than as a super-race, preparing the way for a new kind of savior turned super-hero. "The Superman," he proclaims, "is the meaning of the earth. Let your will say: The Superman shall be the meaning of the earth!"[36]

Nietzsche had a significant influence on esoteric groups and on the development of the modern superhero. Aleister Crowley's prophesies of the "Age of Horus" were greatly influenced by him, and some believe the work of Carl Jung was simply an attempt to systematize Nietzsche's philosophy.[37] It is one of the tragic ironies of history that some of Nietzsche's ideas were appropriated by the National Socialists to promote their Master Race, something Neitzsche himself would surely have deplored.[38]

---

35   Friedrich Nietzsche, *The Antichrist* (Amherst, NY: Prometheus, 2000), part 4, v. 39.

36   Friedrich Nietsche, *Thus Spake Zarathustra* (Whitefish, MT: Kessinger, 2004) Prologue, Sections 1–6.

37   See Richard Noll, *The Aryan Christ:The Secret Life of Carl Jung* (New York: Random House, 1997), pp. 51, 126, 222.

38   Nietzsche himself claimed "the concept of 'pure blood' is the opposite of a harmless concept," in *Twilight of the Idols* (Indianapolis: Hackett, 1997), p. 41.

ALEISTER CROWLEY

One of the most notorious members of the Victorian occult elite was Edward Alexander Crowley, a.k.a. Aleister Crowley, a.k.a. "the Wickedest Man in the World." Not only did Crowley have an enormous influence on the occult, he prepared the way for our modern celebrity-driven culture with his maxim, "Every man and woman is a star,"[39] and his firm belief that there is no such thing as bad publicity.

Crowley was born in 1875 in England. His parents belonged to the Plymouth Brethren, a repressive Christian sect that declared all worldly pleasure (except wealth, of course) to be the tools of the devil. Colin Wilson claims that "[Crowley] spent the rest of his life violently reacting against this view, and preaching—and practicing—the gospel of total sexual freedom."[40] Crowley was a sexual adventurer who eventually turned to the occult, declaring himself the reincarnation of Éliphas Lévi.

In 1898, Crowley was initiated into the Golden Dawn and became a celebrity on the London occult scene. By that time, however, the Order was collapsing and Crowley left it following a series of "magical" battles with McGregor Mathers. He later fictionalized his struggles with Mathers in his seminal occult novel, *Moonchild*. Crowley made a failed attempt to form his own rival order, the *Argentium Astrum* (Silver Star). It was during this time that he devised his famous motto, "Do what thou wilt shall be the whole of the Law," which became the basis of an overarching religious philosophy he called *Thelema*, from the Greek word meaning "true will."

In 1912, Crowley was recruited by Theodor Reuss, head of the Ordo Templi Orientis (OTO), to join the failing quasi-Masonic fraternity. He took the magical name Baphomet (of Templar fame), and became the master of the OTO's British branch. Crowley soon remade the OTO in his own image, developing an elaborate set of sex-magic ceremonies that culminated in a ritual between two male initiates. In the 1920s, he established the infamous Thelemic Abbey in Cefalu, Sicily, from which he was expelled by Italian dictator Benito Mussolini. He later spent time in America, where he attempted to establish the OTO as a legitimate Masonic organization.

---

39   Aleister Crowley, *Book of the Law* (York Beach, ME: Red Wheel/Weiser, 2004), ch. 1, v. 3.

40   Foreword to Sandy Robertson, *The Illustrated Book of the Beast: The Aleister Crowley Scrapbook* (York Beach, ME: Red Wheel/Weiser, 2002), p. 7.

In the end, Crowley's aberrant behavior and notoriety brought him down. Addicted to heroin and booze, perpetually broke and—unkindest of all—sexually impotent, he spent his last days in a boarding house where he died in 1947. The OTO nearly collapsed after his death, but enjoyed a resurgence in the 1960s, finally reestablishing itself in 1971 under the leadership of an avid science-fiction fan named Grady McMurtry.[41]

Crowley claimed to have contacted the original superhero, Horus, while he and his wife, Rose, were living in Cairo in 1904. Reportedly, Rose suddenly went into a trance and began uttering cryptic nonsequiturs like "It's about the Child" and "They are waiting for you." Crowley questioned her about this child and concluded she spoke of Horus. Claiming possession by a spirit named Aiwass, Crowley wrote the *Liber Al*, or *The Book of the Law*, in which he prophesies that the Age of Osiris—the age of kings and churches—is passing and that the Age of Horus will be born in fire and blood. In it, a new race of self-willed supermen will emerge to purge the world of the weak and weak-minded. "Compassion is the vice of kings: stamp down the wretched & the weak," Crowley wrote, "this is the law of the strong: this is our law and the joy of the world."[42]

Although Crowley's prophecy had more to do with his reading of Nietzschean philosophy than with any real understanding of Egyptian theology, it's hard to argue with his insights. Ten years after the *Book of the Law* appeared, the Western world was plunged into a war whose savagery and misery would only be surpassed twenty-five years later when Hitler invaded Poland. At the same time, a new breed of self-willed supermen would enter the popular culture through the pages of *Action Comics*, *Whiz Comics*, and *Detective Comics*. Crowley lived just long enough to see his Horus usher in the New Age, wearing many different masks and fighting under many different names. Unfortunately, Crowley died twelve years before the invention of Spandex.

---

41   George Pendle, *Strange Angel: The Otherworldly Life of Rocket Scientist John Whiteside Parsons* (Orlando, FL: Harcourt, 2005), p. 171.

42   Crowley, *Book of the Law*, ch. II, v 21.

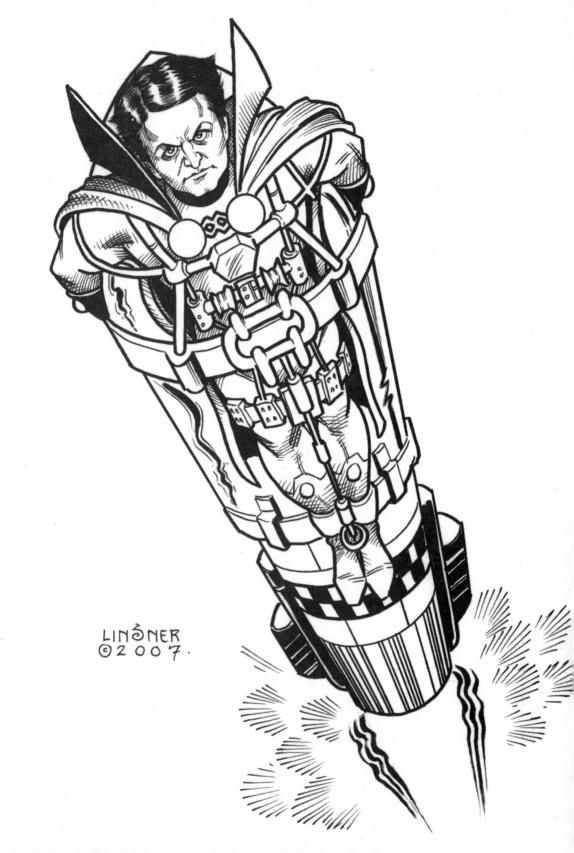

HARRY HOUDINI

Ehrich Weisz, better known as Harry Houdini (1874–1926), was a stage magician who became a real-life superhero. Modeling himself after the legendary French magician Robert Houdin, Houdini began his career at the young age of 17, performing at amusement parks and on the Vaudeville circuit. He soon took his act to Europe, where he became a superstar. Houdini was not only brilliant at prestidigitation; he was also incredibly strong and used his physical prowess in elaborate escape routines in which he broke out of handcuffs, chains, and straitjackets. He was held in such high regard that he was named president of the Society of American Magicians and founded a similar society in London. In *The Secret Life of Houdini: The Making of America's First Superhero*, William Kalush and Larry Sloman reveal that Houdini was also an agent for the British Secret Service.[43] He also became a film star in the 1920 serial *The Master of Mystery*.

Soon after this triumph, however, Houdini suffered the loss of his beloved mother, Cecilia. Distraught over her death, he turned to Spiritualism for comfort. This brought him into contact with Arthur Conan Doyle (of Sherlock Holmes fame), who was dazzled by Houdini's feats, believing them to be the result of supernatural abilities. Houdini denied this, but Doyle would not be dissuaded and later publicized his theories in his 1930 book, *The Edge of the Unknown*. Their friendship ended in acrimony as Doyle continued to champion Spiritualism and Houdini set out to debunk it.

Initially, Houdini was genuinely excited by the possibilities of Spiritualism, but soon recognized the tricks of his own trade being employed by self-professed mediums and psychics—indeed, his wife, Bess, once had a "medium" act. Houdini was enraged by the deception and began a one-man crusade against Spiritualism. He gave lectures exposing the methods employed by phony psychics, at one point offering $10,000 to anyone who could prove genuine psychic phenomena. In 1924, he wrote a landmark exposé against fraudulent mediums entitled *A Magician Among the Spirits*. He even testified before Congress on the subject, calling it "a fraud from start to finish."[44] Houdini returned to performing in 1926, but had lost his edge. He died, aptly, on

---

43   See William Kalush and Larry Sloman, *The Secret Life of Houdini: The Making of America's First Superhero* (New York: Atria, 2006), ch. 6 & 7.

44   See Kalush, Sloman, *The Secret Life of Houdini*, p. 484.

Halloween in 1926, but not before promising his wife that he would escape the bonds of death and return to her.

EDGAR CAYCE

Edgar Cayce (1877–1945), known as "The Sleeping Prophet," was one of America's foremost occult celebrities. He was renowned for his prophecies, medical diagnoses, and religious and philosophic ruminations, which were dictated to an assistant while Cayce was allegedly sleeping or in a trance state. Cayce claimed that the unconscious mind had means of perception that the conscious mind did not. His followers argued that a poorly educated farmboy couldn't possibly have the knowledge of ancient cultures and medicine and philosophy that he displayed, but skeptics countered that Cayce had previously worked in bookstores, and read extensively on the occult and science.[45]

Cayce achieved notoriety for his predictions that Atlantis would rise again in 1968 (it didn't) and that the Atlantean Hall of Records was located beneath the Great Sphinx in Giza (it may be). He also claimed that Atlantis was home to a scientifically advanced society and that, after its destruction, its people fled to Egypt and South America.[46]

The Association for Research and Enlightenment (ARE), created in 1931 to preserve and disseminate Cayce's prophecies and psychic readings, had a major influence on the emerging New Age movement, popularizing occult phenomena like ESP, alternative medicine, meditation, psychic healing, and reincarnation. The ARE is more than a playground for spiritual tourists, however. Two of the world's two most important and influential Egyptologists, American Mark Lehner and Egyptian Antiquities Minister Zahi Hawass, are closely associated with it. Given the eccentric views Cayce held on Ancient Egypt, these associations seem curious until seen in the context of all the esoteric intrigue that, even today, centers in and around Egypt.

---

45 James Randi, *An Encyclopedia of Claims, Frauds, and Hoaxes of the Occult and Supernatural*. (New York: St Martins, 1997), p. 17.

46 Gregory Little and John Van Auken, *Edgar Cayce's Atlantis* (Virginia Beach: ARE., 2006).

PART III

PULP FICTION

CHAPTER 9

LITERARY LUMINARIES

At the same time the occult was infiltrating popular culture, advances in printing technology were creating new forms of mass entertainment. British picture-based "broadsheets," printed woodcuts that addressed current affairs and gossip, spoke to an audience that was predominantly illiterate. These evolved into the "story sheets," sensational prose fiction printed on a single sheet of oversized paper. And these, in turn, evolved into the "penny dreadfuls," so named for their low cost and perceived literary quality. The penny dreadfuls, which appeared sometime in the 1830s, were usually eight pages long and sold to a mostly working-class audience, with salacious titles like *The Smuggler King* and *The Merry Wives of London.* Serial killer Sweeney Todd earned his own title in 1846, and other colorful stars soon emerged, including the occult-themed *Varney the Vampire,* which predated *Dracula,* and Spring-Heeled Jack, the first detective character with a secret identity, who appeared in 1867.

Variations on the penny dreadful appeared in American cities, where they morphed again into long-form prose as the dime novel. This format, which usually featured crude drawings to accompany the crude text, was pioneered by publishers Beadle & Adams during the Civil War, and became especially popular with Union Army soldiers hungry for cheap, accessible entertainment.

Early dime novels fictionalized real-life characters like Davy Crockett, Daniel Boone, Kit Carson, and Buffalo Bill and real-life cowgirl Calamity Jane. The rise of bandits like Billy the Kid and the James Gang, and the subsequent exploits of the ruthless Pinkerton Detective Agency, raised the prestige of lawmen and detectives in the American imagination and made them regulars in the popular press. One early dime-novel hero was Frank Merriwell, a wholesome schoolboy who moonlighted as a detective. Another was clean-living Nick Carter, who first appeared in *New York Weekly* in 1886 and later became a major pulp-fiction star.

The rise of this new mass medium created a new class of writers that specialized in the down-market fiction. The new junk aesthetic—violent, garish, racy, and often racist—found its apotheosis in the 20th century with the rise of comic books. But first, the genre was refined by the hands of master fiction writers—luminaries like Edgar Allan Poe, Arthur Conan Doyle, Jules Verne, H. G. Wells, and Bram Stoker, many of whom were fascinated by the occult.

EDGAR ALLAN POE

Edgar Allan Poe (1809–1849) is perhaps the most important and influential figure in the development of modern genre fiction. Born in Boston to itinerant actor parents, Poe would die young. After being thrown out of the University of Virginia for gambling, he joined the army and was later dishonorably discharged from West Point. Despite this inauspicious beginning, however, Poe displayed a prodigious gift for writing and soon began a career as a literary critic.

Tragedy haunted Poe throughout his career. His marriage to his thirteen-year-old cousin ended in her early death, which critics believe inspired his epic poem *The Raven*, which was published in 1845. An 1840 short-story collection featured his tale *The Fall of the House of Usher*, a classic of the gothic horror genre.

The following year, Poe pioneered the detective story with *The Murders in the Rue Morgue*, which featured the French detective C. Auguste Dupin. His work had a crucial influence on Arthur Conan Doyle, creator of Sherlock Holmes, who claimed, "Each [of Poe's detective stories] is a root from which a whole literature has developed. . . . Where was the detective story until Poe breathed the breath of life into it?"[47] Poe's work also made a lasting impression on Jules Verne, H. G. Wells, and H. P. Lovecraft. Indeed, despite his short and unhappy life, his legacy has had an incalculable influence on almost every writer of genre fiction to follow.

ARTHUR CONAN DOYLE

Arthur Conan Doyle (1859–1930) was not only the creator of the most famous fictional detective in the English language, he was also Spiritualism's most prominent advocate. Born in Edinburgh to Irish parents, Doyle was educated at Jesuit-run schools. When he entered university, however, he renounced his parents' faith and became a spiritual tourist, dabbling in Theosophy, Rosicrucianism, Hermeticism, and Mormonism. He even became interested in fairies, in 1921 writing a book inspired by the Cottingley fairy photographs called *The Coming of the Fairies*. Doyle eventually became an opthamologist and was initiated into the Masonic order.

In 1887, Doyle made his first foray into popular fiction with *A Study in Scarlet*, which featured the debut of Sherlock Holmes. Doyle eventually wrote sixty stories featuring the aristocratic detective. Intellectually brilliant, a master of disguise, and physically adept in the gentlemanly fighting arts, Holmes was very much a superhero. Such was Holmes' prowess that Doyle felt obliged, in 1893, to create a prototype supervillain named Professor Moriarty who was worthy to act as his nemesis (*The Adventure of the Final Problem*).

Following the death of his wife in 1906, and the loss of his son and several other male relatives on the killing fields of the first World War, Doyle turned to Spiritualism for solace. He wrote several books on the subject, including *The New Revelation* (1918), *The Vital Message* (1919), and *The History of Spiritualism* (1926). He became a regular contributor to the Spiritualist magazine, *The Light* and

---

47   "Address before the Poe Centennial Celebration Dinner of the Author's Society, March 1909," taken from Frank S. Frederick, *The Poe Encyclopedia* (Westport CT: Greenwood Press, 1997), p. 103.

traveled the world consorting with mediums, contributing money to Spiritualist organizations like the Society for Psychical Research, of which he became a
member. He later included Spiritualist themes in his fiction, most notably his
1926 novel *The Land of Mists*. Such was Doyle's celebrity that he was named Hon-
orary President at the 1925 International Spiritualist Congress in Paris. Upon his
death, psychic researcher Harry Price wrote in the Spiritualist magazine *Psychic
Research:* "The passing of Sir Arthur Conan Doyle . . . removes the greatest personality Spiritualism ever possessed—or is ever likely to possess."[48]

JULES VERNE

The French writer Jules Verne (1828–1905) is a pivotal figure in the history of
science fiction. His novels married high adventure and heroic fantasy, and anticipated modern technology and space travel in such detail that some today consider
him a prophet. Sci-fi legend Ray Bradbury observes that "we are all, in one way or
another, the children of Jules Verne."[49]

Verne set out to study law, but found himself fascinated by breakthroughs in science and spent most of his free time reading up on geology, engineering, and
astronomy. In 1863, he published his first novel, *Five Weeks in a Balloon*, which
was followed in quick succession by what most consider to be his greatest clas-
sics: *Journey to the Center of the Earth* (1864), *From the Earth to the Moon* (1866),
Twenty Thousand Leagues Under the Sea (1870), and *Around the World in Eighty
Days* (1873).

Verne's fictional science is eerily accurate. *From the Earth to the Moon* tells the
story of a group of scientists who devise a cannon capable of sending a capsule
to the Moon. The Moon-shots are launched from Florida, not far from Cape
Canaveral and, as with the Apollo missions, the returning space craft splashes
down in the Pacific Ocean. In 1886, Verne predicted air travel and a militarily
imposed new world order in *Clipper in the Clouds*. His unpublished work, *Paris
in the 20th Century*, written in 1863, foretold steel skyscrapers, bullet trains, auto-
mobiles, calculators, and even a precursor to the Internet. Needless to say, the

---

48   Harry Price, "Sir Arthur Conan Doyle Obituary," *Psychic Research*, August, 1930.

49   Ray Bradbury's foreword to William Butcher, *Verne's Journey to the Centre of the Self: Space and
Time in the "Voyages extraordinaires"* (New York: Macmillan and St Martin's Press, 1990), p. 8.

manuscript caused quite a stir when unearthed in 1989. Significantly, Verne is believed to have been a Freemason and to have had contacts with both the Rosicrucians and the Golden Dawn.[50]

H. G. WELLS

A hundred years after they were written, Herbert George Wells' science fiction continues to attract audiences in big-budget Hollywood movies. Born in 1866 in England, Wells grew up poor, but distinguished himself as a brilliant student. At the age of 17, he became a teacher and obtained a scholarship to the Normal School of Science in London, where he studied biology under T. H. Huxley, who was nicknamed "Darwin's Bulldog" for his zealous defense of evolutionary theory. Wells wrote extensively on political and scientific topics before trying his hand at fiction.

The continuing power and appeal of Wells' fiction lies in its prescience. In 1895, his first novel, *The Time Machine*, anticipated Einstein's theory of relativity in its portrayal of the breaking of the time barrier. It also offered an inversion of the Vril-ya, presenting a future Earth inhabited by two races: the gentle Eloi who lived above ground, and the bestial cannibalistic Morlocks, who lived beneath it. In 1896, Wells published *The Island of Dr. Moreau*, which anticipated genetic engineering and recombinant DNA. The following year, he offered a character with a kind of superpower in *The Invisible Man*. One year later, *War of the Worlds* became the first popular novel to deal with the theme of interplanetary war, which became a staple topic of superhero comic books.

The First Men on the Moon (1901) was prophetic in its description of the methodology of space flight and *The War in the Air* (1908) foresaw the importance of air forces in combat. Wells combined these two themes in his novel *The Shape of Things To Come* (1933), which was adapted into a remarkably advanced and prophetic film in 1936. *Things to Come* told of a disastrous world war that plunges Europe into a new Dark Age. Civilization is saved by a cabal of Airmen who go underground during the war and return to impose a new technocratic world order. In the film, the Airman Oswald Cabal (Raymond Massey) proclaims a

---

50   Verne's contacts are explored in Michel Lamy's *The Secret Message of Jules Verne: Decoding His Masonic, Rosicrucian, and Occult Writings* (Rochester, VT: Destiny, 2007).

new order based on the "Freemasonry of Science." The Airmen are depicted as superheroes and saviors of humanity, and salvation comes in the form of global federalism. "World government had been plainly coming for some years," Wells wrote, "although it had been endlessly feared and murmured against, it found no opposition anywhere."[51] Wells didn't live to see his prediction come true, and was severely disheartened by the Second World War.

Wells' greatest passion was for the idea of a new world order that offered science as the new religion. He had various contacts with spiritualists like the Theosophists and political radicals like the Fabian Socialists. He soon parted ways with the Fabians, however, and advocated instead an "open conspiracy" of world federalists. In 1928, Wells wrote: "The political world of the Open Conspiracy must weaken, efface, incorporate and supersede existing governments. . . . It will be a world religion."[52] Science fiction was merely Wells' vehicle for popularizing his radical scientific and political ideas. Although he claimed to be an agnostic throughout whole life, books like *Things to Come* reveal the gods to whom he bowed.

BRAM STOKER

One of the best-known Victorian-era occultists was the Irish-born novelist Bram Stoker (1847–1912). Stoker was raised in Dublin and later attended Trinity College. While working in London managing the Lyceum Theatre, Stoker was initiated into both the Golden Dawn and The Societas Rosicruciana. He may also have been a Mason, although this is undocumented.

Stoker is best known for his classic 1897 novel *Dracula*, which popularized the myth of the vampire. The novel has become a metaphor unto itself. Stoker portrayed his Count Dracula as a charming aristocrat with a powerful sexual allure, not as a slobbering ghoul. An entire subculture has sprung up around the vampire myth, fueled by American novelist Anne Rice's hijacking of the theme.

---

51   H. G. Wells, *The Shape of Things to Come: The Ultimate Revolution* (New York: Corgi, 1979 reprint), p. 327.

52   W. Warren Wagar, *The Open Conspiracy: H.G. Wells on World Revolution* (Westport, CT: Praeger, 2001), p. 122.

Several stage plays and film adaptations of the novel have been made, and there was also a popular Marvel Comics series in the 1970s called *The Tomb of Dracula*.

Although *Dracula* is Stoker's best-known occult novel, he also wrote two other highly influential works—*The Jewel of Seven Stars* (1903) and *The Lair of the White Worm* (1911). The first concerned the possession of a young English girl by the evil spirit of an ancient Egyptian queen. Its theme of spiritual transmigration and Egyptian sorcery arose from Stoker's involvement with groups like the Golden Dawn. The novel became the basis for several film adaptations, the best of which is the 1971 *Blood From the Mummy's Tomb*. The second was a novel of pagan revanchism that prefigured Lovecraft, with a cult that worships a giant subterranean worm led by aristocratic Lady March. The book was made into a sexually charged Ken Russell film in 1988.

The gothic atmospheres of Poe, the detective hero of Doyle, the fanciful technologies of Verne, the prescient science of Wells, and the forthright spiritualism of Stoker would all come together in the middle of the next century to provide a fictional backdrop for the superheroes of the "pulps."

CHAPTER 10

THE PULPS

The "pulps," so named for the cheap grade of paper on which they were printed, were the direct descendants of the penny dreadfuls and dime novels. In fact, the term "pulp fiction" has come to define low-quality genre fiction in general. Comics, B-movies, and genre-driven TV shows all have thematic roots in the pulp magazines.

Frank Munsey is generally credited with inventing the "pulp-wood magazine" at the end of the 19th century. Munsey came to New York from Maine to enter the rapidly expanding publishing market. His first offering was an adventure-story magazine called *The Golden Argosy* (later, simply *Argosy*) that first appeared in December 1882. Dime novels were still the preferred format for adventure stories, but pulps had the advantage of qualifying for less-costly second-class postage. The new format evolved quickly to a standard 128-page magazine, with a stapled or glued binding and a coated-stock cover. The early pulps generally featured Western and detective stories, with a smattering of war or high-adventure offerings.

Several publishers entered the burgeoning market, among them Street and Smith, Popular Publications, Culture Publications, and the A. A. Wyn Group (later renamed Ace). Two early pulp firms later became important comic publishers—Dell, founded by George Delacorte, and Fawcett, run by Wilford and Roscoe Fawcett. The pulps laid the groundwork for the comic boom by spawning organized "fandom." Fans formed clubs around favorite titles, genres, and heroes. The Letters pages in the pulps became the *de facto* clubhouses of these early fans. Later, fans of the sci-fi pulps formed influential groups like the Los Angeles Science Fantasy Society, which helped forge an alliance between pulp fiction and the occult.

Pulp publishers compensated for poor paper and printing quality by using colorful, eye-catching cover illustrations. Cover artists like Virgil Finlay, Margaret Brundage, Frank R. Paul, Frank Kelly Freas, and H. J. Ward became stars in their own right, able to sell a magazine solely on the basis of their illustrations. Editors often commissioned a painting first and hired a writer to dream up a story around it.

The pulps did not emerge in a vacuum. American popular culture had always been at odds with its Puritan heritage. In 1919, the 18th Amendment prohibited the sale of alcohol in an attempt to clamp down on the rapid expansion of social and cultural liberalism that followed the First World War. The Volstead Act, as it came to be known, was answered by an explosive reaction that found expression in jazz, illicit booze, and sexually explicit fiction. By default, the pulps became a medium for all types of forbidden expression, including occult themes. Many pulp writers, like Talbot Mundy, were actively involved in the occult; many others were fascinated by it.[53] Pulp heroes all tended to live on the edge of cultural correctness and seemed to delight in testing social norms.

HARD-BOILED

One of the earliest pulp heroes was the aristocratic detective Nick Carter, who first appeared in *Nick Carter Weekly* in 1886. Carter became the top sleuth for Street

---

53 See Ron Goulart, *Cheap Thrills: An Informal History of the Pulp Magazine* (New Rochelle, NY: Arlington House, 1972), p. 37.

and Smith. His yarns usually involved rescuing some posh young deb from the depredations of mobsters, sickos, perverts, and cultists. Carter survived in one incarnation or another into the 1960s, when he became a James Bond-type spook. Street and Smith launched *Detective Story Magazine* in 1915, which was so popular it earned itself a weekly release schedule and spawned a host of clones.

In 1920, *Black Mask*, one of the most important detective pulps, debuted—created, strangely enough, by the legendary social critic H. L. Mencken. *Black Mask* heralded the arrival of the hard-boiled detective—bare-knuckled heroes like Carroll John Daly's Race Williams—and paved the way for the more aggressive superheroes of DC Comics. Dashiell Hammett's classic Sam Spade novella *The Maltese Falcon* and Raymond Chandler's early Philip Marlowe yarns both appeared in it.[54]

TARZAN

The first true superstar to emerge from the pulps, however, was Edgar Rice Burrough's Tarzan, who first appeared in the October 1912 issue of *All Story*. Tarzan was actually young Lord Greystoke, scion of an aristocratic family marooned in the jungle after a mutiny at sea. Tarzan, whose name means "Skin-Boy," becomes the surrogate son of a gorilla named Kala, whose own baby had died. The *Tarzan* series was an enormous hit, spawning over eighty-eight film adaptations, starting with a series of silent films in 1918. The definitive Tarzan film series began in 1932 with *Tarzan the Ape-Man*, featuring Olympic swimmer Johnny Weismuller in the title role.[55]

Tarzan has also been a major comic character since 1931. Both Marvel and DC have had a crack at him, among several others. Alan Moore has included him (under a different name) in his Victorian-era superhero series, *The League of Extraordinary Gentlemen.*

---

54 Hammett created the comic strip *Secret Agent X-9* with future *Flash Gordon* artist Alex Raymond in 1934, featuring a dashing superspy and master of disguise. In many ways, X-9 was a direct prototype for James Bond.

55 Weismuller played Tarzan in twelve films, and was later replaced by several lesser-known actors. More recently, Disney had a major hit with an animated adaptation of the character. Two direct-to-video sequels and an animated TV series soon followed. More recently, Disney adapted their film as a Broadway musical.

Burroughs reportedly based Tarzan on the myth of Romulus and Remus, the legendary founders of Rome. He presented Tarzan as an idealized man, a noble savage free of the corruption of civilization—almost, in fact, Christlike. Burroughs inserted religious and esoteric themes in many of his other characters as well, and occult themes are woven throughout the Tarzan stories. Artist Hal Foster explicitly introduced themes from the ancient mysteries into his *Tarzan* newspaper strip in the famed "Egyptian Saga" storyline, in which the hero encounters a "lost world" of ancient Egyptian descendants. An injured Tarzan is mystically restored by a priestess of Venus, who believes him to be an incarnation of Thoth, god of the apes. He undergoes an occult initiation in the temple of Isis, passes a series of tests to prove his kinship to the sacred beasts, and is finally greeted by the Egyptians as an avatar of the god.[56] Foster's next strip, *Prince Valiant,* still runs to this day. A knight in the mythical court of King Arthur, Valiant's mentor is Merlin, history's most famous wizard. Of course, the Arthurian mythos was of particular interest to 19th-century occultists.

GLADIATORS: THE PULP SUPERHEROES

The Thirties were a miserable time for America. Urban violence, mass immigration, the Depression, and political radicalism at home and abroad kept Americans in a state of fear and anxiety. Prohibition empowered organized crime. Corruption and graft compromised local and state authorities. The tentacles of the syndicates reached deep into labor and municipal unions, social institutions, and even into the Catholic Church. As the worries of the American public grew, so did the need for comforting fantasies of powerful, decisive men who could set things right. Pulp heroes got more powerful and more outlandish as publishers competed for readers. As Les Daniels wrote, "the rise of superheroes like the Shadow, Doc Savage, Spider and the others coincided with the downfall of public figures in the Depression."[57]

In a sense, the superhero became a historical necessity in America. As Les Daniels wrote: "The rise of crime in the US and the emergence of dictators in Europe

---

56   Hal Foster, *Tarzan*, November 20, 1932–March 5, 1933.

57   Les Daniels, *DC Comics : A Celebration of the World's Favorite Comic Book Heroes* (New York : Billboard Books, 2003), p. 14.

were also regarded by the pulp publishers and their writers as forces that could be combated only by men of supernormal powers."[58] The model for the pulp hero who could save this ailing world was supplied by sci-fi novelist/social critic Philip Wylie in his novels *The Gladiator* (1930) and *The Savage Gentleman* (1932).

The Gladiator told the story of Hugo Danner, a professor's son subjected to his father's genetic experiments. Hugo develops superpowers—he can jump "higher'n a house" and run "faster'n a train," (as opposed to being "able to leap tall buildings in a single bound" or "more powerful than a locomotive")—but is unable to find a constructive outlet for them. Danner excels at football and on the battlefield during World War I, but is persecuted when he demonstrates his powers while rescuing a person trapped in a bank vault, and becomes discouraged while working in politics. His isolation leads him to join an archaeological expedition in South America, where he is struck by lightning and killed after cursing God.

Wylie's fiction is fairly downbeat and pessimistic, reflecting his dim view of American society. He seemed to think that human society was not ready to accept a superman, and that superpowers could only lead to isolation. Although *The Gladiator* may not sound like much today, but it electrified young readers in 1930, particularly the future creators of Superman.

After *The Gladiator*, pulp heroes began to acquire superhuman powers. Some of them did so by scientific means, others through the occult arts. The time for ordinary human abilities was past; so was the time for ordinary street clothes. Boredom with look-alike private eyes led to the development of garish outfits, which also helped to distinguish, and therefore market, the individual heroes. No one could confuse characters like the Shadow, Doc Savage, the Avenger, the Spider, or Black Bat with Nick Carter or Philip Marlowe. A quick glance at the cover told readers exactly what kind of adventure to expect.

THE SHADOW

It was in this atmosphere that America's first superstar crimefighter, the Shadow, arose. The Shadow appeared in 1930 as a narrator/announcer on a radio mystery program, but soon became a character in his own right with his own radio adventures and a pulp magazine published by Street and Smith. The Shadow was a sort

---

58   Les Daniels, *Marvel: Five Fabulous Decades of the World's Greatest Comics* (New York: Abradale, 1991), p. 21.

of gothic variation on costumed characters like the Scarlet Pimpernel and Zorro. The Shadow dressed all in black, punctuated with menacing splashes of red. A fedora and scarf obscured most of his face so the only visible features were his piercing eyes and aquiline nose. He was merciless, dispatching his foes with twin .45 automatics. He struck terror into the hearts of fictional criminals, satisfying the need for bloody vengeance felt by many urban Americans during the chaos of the Depression. He also possessed mystical powers learned during his travels in the Orient, including the ability to "cloud men's minds."

The Shadow was created by Walter Gibson, who wrote under the alias Maxwell Grant. A prolific author, Gibson had a deep and abiding interest in occultism and wrote onstage patter for magicians like Houdini, Blackstone, and Thurston, as well as works on mysticism and divination. He drew on all these interests to create the Shadow, molding a character who was a "mystery in himself." The Shadow combined Houdini's penchant for escapes with the hypnotic power of Tibetan mystics and the stage magicians' talent for creating illusions. "Such a character," he notes, "would have unlimited scope when confronted by surprise situations, yet all could be brought within the range of credibility."[59] Gibson was also inspired by Rene Lupin, a master of disguise from the French pulps.

The Shadow was featured in two feature films, in 1937 and 1938, as well as a 1940 serial starring Victor Jory. Street and Smith launched a *Shadow* comic quite late in the game (1949) and DC Comics revived the character in 1972, and again in 1985. An unfortunate film made in 1994 proved him a hero for a bygone age. But in his prime, the Shadow inspired a horde of masked and/or superpowered avengers. It's safe to say that without the Shadow there never would have been a Batman.

DOC SAVAGE

As the Shadow is the most obvious precursor of Batman, so Doc Savage is the most immediate inspiration for Superman. Doc Savage was also inspired by a Philip Wylie novel, *The Savage Gentleman*. Nicknamed the "Man of Bronze" (as opposed to the "Man of Steel"), the character first appeared in *Doc Savage Magazine* #1 in 1933. Writer Lester Dent (writing under the alias Kenneth Robeson) aptly described him as having "the clue-following ability of Sherlock Holmes, the

---

59   William V. Rauscher, *Walter B. Gibson: Wizard of Words* (Woodbury, NJ: Mystic Light Press, 1996).

muscular tree-swinging ability of Tarzan . . . and the morals of Jesus Christ"[60]
The first issue's cover pictured the hero standing in a Mayan ruin, reinforcing the occult and mystical overtones of his milieu.

Doc Savage's origin is pseudoscientific in nature. Like the Gladiator, he is trained by scientists to perform at peak human efficiency. But he also travels to Tibet for the prerequisite study of yoga and hypnotism. Savage then inherits a vast fortune, makes his headquarters on the 86th floor of the Empire State Building. Like the Shadow, he and his entourage fight against evil. He also uses his fortune to invent all sorts of technological gadgets, including then-fanciful items like telephone answering machines, night-vision goggles, and automatic handguns. Doc Savage was popular in the Thirties, and enjoyed a renaissance in the Sixties with a series of paperback reprints. He appeared sporadically in other media—comics, radio, even a 1974 feature film. But, like the Shadow, Savage is essentially a relic of the Pulp Age, made irrelevant by commercial air travel and mass media. The Shadow and Doc Savage were followed by copy-cat heroes like the Whisperer, the Avenger, the Spider (cited by Stan Lee as an inspiration for Spider-Man), the Phantom Detective, the Ghost, the Black Hood, Captain Satan, even a female superhero called Domino Lady. As competition increased, these pulp superheroes became ever more flamboyant.

Ironically, all these masked heroes existed on the fringes of the mainstream society they had come to save—masks were for crooks, not lawmen. The pulp superheroes were dangerous, in marked contrast to the wholesome comic book superheroes that came later. They were usually men of science who fight against occult enemies, despite their own occult "mental powers." Sorcerers and witch doctors were common enemies of the Shadow and Doc Savage. By contrast, the comic-book superheroes of the 1940s were often occult-powered creatures who spend a great deal of their time fighting against evil men of science. World War II brought both undreamed of destruction and unparalleled technological advance. The quaint old pulp heroes, with their Theosophical hoodoo and pseudo-scientific gadgets, were no longer relevant. It was time for new gods.

---

60   Quoted in Goulart, *Cheap Thrills*, p. 78.

AMAZING STORIES

Sci-fi was being published in the pulps "years before they knew what to call it."[61] Hugo Gernsback, a wealthy Jewish immigrant with a degree in electrical engineering, pioneered the genre in his pulp *Amazing Stories* in 1926. He called the stories "Scientifiction" which he described as "the Jules Verne, H. G. Wells, Edgar Allan Poe type of story."[62] Gernsback's engineering background ensured that *Amazing Stories* placed a heavy emphasis on gadgetry, in turn influencing other tech-geek magazines like *Popular Mechanics*. Gernsback is considered so vital to the development of science fiction that sci-fi's highest literary award, the Hugo, is named for him.

For young dreamers mired in the misery of the Great Depression, *Amazing Stories* offered a compelling vision of the future. "World of Tomorrow" propaganda became an important government tool for keeping citizens looking beyond the trying times of the Thirties. The yarns in *Amazing Stories* and its imitators often depict a future free from poverty and disease, leaving readers free to worry about more exotic dangers like space aliens and mad scientists.

In 1928, *Amazing* featured Philip Nowlan's first Buck Rogers story and, later, the first stories by sci-fi pioneer E. E. "Doc" Smith (*The Skylark of Space*). Smith's stories of space-faring brotherhoods had a significant influence on comics in the 1950s, especially *Green Lantern* and *The Legion of Super-Heroes*. Gernsback launched *Scientific Detective Monthly* in January 1930, introducing the first of the modern invincible crime fighters, "Miller Rand, the Electrical Man," a clear progenitor of Marvel Comic's later Iron Man.

Many prominent sci-fi writers—Arthur C. Clarke, Robert Heinlein, Isaac Asimov, and Ray Bradbury—got their start in the sci-fi pulps and went on to influence both comics and the movies. The imagery and art of the sci-fi pulps had a huge impact on comic artists, who often recycled images directly from the pulps to the comics. The flying spacemen often portrayed on the covers of sci-fi pulps like

---

61   Goulart, *Cheap Thrills*, p. 159.

62   Peter Haining, *The Classic Era of American Pulp Magazines* (Chicago: Chicago Review Press, 2001), p. 156.

Amazing, Startling Stories, and *Thrilling Wonder Stories* prefigured superheroes like Superman and Captain Marvel. As the new comic Olympians grew in popularity, however, they did so at the expense of the sci-fi pulps.

WEIRD TALES

As the comics continued to peel away their readership, the sci-fi pulps responded by adding sex and horror to the mix. Sci-fi covers went from portraying future technocratic wonders to hosting a bevy of beauties bedeviled by bug-eyed monsters. In fact, the industry found that "pulp" and "horror" were two words that went together beautifully—or more accurately, hideously. Horror and pulp fiction consummated their ghastly marriage in *Weird Tales,* first published in 1922 by Clark Henneberger, an obsessive Edgar Allen Poe fan who saw opportunities in the pulp market for fantasy and horror.

Weird Tales was nothing if not transgressive. Occult-themed tales leavened with strong sexual and countercultural content were its stock in trade. The magazine exuded a decadent aura, with nudity and depictions of occult activity featured in cover art. *Weird Tales* floundered commercially in its infancy, but soon achieved notoriety when a tale about necrophilia (C.M. Eddy's "The Loved Dead") got the magazine banned in 1924.

Weird Tales popularized the occult detective sub-genre with series like Seabury Quinn's Jules De Grandin stories. It also gave birth to the sword-and-sorcery genre—particularly the *Conan* tales of Robert E. Howard—and a new kind of ritualized occult horror typified by the arcane writings of H. P. Lovecraft and Clark Ashton Smith. As if all this weren't enough, it also acted as the launching pad for the careers of Fritz Leiber (*Fahfrd and the Grey Mouser*) and Robert Bloch (*Psycho*).

Weird Tales became notorious for its sexy and surreal cover paintings, particularly those of Chicago housewife Margaret Brundage. Fiorello LaGuardia chased Brundage's naked women off *Weird Tales'* covers, only to unleash a parade of occultic images far more damaging to impressionable minds than a little naked flesh. Hannes Bok decorated the publication's covers with chthonic tableaux that seemed like photos from the depths of hell. J. Allan St. John, who worked in a lush and impressionistic fantasy style similar to legends like Arthur Rackham and Edmund Dulac, followed suit.

Like any successful pulp, *Weird Tales* inspired a host of imitators. *Ghost Stories*, from MacFadden Co., claimed to publish "true" ghost stories; *Tales of Magic And Mystery* (1927) specialized in stories of the occult and featured articles by Howard Thurston;[63] *Strange Tales* (1931) and *Strange Stories* (1939) unleashed hastily written tales of occult horror[64] and *Unknown* (Street and Smith) treated the occult as "a kind of science operating under it own laws."[65] Although *Weird Tales* and its occult-oriented progeny fell by the wayside during the idyllic Eisenhower years, they had an incalculable influence on horror, sci-fi, and comic books, as well as on Neopaganism and the occult in general.

Like the comics (and rock 'n' roll, and video games), the pulps fell under the scrutiny of the censors. In the early 1930s, President Herbert Hoover sought to divert attention from his disastrous economic policies by forming the Committee on Recent Social Trends, which set about investigating moral turpitude in the pulps. The American public was more concerned with staving off financial ruin, however, so when the effort went nowhere, moral guardians like Fiorello La Guardia took up the cause and were more successful. "By the start of the 40s, with the nation on the verge of war, there was a kind of moral backlash," says Harry Steeger, "it was the social pressures that killed off the pulps."[66] But it was also economic pressure. The pulps were pushed off the racks by comic books aimed at younger readers and paperback books aimed at older ones.

The pulps never really died, however. They simply morphed into post-war magazines like *Man's Life* and *Stag*, many of which morphed again into the skin mags of the late 1960s, inspired by the efforts of a young midwesterner named Hugh Hefner. And vestiges of the pulps still linger in the form of digest-sized story magazines like *Analog*, *Asimov's Science Fiction*, and *Ellery Queen's Mystery Magazine*.

---

63 *Tales* editor Walter Gibson would soon become famous for his work on the Shadow. See Haining, *Classic Era*, p. 116.

64 *Strange Stories*, helmed by future *Superman* editor Mort Weisinger, featured a regular column entitled "The Black Arts," written by one Lucifer, who claimed to be a "Famous Authority on Witchcraft and Black Magic." *Strange Tales* included a letters column called "The Cauldron" that acted as "a Meeting Place for Sorcerers and Apprentices." Haining, *Classic Era*, p. 121.

65 Haining, *Classic Era*, p. 124. Sci-fi scribes like Robert A. Heinlein (*Starship Troopers*) and Theodore Sturgeon (*Star Trek*) also dabbled in the dark arts in *Unknown's* pages, as did future *Conan* chronicler L. Sprague de Camp.

66 Haining, *Classic Era*, p. 152.

CHAPTER 11

RACONTEURS

In their heyday, the pulps attracted a wide range of authors, with a wide range of talent and varying degrees of interest in the occult. Among them were luminaries like Edgar Rice Burroughs, fantasy giants like H. P. Lovecraft and Robert E. Howard, and serious occultists like Dion Fortune and Sax Rohmer. All of them contributed spiritually and materially to the coming comic craze by combining heroic fiction with themes taken from the ancient mysteries.

EDGAR RICE BURROUGHS

Edgar Rice Burroughs (1875–1950) is a pivotal figure in the development of the superhero. And although it is unclear what direct associations he may have had with occult or esoteric groups, it is certain that his work is rife with mystical themes.[67] Scion of a middle-class Masonic family, Burroughs left home after high school to seek adventure. He worked on a cattle ranch, did a stint in the military, and held a series of menial jobs, until boredom and financial pressure finally inspired him to try his hand at writing. He sold his first story, "Under the Moons of Mars," to *All-Story Magazine* in 1912.

Burroughs' Mars yarns are alternately known as the *John Carter, Warlord of Wars* series or, among hardcore fans, the *Barsoom* series. What is most remarkable about the stories is that Carter reaches the red planet, not by rocket, but by using the occult art of astral projection. He describes this mystical process: "I closed my eyes, stretched out my arms toward the god of my vocation and felt myself drawn with the suddenness of thought through the trackless immensity of space."[68] Not only can Carter astrally project himself into space, he is also immortal. Because of the lighter gravity on Mars, he is a superman there, and becomes a warlord when he marries the Martian princess Dejah Thoris.

Fritz Leiber commented on the esoteric roots of Burroughs' space-faring hero, saying: "I got the impression that Edgar Rice Burroughs had found in Theosophy a rich source of background materials for his *Mars* books; his chief job seemed to have been adding canals and atmosphere plants."[69] Leiber also notes other themes in the *Mars* stories that were initially popularized in Theosophist literature, including "instantaneous interplanetary travel by thought power; each planet having its characteristic ray . . . and airships held aloft by tanks of these rays; Methuselah-size lifetimes of one thousand years . . . creation of phantom and living matter by thought power . . . and finally the oppression and persecution of wise freethinkers by an evil priesthood." Sword-and-sorcery legend L. Sprague De Camp added that "altogether life in the Theosophical Atlantis resembles nothing

---

67   Whatever Burroughs' enthusiasms, he seems to have kept them in his novels. Burroughs had no known association with any occult groups or secret societies (unless, of course, they were *truly* secret societies). Yet noted anti-cult activist Carl Raschke, Dean of Religious Studies at the University of Denver, goes so far to claim that writers like "Edgar Rice Burroughs, progenitor of the Tarzan and Jane tales, were practicing occultists." See Carl Raschke, *Painted Black: From Drug Killings to Heavy Metal Music* (San Francisco: Harper & Row, 1990), p. 183.

68   Edgar Rice Burroughs, *A Princess of Mars* (New York: Modern Library, 2003 edition), chapter 2.

69   In an article entitled "John Carter: Sword of Theosophy," which ran in the fanzine *Amra* in 1959. Leiber noted that a pamphlet on Theosophy's alternative history "sounded to me very much like good old Barsoom with its green men, white priests, levitating battleships, egg-laying princesses, and all the rest."

so much as life on Mars as pictured in the Martian novels of Edgar Rice Burroughs."[70] Burroughs himself claimed that all of the Martian races descended from the "Tree of Life," a term borrowed from the Kabbalah.

Later in the same year that the *Mars* stories appeared, Burroughs turned the pulp world on its ear with the publication of his novella, *Tarzan of the Apes*. Tarzan was a huge hit and brought Burroughs all sorts of merchandizing opportunities. He formed his own company, and aggressively licensed his characters to radio, movies, comics, and all manner of enterprises. A pioneer of saturation marketing, he provided a model for later companies like Disney and DC Comics. As *The New York Times* noted "before Tarzan, nobody understood just how big, how ubiquitous, how marketable a star could be."[71]

Following the success of *Tarzan* and *John Carter*, Burroughs introduced the *Pellucidar* novels, starting with *At the Earth's Core* in 1922. In this tale, a group of scientists discover Pellucidar, a world inhabited by dinosaurs and—believe it or not—psychic pterodactyls inside the Earth's crust.[72] Burroughs even sends Tarzan to Pellucidar in 1930 in *Tarzan at the Earth's Core*. Later, he introduced the *Carson of Venus* books, starting with *The Pirates of Venus,* first serialized in *Argosy* in 1932. This series stars astronaut Carson Napier, who, like Carter, has occult powers—in this case, telepathy. All these psychic supermen seem to reflect Burroughs' straining toward a new race, one that is both physically powerful and morally upright, and possessed of extrasensory, occult powers that set them apart from the rest of humanity.

SAX ROHMER

For some bizarre reason best left to sociologists, the Chinese became the favorite villains of the pulps. Baddies like Shu Ling, Yow Sum Gay, Wu Fang, and Chang Ch'ien regularly wrought havoc in magazines like *Dime Detective* and

---

70   Excerpted in Dale R. Broadhurst, "John Carter Beginnings?" *ERB Zine*, vol. 1107, no pagination.

71   John Talieaferro, "Tarzan Forever: The Life of Edgar Rice Burroughs, Creator of Tarzan," *The New York Times*, April 4, 1999.

72   In 1924, Burroughs wrote a similar novel, *The Land That Time Forgot*, a story about a hidden Antarctic island called Caprona. The island is heated by thermal waters and is also inhabited by dinosaurs and other prehistoric animals.

Spicy Mystery. The granddaddy of all Asian arch-villains, Fu Manchu, was created by Englishman Arthur Sarsfield Ward (1883–1959), writing as Sax Rohmer. Fu Manchu is an occult-oriented character whose existence Rohmer describes as a danger to the entire white race.[73] He heads a network of Chinese secret societies bent on destroying Western civilization. His nemesis, Sir Denis Nayland Smith, is a blatant Sherlock Holmes knockoff, complete with his own Watson, Dr. Petrie. However offensive their racist edge today, the *Fu Manchu* books were a huge hit in their time and inspired a horde of imitators, several film adaptations, a Republic Pictures serial, a radio program, a comic strip, and even a short-lived television serial. Rohmer was not some jingoistic, ethnocentric nativist, however. He was a worldly, erudite man completely immersed in the occult. Rising above humble beginnings, he developed an early interest in writing and in 1903, at the age of twenty, netted his first sale ("The Mysterious Mummy," *Pearson's Magazine*). He took his pen name from the Old English *sax*, meaning "sword," and *rohmer*, meaning "roamer."

As a youth, Rohmer, like many of his time, had a deep-seated fascination with ancient Egypt. Indeed, Peter Haining records that Rohmer is "most clearly remembered for his knowledge of Egyptology and as a practitioner of its rites."[74] Rohmer's introduction to the Egyptian rites came by way of his family doctor, Dr. R. Watson Councell, who reportedly initiated him into the Rosicrucian Society. In 1925, Rohmer wrote an introduction for Councell's book *Apologia Alchymiae*, reportedly the only introduction he ever wrote for another author's book.

Rohmer's involvement with the occult was extensive.[75] He joined the Golden Dawn and wrote occult-themed works, including stories like "Brood of the Witch Queen" (1918), "Grey Face" (1924), and "The Green Eyes of Bâst" (1920), and books like *The Romance of Sorcery* (1913). Through his work with the occult,

---

73   Sax Rohmer, *The Insidious Dr. Fu Manchu* (New York: Dover, 1997 reprint), chapter 13.

74   Peter Haining, ed., *The Magicians: The Occult in Fact and Fiction* (New York: Taplinger, 1972), p. 149.

75   According to one biographer, Rohmer's wife "was psychic and Rohmer himself seemed to attract metaphysical phenomena — according to a story, he consulted with his wife on a ouija board as to how he could best make a living. The answer was 'C-H-I-N-A-M-A-N'." Rohmer also spent a great deal of time with Harry Houdini, trying like Doyle to ascertain whether the magician possessed superhuman powers. The two became friends, but Houdini apparently found Rohmer's studies to be intrusive. See "Sax Rohmer, Classic Reader Biography," *classicreader.com*.

Rohmer came to believe that "a great new adept" was coming—one who would "pour the light of the East into the Darkness of the West." [76]

Of course, this fascination with superhuman powers brings us right back to the comic books. And it is through Marvel Comics that Rohmer's work was introduced to a new generation. In 1972, Marvel bought the rights to *Fu Manchu* and assigned two of its most mystically minded creators to update the property. Capitalizing on the Kung Fu craze inspired by Bruce Lee, Steve Englehart and Jim Starlin created "Shang Chi, the Master of Kung Fu" in 1973 (*Marvel Special Edition* #15). Shang Chi, the son of Fu Manchu, rebels against his father and joins the British Secret Service to combat the paternal villain's quest for world domination. The series, which greatly mitigates the racist tinge of Rohmer's original tales, was a big hit and ran for ten years. Shang Chi survives as a Marvel character, although the company gave up rights to the original Rohmer characters. [77]

Sorcery was an ever-present theme in the pulps, but a new generation of writers would move beyond the usual witch-doctor/murderous cult riffs and make the occult the focus of their fiction. Coincidentally, the three leading lights of this movement—H.P. Lovecraft, Robert E. Howard, and Dion Fortune—would lead unhappy lives and die before their time. But their work would become the entry point for serious exploration of mystical themes in popular fiction.

H. P. LOVECRAFT

No investigation of the occult roots of pulp fiction would be complete without some mention of Howard Phillips Lovecraft (1890–1937). Lovecraft had a knack for conveying pure, existential terror unmatched by any other writer in the genre. Born the last scion of an old aristocratic family, Lovecraft lived and worked in obscurity. Left penniless by a father driven mad by syphilis and a grandfather who squandered the family's fortune, he was haunted by images of decay and degeneracy throughout his life.

Lovecraft was a child prodigy who exhausted his grandfather's library at a very early age. He began to write—first, nonfiction articles for a variety of magazines,

---

76   Haining, *The Magicians*, p. 150.

77   *Hulk* director Ang Lee is reportedly developing a *Shang Chi* film as of this writing.

LINSNER ©2007.

and eventually stories for pulp magazines. His career in the pulps brought him into contact with writers like Clark Ashton Smith and Robert E. Howard, both of whom he kept as correspondents. He is most famous as a writer of horror stories for *Weird Tales*.

Lovecraft was heavily influenced by Edgar Allan Poe and an Anglo-Irish fantasy writer named Lord Dunsany. When it comes to pure imaginative power, however, Lovecraft has no match. He constructed a coherent, overarching "mythos" that runs throughout all of his (non-serial) stories, complete with a fictional satanic bible, *The Necromonicon*, that many readers believe to this day is a real book.[78] To enter Lovecraft's imaginative world is to enter a world of unending nightmare that is crystalline in its lucidity and luminous in its clarity.

Though Lovecraft insisted that he was a scientific rationalist, he constructed a complex cosmology of hideous extraterrestrial beings that once ruled the Earth. With the rise of man, these chimeras go into hiding, and begin preparing for the day when they will reemerge and take possession of the planet once more. Creatures with names like Chthulu and Nyarlathotep gather human acolytes to worship them as gods in rites replete with blasphemy and depravity. Lovecraft's descriptive powers are so effective that many readers seriously question his self-professed mechanistic atheism.

Many researchers have speculated that Lovecraft had extensive contacts with esoteric and occult organizations like the Theosophists or the OTO. Aleister Crowley's disciple Kenneth Grant, for instance, has written extensively on the parallels between Lovecraft's and Crowley's work.[79] Lovecraft has featured prominently in occult conspiracy theory, with some writers claiming that he was actually in contact with demonic spirits and wrote his numinous tales under their direction. Occultist Tracy Twyman maintains that Lovecraft's stories are adaptations of the stories of the so-called Nephilim, or fallen angels, from the ancient Book of Enoch. [80] And mercenary-turned-pulp writer E. Hoffman Price

---

78   Several *Necronomicon* forgeries have, in fact, surfaced over the years. See Alan Cabal, "The Doom that Came to Chelsea" *New York Press*, vol. 16, issue 23.

79   See Kenneth Grant, *Hecate's Fountain* (London: Skoob Books, 1995).

80   Tracy Twyman, "Dead But Dreaming: The Great Old Ones of Lovecraftian Legend Reinterpreted as Atlantean Kings" from *The Arcadian Mystique: The Best Of Dagobert's Revenge Magazine* (Portland, OR: Dragon Key Press, 2005).

introduced Lovecraft to several occult and Theosophical concepts during their extensive correspondence.[81]

Lovecraft had a marked influence on the horror and sci-fi genres, and many popular writers have tried to replicate his Cthulu Mythos in their tales. He also had a strong influence on comics writers like Gardner Fox and Alan Moore. It's interesting to note that legendary DC Comics editor Julius Schwartz began his career as Lovecraft's literary agent.

ROBERT E. HOWARD

Robert Ervin Howard (1906–1936) was born the only child of a Texas country doctor and a sickly mother. A voracious reader, he developed an early interest in boxing and weight lifting that found expression in his writing for the adventure pulps and boxing magazines. An early interest in ancient history led to a lasting fascination with barbarian tribes like the Picts of ancient Scotland. He was also a fan of occultic fiction of magazines like *Weird Tales*, and began a long-lasting correspondence with H. P. Lovecraft, joining what came to be known as The Lovecraft Circle, a precursor of later sci-fi societies and organizations.

Howard became a successful writer for the pulps, contributing to magazines like *Argosy, Spicy Adventure,* and *Strange Detective.* He invented warrior heroes like Bran Mak Morn, Kull the Conqueror, and Solomon Kane whom he set against the machinations and conjurings of wizards and warlocks, and a host of demons, monsters, and spirits. His signature character, Conan the Cimmerian, appeared in the story "The Phoenix on the Sword" in the December 1932 issue of *Weird Tales*.

It's unclear why Conan became so much more popular than his other characters, who were expressions of the same essentially Nietszchean ethos. Howard explained in a letter to a fan that "Conan simply grew up in my mind . . . . He simply stalked full grown out of oblivion and set me at work recording the saga of his adventures." He wrote to Clark Ashton Smith: "I have sometimes wondered if it were possible that unrecognized forces of the past or present—or even the

---

81　John Carter, *Sex and Rockets: The Occult World of Jack Parsons* (Los Angeles: Feral House, 2004), p. 60.

future—work through the thoughts and actions of living men." Indeed, writing Conan's adventures became a total preoccupation for Howard. "The character," he claimed, "took complete possession of my mind."[82] Conan became a huge success, but Howard did not enjoy the fruits of his labors for long. Distraught over the death of his mother, he committed suicide in 1936.

Conan, however, lives on, and Howard's work has had an incalculable effect on popular culture. The spirit of Conan has informed many other rough-edged superheroes, and even J.R.R. Tolkien acknowledged him as an influence. The sword-and-sorcery genre itself, however, did not play well in comics until the early 1970s. With superheroes slipping in the marketplace, Marvel licensed Howard's characters in hopes of tapping into the fantasy craze of the late 1960s. As before, it was Conan who hit the jackpot. In 1982, the John Milius film *Conan the Barbarian* launched the career of Austrian muscleman Arnold Schwarzenegger. The film was a hit, but its dismal 1984 sequel, *Conan the Destroyer,* killed the franchise in its infancy. Two totally unfaithful cartoon series appeared in the 1990s, followed by a short-lived action series in 1997 that tried to cash in on the success of the campy series, *Hercules: The Legendary Journeys.*

DION FORTUNE

British author Dion Fortune provides our strongest link between the occult underground and the pulps. Born Violet Mary Firth in 1890 to a Christian Science family in Wales, Fortune reported mystical visions at an early age. In her teens, she studied occultism under Dr. Theodore Moriarty and developed an interest in psychoanalysis, particularly the occult-tinged teachings of Carl Jung. Said to be a "natural psychic," she was credited with powers of clairvoyance and astral projection, and the ability to read Edgar Cayce's Akashic Records. She also claimed to be in direct contact with the Ascended Masters, who she said aided her in her writings.

Fortune was initiated into the Golden Dawn in 1919, but later became disenchanted with the "bare bones" approach to occultism taught by McGregor Mathers. In 1922, she formed a new society called The Society of the Inner Light

---

82   Quotes excerpted from Rusty Burke, "A Short Biography of Robert E. Howard," *The Official Robert E. Howard Site,* p. 11, *rehoward.com.*

and later joined the Theosophical Society. She was a prolific writer of what she considered to be practical and accessible works on the occult, among them *The Esoteric Philosophy of Love and Marriage, Sane Occultism, The Training and Work of an Initiate,* and *Practical Occultism in Daily Life.* She befriended Aleister Crowley, corresponded extensively with him, and wrote eloquently of their friendship in *The Mystical Qabalah* (1935), which many consider to be her masterpiece.

Fortune also tried her hand at fiction and created the occult detective Dr. Taverner, who first appeared in the British pulp, *Royal Magazine,* in the early 1920s, basing the detective on her own mentor, Dr. Moriarty. These stories were later reprinted in the collection *The Secrets of Dr. Taverner.* She also wrote a series of occult novels, including *The Demon Lover,* a cautionary tale about the dark side of occultism, *The Sea Priestess, The Winged Bull,* about sex magic and occultism in the British military, and *Moon Magic,* in which she embedded many actual spells and rituals used in the Society of the Inner Light.

As if all this weren't enough, Fortune claimed to have become a kind of real-life superhero with her participation in the "Magical Battle of Britain" during World War II. Fortune gathered a number of witches and occultists from across the United Kingdom in order to cast spells of protection to stave off a German invasion.[83] This effort, which became legendary in occult lore, allegedly left her in a weakened state. She died of leukemia in London in January 1946.

JACK PARSONS: ROCKETMAN

The rise of science fiction and fantasy fandom would play a crucial role in the development of comic book culture. Several clubs would form that would allow fans and creators to meet and exchange ideas, and eventually would lead to creation of the sci-fi and comic book convention circuit. The rise of this network closely mirrored the rise of the neopagan and occult movements of the mid–20th century. In fact, many of the leading figures in fandom were also deeply involved in occult activity. As former Eclipse Comics publisher and occult author Catherine Yronwode, put it, "Neopaganism would never have gotten started without the rise

---

83   See Dion Fortune, Gareth Knight, ed., *The Magical Battle of Britain* (Oceanside, CA: Sun Chalice, 1993).

of Science Fiction and comics fandom."[84] One figure who straddled both worlds would also play a crucial part in development of the real-life "World of Tomorrow."

Jack Parsons (1914–1952) combined his love of sci-fi with a prodigious knack for chemistry and became one of the founding fathers of the Space Program. Parsons was an avid reader of pulps like *Amazing Stories* and had a particular love for Burrough's *John Carter* stories. From an early age, he experimented with explosives, a hobby that eventually led to his invention of solid rocket fuel. He played a major role in the development of the Apollo space program and in the formation of Jet Propulsion Laboratories—indeed, some have joked that the initials JPL actually stand for Jack Parsons' Laboratories.

Jack Parsons was also an avid practitioner of Thelema, and a regular correspondent with Aleister Crowley. Some even claim he recited Crowley's "Hymn to Pan" before every rocket launch. His family estate in Pasadena became the site of the Agape Lodge of the OTO; offerings collected there provided Crowley with one of his few sources of income in his declining days.

In addition to his work with the OTO and his scientific pursuits, Parsons also had contacts with the Los Angeles Science Fantasy Society, the forerunner of modern fandom. The LASFS grew out of Hugo Gernsback's Science Fiction League and eventually hosted weekly meetings where writers and fans mingled. Parsons gave talks on rocketry at LASFS meetings and befriended several future sci-fi legends, among them Ray Bradbury, Robert A. Heinlein, German sci-fi pioneer Fritz Lang, and Vril Society theorist Willy Ley.

Parsons' circle of sci-fi writers grew to include L. Ron Hubbard, with whom he undertook the infamous "Babalon Working" in January 1946. This ritual, which earned them both a place in occult conspiracy-theory lore, was inspired by Crowley's writings, particularly his novel *Moonchild*. Hubbard and Parsons sought to summon the Scarlet Woman, whom Parsons saw as an incarnation of the Whore of Babylon. His goal was to mate with her and conceive the Moonchild—the future Antichrist.[85] When informed of the working, Crowley himself exclaimed: "I

---

84   Telephone interview with Catherine Yronwode by this author, October 26, 2006.

85   The two went into the desert and muttered chants based on Crowley's writings. Not long after, a redhead named Marjorie Cameron showed up at the Agape Lodge, which Parsons saw as proof that the ritual had worked. Parsons and his Scarlet Woman never had any children, however—never mind moonchildren.

get fairly frantic when I contemplate the idiocy of these goats."[86] Not long after the Babalon Working, Parson's friendship with Hubbard faltered and Hubbard went on to found his new occult religion, Scientology, in 1950.[87] Parsons later fell on hard times, and his OTO activities earned him some unwelcome attention from the federal government. He developed an addiction to methamphetamines and cocaine, eventually lost his security clearance. Parsons would die in a laboratory accident in 1952 that some claim was murder.

Parsons' favorite novel, Jack Williamson's *Darker Than You Think*, was originally serialized in *Unknown* in 1940. A powerful and chilling work even today, the book tells the story of journalist Will Barbee, who stumbles across a worldwide cult of shape-shifting witches bent on world domination. Barbee's own occult powers are awakened by a seductive redhead named April Bell, and he soon realizes that he himself is the prophesied "Child of Night"—the "Black Messiah" that will lead the witches out of the shadows and into the halls of power. The story ends, not with the obligatory defeat of the forces of darkness, but with their rise to power. Parsons was fascinated by the book's description of a magickal race that doesn't want to coexist with mankind, but wants to dominate it completely and covertly. It's hard not to find echoes of Williamson's theme of an occultic super-race—which is, in itself, an echo of Bulwer's *Vril*—throughout Parsons' Thelemic writings.

By mid-century, the cross-pollination between sci-fi, fantasy, and occultism had flowered and borne fruit, but the pulps were beginning to fade. The emerging superheroes would need a new place to grow and a new, fresh audience as well. The dingy monochromatic pages of *Amazing Stories* and *Weird Takes* would have to give over to a new and colorful format so the new gods could truly come into their own.

Oh, before we go on it's probably important to note that Jack Parsons' birth name was "Marvel."

---

86   Lawrence Sutin, *Do What Thou Wilt: A Life of Aleister Crowley* (New York: St. Martin's, 2000), p. 414.

87   For the definitive story on Parsons and Hubbard, see Pendle, *Strange Angel* pp. 252-279. See also Miller Russell, *Bare-Faced Messiah* (New York: Henry Holt, 1988), p. 132.

PART IV

THE NEW GODS

CHAPTER 12

FAMOUS FUNNIES

Like so many "uniquely American inventions," the modern comic strip was actually born in England. As early as 1731, cartoonist-turned-fine-artist William Hogarth was using sequential pictures to tell stories, first in his cautionary tale on easy virtue, *A Harlot's Progress,* and then with an eight-panel sequel called *A Rake's Progress,* which warns of the dangers of drinking and whoring. In fact, cartoon features, modern political cartooning, and word balloons all first surfaced in 18th-century England. Cartoons were originally used for political propaganda in newspapers, but many cartoons and strips were printed onto single sheets that were sold on the street.[88]

---

88   For the definitive history of early English comics, see Denis Gifford, *International Book of Comics* (London: Crescent Books, 1984).

Cartoons migrated to America and got their start in *The New York World* in 1893. Two years later, Richard Outcault's pioneering strip *Hogan's Alley* appeared in the *Sunday World,* inaugurating the modern Sunday comics.[89] Outcault, considered the father of modern comic strips, was the first to use panels and speech-balloons together, and introduced color to the strips.[90]

Comics got off to a rocky start in America. Christian busybodies attacked them for promoting hilarity on the Sabbath.[91] *Hogan's Alley* was also criticized for its portrayal of immigrant squalor, leading Outcault to create Buster Brown, a more socially acceptable, middle-class sprite who was later appropriated by the Brown Shoe Company for its logo. Despite these early setbacks, however, comic strips survived and thrived. *Mutt and Jeff,* the first major daily strip, created by Bud Fisher in 1907, ran uninterrupted for an astonishing seventy-five years. Mutt and Jeff were the cover stars for *Famous Funnies* #1, the series often inaccurately cited as the first American comic book. The duo also became major stars for the All-American Comics Co., the firm that later would bring pagan gods out of the history books and into the funny books.

Other classic strips include George McManus' *Bringing Up Father*, Chic Young's *Blondie*, Frank King's *Gasoline Alley,* George Herriman's *Krazy Kat*, and *The Katzenjammer Kids,* created by Rudolph Dirks. These strips became wildly popular and have since become American icons. They were immediately tapped for licensed merchandising, a process that eventually led to the creation of the modern comic book. Cartoonists were major celebrities in those days, and many made personal appearances on the Vaudeville circuit. Winsor McKay, creator of *Little Nemo in Slumberland* and one of the very first motion-picture animators, was so talented that he could reportedly draw detailed images and simple animations while addressing an audience. He was also, incidentally, a dedicated Freemason.[92]

Like the first comic strips, what we call "comic books" were originally developed in England by collecting reprinted comic panels and strips. Caricature magazines

89   In a strange synchronicity, Outcault's name (originally Altgelt) bears an uncanny etymological similarity to "occult."

90   Outcault's star, The Yellow Kid, was the source of the term *yellow press*, which was coined to describe the type of unethical journalistic practices in *The World.*

91   Around the same time, those same busybodies worked to ban the sale of ice cream sodas on the Sabbath, leading to the invention of the Sundae.

92   John Canemaker, *Winsor McCay: His Life and Art* (New York: Abbeville, 1987), p. 32.

like *McLean's Monthly Sheet of Caricatures* appeared early in the 19th century. *The Comic News* appeared in the 1860s and *Funny Folks* premiered in 1874, followed by *Comic Cuts* (1890) and *Illustrated Chips* (1891). *Ally Sloper's Half Holiday* became the first true comic book, published in May 1884.[93]

In America, comic-strip characters became vehicles for licensing almost as soon as they appeared, and comic books were initially a part of that phenomenon. Most of the earliest comic books were collections of reprints from the funny pages, used as lucrative promotional items for gas stations, toy stores, and soap companies. When the Depression hit, the publishing industry took it hard. A struggling salesman named Max Gaines made a deal with the Eastern Color Printing Co. to produce a comic book called *Famous Funnies,* which he presented as a promotional item to stores and manufacturers. The first issue sold out, inspiring other publishers to snap up every available newspaper strip for reprinting.

Comic books were gravy for almost everyone involved. They were cheap to print and gave printing companies a lucrative way to keep newspaper presses running in hard times. They gave the industry a new revenue stream and advertisers a new way to attract customers. Kids loved the content and parents appreciated them keeping the kiddies occupied on Sunday afternoon.

HIGH ADVENTURE

Although most of the early comic strips were humorous, adventure strips were not long in coming. One of the first, Harold Grey's *Little Orphan Annie,* appeared in 1924. Popeye, the marble-mouthed sailor man, was a superhero prototype who premiered in E. C. Segar's *Thimble Theatre* strip in 1929. Roy Crane's *Wash Tubbs* began as a humor strip in 1924, but evolved into a globetrotting high-adventure strip with the addition of Cap'n Easy in 1929. Chester Gould's hard-boiled *Dick Tracy* made its debut in 1931, complete with sci-fi elements and outlandish villains that inspired later comic-book supervillains.

More recognizable superheroes found their way into the funnies. Buck Rogers drifted in from the pulps and became the star of the first sci-fi strip in 1929. *Flash Gordon,* created by Alex Raymond, appeared five years later. Both had a huge

---

93   Gifford, *Book of Comics,* pp. 14–15.

impact on superheroes, particularly in the late 1950s, and were frequently adapted into other media. *Mandrake the Magician*—often called the first true super-hero—was conjured into the physical plane by Lee Falk in 1934. Two years later, Falk summoned the Phantom, who created the visual model of the superhero in his form-fitting bodysuit, nifty skull logo, and eyemask. The Phantom, called "The Ghost Who Walks," was essentially a circus-costumed version of Tarzan—the nearly dead son of a British sea captain who is restored to health by a tribe of pygmies. A harbinger of things to come, the Phantom establishes a hereditary secret society whose members are sworn to "fight all forms of piracy, greed, and cruelty."

DIRTY DEALINGS

The idealistic fantasy of the early comic heroes came face-to-face with real vice during Prohibition. Mobsters were looking for new sources of revenue. Because of their high volume and low cost, comics became an ideal tool for organized crime to launder money through the strictly cash-and-carry news-stand business. The Mob quickly extended their hold on distributors as well. As Jones writes: "The volume of product and cash opened up new opportu-nities for many of the standby residual benefits—money laundering, cash skimming, smuggling."[94] Indeed, politicians like Thomas Dewey and Fiorello La Guardia went after the pulps, not just for their moral transgressions, but because of their financial relationship to the rackets. Many publishers did have cozy relationships with the Mob, both in business and social settings. Many others ran their businesses with ethical standards hardly better than those of gangsters. The irony is that, while comics and pulps helped criminal gangs financially, they also popularized the vigilante heroes bent on bringing them down.[95] This paradox created a strange symbiotic relationship between the mobsters and the new gods.

---

94 Gerard Jones, *Men of Tomorrow: Geeks, Gangsters, and the Birth of the Comic Book* (New York: Basic, 2004), p. 163.

95 The same was true for pornography. Tijuana Bibles, pornographic comic books featuring char-acters from famous cartoons and comic strips, were produced and printed by comic book artists and publishers, then distributed by the crime syndicates.

FOUNDING FATHERS

The pulps not only provided the comics with most of their heroes and themes, they also provided the industry with most of its key personnel, most notably Harry Donenfeld, godfather of DC Comics, and Martin Goodman, founder of Marvel Comics.

Donenfeld started his career as a salesman for a printing company, but soon moved into publishing. He formed an alliance with the distributor Eastern News, which had connections to both legitimate business interests and the mob. Eastern handled feminist and Spiritualist magazines, as well as purported health journals like *Sex Monthly,* catering to the forbidden tastes of a hypocritical American popular culture that couldn't acknowledge its appetite for booze, porn, radical politics, and alternative spirituality. Donenfeld used his extensive business, government, and Mafia connections to keep the business growing, to the point, Gerard Jones writes that, "Margaret Sanger's condoms, Hugo Gernsback's science fiction, and Frank Costello's whiskey could ride together on trucks and on trains and through post offices where the inspectors were on the take."[96]

Donenfeld built an empire that included *Paris Nights* and *Pep!* and earned him a reputation as a pornographer in a time when any hint of nudity could cause a magazine to be taken off the stands and its publisher yanked into court. When publishers began to test these social boundaries, Donenfeld was, predictably, on the cutting edge. He paid his artists well and they delivered what discerning gentlemen wanted.

The government crackdown on the Mob in 1936 encouraged publishers with shady connections to legitimize their businesses. Donenfeld was in a particularly vulnerable position because of his relationship with organized crime and the high visibility of his sexy *Spicy* pulps. Convinced that he needed to find a safer line of work, Donenfeld turned to comic books as a safe and profitable alternative.

If Harry Donenfeld was a rakish opportunist, Martin Goodman, founder of Marvel Comics, was a true believer—a pulp fan turned pulp salesman turned pulp publisher. He formed his first company, Western Fiction Publishing Co., with future Archie Comics publisher Louis Silberkleit. His business strategy was

---

96 Jones, *Men of Tomorrow,* p. 163.

to capitalize on popular titles by publishing knock-offs of them. In 1936, he put out a series starring a blond Tarzan called *Ka-Zar*. In 1938, he played off of *Amazing Stories* with a series *Marvel Science Stories*. The success of *Unknown* and *Weird Tales* inspired him to launch two "shudder pulps"—*Mystery Tales* and *Uncanny Tales* that featured endless retellings of the old girl-tortured-by-fiend yarn.

When the pulps began to flounder, Goodman, convinced that "comic magazines" were the wave of the future, began to run strips in his pulps to test the waters. In 1939, he founded *Marvel Comics #1.* whose success would launch an empire.[97] Alarmed by the rise of fascism in Europe, Goodman prompted his young editor Joe Simon and his partner Jack Kirby to come up with a patriotic spin on the popular hero Captain Marvel. They called him Captain America. After a brief legal skirmish over similarities between this hero and a previous character named the Shield, the Captain became a major hit. The world was ready for new gods—and the new gods were ready for the world.

---

97   Many historians refer to Goodman's company in the 40s as Timely. However, Timely was merely one of the many shell companies that Goodman operated. For simplicity's sake, Goodman's firm will be referred to as Marvel, whether in its 40s, 50s, or 60s incarnation.

CHAPTER 13

WHO WILL SAVE US?

All superheroes are essentially savior figures. Unlike religious saviors, however, superheroes offer salvation as a tangible, unambiguous event. They exist, quite simply, to save others from physical danger—which explains their enduring appeal. Tales of their exploits address real anxiety and satisfy a deep need. The childhood need for a father or big brother to shield us from harm and solve our problems is an impulse we all feel. That is why superheroes traditionally enjoy greater popularity—with children *and* adults—in times of national stress. Children are remarkably sensitive to existential threats and they often internalize their parent's anxieties. And adults often feel as vulnerable as children when confronting the fear of war or economic hardship.

Young children have a magical worldview. Because they don't understand the physical processes of the everyday world, they tend to perceive their environment as supernatural. This is true even in older children, though many may deny it if pressed. Because superheroes were originally aimed at an audience of children, they are all essentially *magical*, with no basis in science or ordinary reality. Even if heroes like Spider-Man or Green Lantern draw their powers from technology, the actual scientific explanation for those powers is simply window dressing. If you are bitten by a radioactive spider, chances are good you'll get a horrible rash, go into toxic shock, and then die—not wake up the next morning and start climbing up walls. Themes of mutants, androids, and cyborgs speak to social and spiritual impulses, not science.

As America struggled to emerge from the Great Depression, the symbols and stories of the old gods reentered American culture. In the comic books, these gods and heroes of antiquity truly came alive and helped inspire America to regain its strength. This return of the old gods collided head-on with huge leaps forward in science and technology. At the same time, genetics prompted scientists to ponder the possibility of improving the race through genetic manipulation. Credible ideas about space travel were propounded to a public many of whom still believed there was intelligent life on Mars and Venus. Science, philosophy, religion, and the occult all merged in a general yearning to overcome intractable human problems and improve mankind's future.

This yearning also had a dark side, however, that manifested in ethnocentric politics, racial hatred, and fascism. These dark impulses turned the occult striving toward the "New Man" into murderous political movements that, unfortunately, claimed justification from the same texts that gave rise to the modern superhero. The parallels have not gone unnoticed and some social critics today feel that the superhero myth is irredeemably fascist.

It was this yearning that inspired the young writers who created the superheroes from antecedents in the pulps, mythology, religion, and folktales. In fact, most superhero figures fall into a handful of archetypal categories drawn from origins in the ancient mysteries.

MAGIC MEN

Wizard archetypes are as old as fiction itself. Thoth, Egyptian lunar god and patron of magic and science, was perhaps the first Wizard archetype. Thoth was also the patron deity of Aleister Crowley's *magnum opus* on the Tarot, which he called *The Book of Thoth*. The melding of Thoth and his Greek counterpart Hermes gave the world Hermes Trismegistus, Thrice-Great Hermes, the patron of all magical arts and sciences in the pagan world. This tradition, known simply as Hermeticism, was powerful and influential enough to survive centuries of brutal and bloody suppression by the Catholic Church and enjoy a revival among the alchemists of the Middle Ages, who saw themselves as heirs to the Hermetic tradition.

Few people realize, however, that explicitly magical characters are actually the earliest examples of modern superheroes. In fact, it can be argued that all super-heroes are essentially magical, since most of their powers have no basis in real science. Early superheroes like Captain Marvel, Phantasmo, and Green Lantern were unambiguously magical in origin, drawing on themes taken directly from the pulps.

Wizards functioned as shamans and medicine men, teachers and priests, and often as chieftains in ancient tribal societies. Three of the most famous sorcerers in Western culture are the Three Wise Men, from the Gospel of Matthew. These magi were Zoroastrian astrologers said to have prophesied the coming of Christ, whom they found in the manger at Bethlehem. The most famous sorcerer of all time, however, is Merlin, the mage from the King Arthur myths.

Merlin is usually portrayed as the wise wizard of Uther Pendragon's court who raises and tutors young Arthur to be King of the Britons. Many of the Arthu-rian romances are told from Merlin's point of view, and Merlin seems to be the archetype for both Gandalf the White in J.R.R. Tolkien's *Lord of the Rings* trilogy and Obi-Wan Kenobi in the *Star Wars* dramas. A less-acknowledged inheritor of Merlin's mantle is Q, the master of technological wonders in the James Bond films, whose role is very much like that of Merlin in the Arthurian tales—a scold-ing paternal figure who is also the source of the ingenious tricks and gadgets that regularly save the day. Likewise, Obi-Wan Kenobi can be seen as a Christlike, sci-fi Merlin who sacrifices himself to save Luke and Leia and their companions. Obi-Wan and Q (like Gandalf) are both members of a brotherhood—in Obi-Wan's case, the suppressed Jedi, in Q's, the Secret Service.

Of course, the most popular magus today is Harry Potter, created by J. K. Rowl-ing. In a time when most children can't be bothered to read anything, Rowling has created a series of runaway bestsellers devoured by millions of young readers the world over. Sociologists have wasted volumes trying to explain Harry Potter's unprecedented success, when they need not have looked far at all. The answer lies in the hearts and imaginations of all insecure young children (and adults) who want to believe that they—like Harry, Ron, and Hermione—have latent magical powers that can help them negotiate the horrors of adolescence (and life). And as we'll see later, Harry has a direct ancestor in the comics.

MANDRAKE THE MAGICIAN

The character generally seen as the comics' first superhero is Mandrake the Magician. Created by Lee Falk in 1924, Mandrake didn't find his way into the funny pages until a decade later. True to form, Mandrake studied with ascended masters in Tibet, and returned to the West to ply his trade as a stage performer. Along the way, he picked up a sidekick named Lothar, an African prince who acted as Mandrake's personal bodyguard, and is generally acknowledged as the first heroic black character in American comic strips.

In his early adventures, Mandrake is an occult magician who uses hypnotic suggestion to convince others he is a true conjurer. Falk incorporated many interesting occult themes into his storylines. Mandrake fights a death cult in 1935 in *Kingdom of Murderers*, and masters the arcane art of inter-dimensional travel a year later in *Mandrake in the X Dimension*. In *Mandrake on the Moon* (1938), the magician discovers that the ancient Atlanteans escaped and built a new civilization of domed cities on the dark side of the Moon. Starting in 1939, Mandrake strips were reprinted in magazine format in *Magic Comics*. Mandrake never hit the big time outside the funny pages, however, despite attempts at a movie serial (1939), a radio program (1940), a TV series (1954), a TV movie (1979), and a TV cartoon (1986).

Mandrake did, however, inspire a whole host of warlocks in both comics and the strips. The first costumed character that can be definitively called a superhero is the Phantom Magician, who first appeared in Mel Graff's syndicated comic strip *The Adventures of Patsy* in 1935. As comics historian Dick O' Donnell notes, the Phantom Magician "was clad in the outfit of tights, cape, and domino mask favored by so many later adventure heroes, including the Phantom and Superman and Batman."[98] Although Phantom Magician appeared in only one *Patsy* storyline, he caught the attention of *Mandrake* creator Lee Falk, whose next hero also donned a mask and costume.

Another supermagus character inspired by Mandrake is DC Comic's Zatara, created by Fred Guardineer. Like Superman, Zatara premiered in the first issue of *Action Comics*. DC seemed to have high hopes for Zatara and allowed him to push Superman off the cover of *Action* for several issues. Like Mandrake, Zatara is essentially a hypnotist who casts spells by gniklat drawkcab.[99] He vanished in a puff of smoke in 1950, replaced by his sexy, scantily-clad daughter, Zatanna. Perhaps seeking favor with some dark god, writer Alan Moore ritually sacrificed Zatara in the pages of *Swamp Thing #50* in 1986.

Possibly the first female superhero to pop up in the funny pages is Fantomah, Mystery Woman of the Jungle. Created by Barclay Flagg, Fantomah first appeared in Fiction House's *Jungle Comics #2* in 1940. Like so many other characters, Fantomah acquired her magical powers through a previous incarnation in ancient Egypt. She was a shape-shifter whose favorite trick was to transform herself into a blonde-haired, skull-headed freak when danger threatened. Apparently, Fantomah's readers felt threatened by this disconcerting and ugly metamorphosis, because she later morphed into a more sexy, kittenish character. Nonetheless, she is true to the type in that magic and the occult are crucial to her status as superhero.

DOCTOR OCCULT

Perhaps the clearest progenitor of the modern superhero is Jerry Siegel and Joe Shuster's mystic hero, Doctor Occult, who first premiered in *New Fun #6* in 1935. Doctor Occult started out as a traditional ghost detective, but underwent a startling transformation in 1936. As historian Les Daniels notes, the Doctor "developed immense strength and began flying around in a red and blue outfit.

---

98 Dick O'Donnell, "It's Magic," in *The Comic Book Book* (New Rochelle, NY: Arlington House, 1973), p. 146.

99 (talking backward)

He thus served as a prototype for the unpublished Superman."[100] For some reason, Siegel and Shuster later changed his name to the less-objectionable "Doctor Mystic."

Here, then, is our missing link in the evolution from Theosophy and the Golden Dawn to Spider-Man and the Flash. In *The Comic Book Book,* Dick O'Donnell unequivocally declares that "students of the history of comics must regard the Occult-Mystic figure as a definite prototype of Superman, performing many of the feats Superman later performed, but doing so by supernatural rather than superscientific means."[101] It is highly significant that the character who becomes the definitive archetype of the modern superhero is brought into the world by the same men who created the obscure "Doctor Occult," and that Superman bears such a strong, if unacknowledged, resemblance to his mystical progenitor. In point of fact, the name of Superman's home planet, "Krypton," stems from the Greek word *kryptos* meaning 'hidden' or 'secret.' The Latin translation of *kryptos* is "occult."

100 Les Daniels, *DC Comics: A Celebration of the World's Favorite Comic Book Heroes* (New York: Billboard Books, 2003), p. 44.

101 O'Donnell, "It's Magic," p. 157.

CHAPTER 14

THE MESSIAHS

Some historians note that the long-awaited Jewish Messiah was an Earthly king—very much a man of the world and not necessarily of the spirit. The term itself, which means simply "anointed," was bestowed on a number of other characters in the Old Testament. Jews believed that the Messiah would be a descendant of King David who would lead them out of captivity and restore Jewish rule in Palestine. By that description, the first prime minister of Israel, David Ben Gurion, is as much a Messiah as anyone. Yet, say the word "Messiah" and the first thing that pops into most people's minds is "Jesus Christ."

The Messiah of the funny pages is a noble, self-sacrificing hero who acts to save others out of a sense of altruism. Superman, of course, is the first and foremost of this type; Spider-Man is another. The Messiah superhero became so wildly popular because he addressed deep-seated anxieties in American life. Fascism, corporate corruption, and organized crime had grown to such a degree by the late 1930s that they seemed both overwhelming and intractable. Superman rose from the ranks of the common man to counter these threats. Of course, DC editors quickly blanderized him and inspired thousands of impotent saviors that diluted the force of the archetype.

The archetype remains a popular figure, nonetheless. Though contemporary writers have worked hard to make Superman and other messianic characters interesting and relevant, it's often difficult for readers to relate to a character who uses his powers for purely altruisistc purposes, not for personal gain. Indeed, salvation through Christ's sacrifice on the cross makes sense only to those completely committed to the Christian faith. For many, it's hard not to see these characters as fundamentally deluded, or at least severely misguided. In the mythic realm of comic books, however, the laws of human nature are often suspended, and Messiahs can arise who need not be anointed by God to save his people or humanity in general.

SUPERMAN

Superman, who made his debut in *Action Comics* #1 in 1938, is one of the world's most popular and enduring Messiah characters. Created by two young cartoonists from Cleveland named Jerome Siegel and Joseph Shuster, Superman has been the subject of countless thousands of comic books and comics strips, a movie serial, a popular radio show, several TV cartoons and live action series, toys, games, and enough memorabilia to stretch from Earth to the Moon.

Superman was not an overnight success, however. Siegel had created him several years before his comic debut, but had no luck promoting him to the newspaper syndicates or the fledgling comic-book publishers, who rejected the character as too fanciful. Finally, DC publisher Harry Donenfeld bought the character outright for $200 and Superman became an immediate hit, inspiring thousands of imitators. In many ways, it can be said that all subsequent comic-book superheroes are, in fact, variations on Superman.

Superman is Kal-El, the last son of Krypton, sent into space as an infant by his scientist father when his home planet explodes. His space-capsule lands in the Midwestern town of Smallville, where it is found by an elderly couple named

Kent who name the baby Clark and raise him as their own. Clark, who from the start displayed amazing strength, leaves Smallville for Metropolis and goes to work as a reporter for *The Daily Planet*. In times of crisis, he dons his blue-and-red costume and uses his powers—flight, superstrength, and x-ray vision—to fight for truth and justice.

At his core, Superman is a Messiah in the Biblical tradition, who can also be seen as a metaphor for American Jewish assimilation. The destruction of Krypton is an apt metaphor for the Diaspora, as well as for the assault on European Jewish communities that prompted their mass emigration to North America in the late 19th century. In Michael Chabon's novel about the comics industry, *The Amazing Adventures of Kavalier & Clay*, a Jewish character comments on Clark Kent's secret identity: "Superman, you don't think he's Jewish? Coming over from the old country, changing his name like that. Clark Kent, only a Jew would pick a name like that."[102] Superman's identity as one of the People of the Book is cemented when he takes a job as a reporter and pledges himself to fight the good fight.

Jerry Siegel had a more esoteric vision of his Superman than merely a new King David, however. Les Daniels notes that Siegel "must also have been aware of the analogies with Jesus," pointing out that Superman was "a man sent from the heavens by his father to use his special powers for the good of humanity."[103] Other writers also noted these Christlike characteristics and played on them as they developed similar characters. Writer Kurt Busiek called his version of Superman "the Samaritan" in his series, *Astro City*. *National Lampoon* ran a strip called *Son O' God* that parodied Jesus as a Superman-like hero complete with red cape and art by DC Comics star Neal Adams.

In the early issues of *Action Comics*, however, Superman is not the smiling, idealized Apollo he later becomes. He's a pissed-off crusader who fights for the common man against the corruption of the power elite. Many of his early adventures touch on occult and mythological themes. He meets Cleopatra (*Action #14*), fights to protect the Great Pyramids (*Action # 56*), stands alongside Atlas and Hercules (*Superman #28*), and encounters an extra-dimensional imp with magical powers called Mr.

---

102 Quoted in Jay Schwartz, "Jews and the Invention of the American Comic Book," *Jewish News Weekly of Northern California*, Oct. 21, 2005. Similarly, "Kal-El" has a distinctly Hebraic sound. Like Moses, young Kal-El is put into a small craft and found by kindly Gentiles. His escape to Earth from Krypton is an eerie foreshadowing of the coming Holocaust, when parents sent their children out of Europe to save them.

103 Daniels, *DC Comics*, p. 81.

Mxyztplk (*Superman* #30). The source of his power is the Sun, which ties him to solar gods like Horus and Mithras, as well as Biblical characters like Samson and Elijah. These divine aspects of Superman's character only increased over the years. Historian Bradford Wright notes that "Superman's comic books developed into a fantastic mythos that owed less and less to any standard of reality. Superman's powers, daunting enough to begin with, grew to staggering, godlike dimensions."[104]

These "godlike" powers became a major news story in 1992 with the cynical "Death of Superman" publicity stunt. In this storyline, Superman is killed by an alien called Doomsday and spends several issues in a kind of limbo while a bunch of tedious substitutes try to fill his shoes. Reinforcing his Biblical dimension, Superman dies and rises again, complete with a Christlike mane that most traditionalists hated. Driving home the parallel, the cover of the graphic novel *Death of Superman* (1993) features a garish and tasteless tribute to Michelangelo's *Pietà*, with Lois Lane cast in the role of the Virgin Mary.

One curious footnote to the Superman saga has played out outside the comic pages. A series of tragic events—the mysterious death of TV Superman George Reeves in 1959, the horrible accident that left Superman Christopher Reeve a quadriplegic, the subsequent death of his wife from cancer, and the serious illnesses of *Superman III* stars Margot Kidder and Richard Pryor inspired talk of a "Curse of Superman."[105] Despite the purported curse, however, Superman is still a popular character and continues to earn millions for his owners. Chaos magician Grant Morrison hit the top of the charts with his 2005 *All-Star Superman* series. 2006's *Superman Returns*, while not quite the earth-shaker Warner Bros. hoped for, earned a whopping $390 million worldwide, the Caped Crusader is the star of the successful *Justice League* cartoon series, and Superboy is the star of the 2006 CW network series *Legion of Super Heroes*. Superman even bridged the gender gap with two hit TV series that captured a female audience—*Lois and Clark: The New Adventures of Superman* and *Smallville*. These shows proved that, if handled correctly, the new gods can appeal to a wider

---

104 Bradford W. Wright, *Comic Book Nation* (Baltimore: Johns Hopkins University Press, 2001), p. 60.

105 Many believe that Reeves was murdered and this controversy became the theme of the 2006 film *Hollywoodland* with Ben Affleck. Superman Christopher Reeve was severely injured in a horse-riding accident. His wife Dana died of lung cancer in 2006, though she was not a smoker. Margot Kidder (Lois Lane) suffered severe mental illness and Richard Pryor succumbed to multiple sclerosis. Hollywood gossip was such that some prominent actors reportedly refused roles in the 2006 film *Superman Returns*.

audience as "the ultimate expression of human aspirations to power and pure freedom."[106]

CAPTAIN MARVEL

Fawcett Publishing's Captain Marvel, who debuted in *Whiz Comics* #1 in 1940, played the role of pagan Sun god to Superman's more traditional Davidic Messiah. Created by writer Bill Parker (who studied classical literature in college) and artist C. C. Beck (the son of a Lutheran pastor), Captain Marvel was Superman's most serious competition in the marketplace. In fact, *Captain Marvel Adventures* far outsold *Superman* in the hero's heyday, and Captain Marvel was the first superhero to be adapted to film in 1941 (*The Adventures of Captain Marvel*). DC Comics rightly saw Captain Marvel as a serious market threat.

In many ways, Captain Marvel is a more fascinating character than Superman. He is not an actual individual, but a magical entity into which young Billy Batson transubstantiates when he utters the occult incantation, "Shazam!"—the name of the wizard who granted Batson his powers, and an acronym for the ancient deities who lend the Captain their powers.[107]

Batson's transfiguration strongly resembles a Masonic, or secret-society, initiation. In the first Captain Marvel story, Billy, a homeless orphan, is led by a mysterious stranger into an abandoned subway tunnel, recalling initiations performed in ancient times. Out of nowhere, a driverless subway car decorated with arcane symbols appears and Billy and the stranger climb aboard. They then enter an ancient hallway lined with statues depicting the seven deadly enemies of man: pride, envy, greed, hatred, selfishness, laziness, and injustice. Billy enters a throne room and his mysterious companion vanishes.

Billy then encounters an ancient wizard, Shazam, who conjures an inscription on the wall behind him out of the names of six deities. Billy speaks this magic word, is struck by a bolt of lighting, and magically transfigures into Captain Marvel,

---

106 Les Daniels, *Comix: A History of Comic Books in America* (New York: Outerbridge, 1971), p. 11.

107 Solomon, a Biblical figure revered by occultists and Freemasons, who grants his wisdom; Hercules, who grants his strength; Atlas, who grants his stamina; Zeus, who lends his power; Achilles, who adds his Courage; Mercury, who shares his speed.

resplendent in red, white, and yellow cape and costume—solar colors all. The wizard is then crushed by a slab of stone and his Kenobi-like wraith immediately emerges and lights an eternal flame in a ceremonial urn, symbolizing the death and transformation of Osiris and the birth of Horus, the new Sun King. Shazam instructs Captain Marvel to go out and fight against evil and injustice. One of Marvel's nemeses is Black Adam, whose name is an approximate cipher for "Egyptian Man."[108]

By the 1940s, Captain Marvel soon found himself surrounded by his own pantheon, including Captain Marvel Jr. (*Whiz Comics* #25),[109] Mary Marvel (*Captain Marvel Adventures* #18), several Lieutenant Marvels, an Uncle Marvel, and even a Marvel Bunny. The Captain, Captain Jr., and Mary often appeared together in adventures, mirroring the Egyptian holy family of Osiris, Isis, and Horus. The fact that Mary Marvel is Billy Batson's lost twin sister helps cement the Osiris-Isis connection.

In 1953, after thirteen lucrative years, Fawcett finally canceled the Captain Marvel series, prompted by decreasing sales and a series of infringement lawsuits by DC Comics. But the story doesn't end there. Fawcett let the trademark on Captain Marvel lapse and Marvel Comics snapped it up in 1968, only to fumble the ball. Their sci-fi oriented Captain Marvel went through a series of incarnations, resulting in mostly forgettable adventures. The strip enjoyed its greatest success under artist/writer Jim Starlin, a lapsed Catholic obsessed with mysticism, magic, and death. Starlin pitted Marvel against Thanos, an alien tyrant who worships death as his lover. Death later came for Starlin's hero in a 1981 graphic novel entitled *The Death of Captain Marvel,* whose cover also featured a parody of the *Pietà,* with the Captain as Christ and Death as the Virgin.

DC acquired the Captain Marvel character from Fawcett and resumed his title (named *Shazam,* for legal reasons) in the 1970s. C. C. Beck was hired to do the art but soon left in protest over the juvenile scripts he was given to illustrate. After a strong start, the title floundered. In 1974, *Shazam* premiered as a live-action pro-

---

108 "Black" is a rough translation of the ancient name for Egypt, *Kemet*; Adam means "man." In Black Adam's case, SHAZAM stood for the patron deities Shu (Sky God), Heru (Horus), Amon (Amen, king of the gods), Zehuti (Thoth), Aton (Sun), and Mehen (an Egyptian board game).

109 Daniels, *DC Comics,* p. 86. Junior's adventures were drawn by the talented Mac Raboy, who also created the magical character Doctor Voodoo, a knock-off of Doctor Occult. Raboy's elegant art gave Junior's adventures a particularly enchanting mystique. One of Junior's most famous admirers was Elvis Presley, who borrowed his hero's hairstyle and costume for his stage attire.

gram on CBS to a new generation of Marvel fans, but the Captain was presented as a typically bland 70s TV hero. This Captain Marvel didn't fight reincarnated Egyptian deities or Nazi robots. He simply showed up when things got too tense with some tedious band of small town toughs. Yet somehow the show lasted for three seasons. As if to signal viewers as to Marvel's true occult nature, a ritual drama of Isis was programmed directly after the show in 1975.[110]

CAPTAIN CLONES

After the runaway success of Captain Marvel, it was inevitable that other mythological and religious characters would follow. Samson was pulled from the Book of Judges and put to work in Fox's *Fantastic Comics* in 1939; Hercules became a star in Quality's *Hit Comics;* American icon Uncle Sam helped lick the "Japanazis" in Quality's *National Comics,* and publishing giant Dell created its first superhero in the explicitly occultic character, Phantasmo.

Ominously known as "Master of the World," Phantasmo made his first appearance in *Funnies* #45 in 1940. He was identical in appearance to Quality's Hercules (and Doctor Occult)—a nearly naked man wearing boots and briefs, and a cape with a folded shirt-collar. Phantasmo spent twenty-five years in Tibet, where Grand High Lamas (read: Blavatsky's Great White Brotherhood) schooled him in the mystic arts. He can grow to enormous size, fly, become invisible, pass through solid matter, and separate his astral form from his physical body. Another clone, Flash Lightning (*Sure-Fire Comics* #1), received his superpowers "from the Old Man of the Pyramids in Ancient Egypt . . . in order that he might save the world from destruction by crime." Flash's chest logo—a pyramid with three lightning bolts bursting from it—signalled readers to his occult origin.

Another early superhero clone with mythological undertones is Sub-Mariner, created by artist Bill Everett. Sub-Mariner first appeared in *Motion Picture Funnies Weekly* in 1939 and made an appearance in *Marvel Comics* #1 in the same year. Sub-Mariner is the half-human, half-merman ruler of an "undersea kingdom" (later Atlantis) who has an ambivalent relationship with surface folk. He doesn't

---

110   *The Secret of Isis* featured Joanna Cameron in the title role as a schoolmarm who finds a magical amulet that grants her the powers of Isis. Isis, very much a Wonder Woman clone, faltered after a slightly promising debut and soon lapsed into trite storylines.

look fully human (Daniels suggests he has the appearance of "an elemental spirit who possesses magical talents."[III]), but rather has elfin features—arched brows, pointed ears, and a severe coif that was borrowed by Mr. Spock in *Star Trek*. Subby hated surface-dwellers, but especially the Nazis. In fact, in 1940, he takes out a Nazi submarine over a year before the U. S. entered the war (*Marvel Comics #4*). Like Marvel's other Golden Age gods, Subby went into exile after the war, but returned in *Fantastic Four #4* in 1962, when a nuclear test destroys Atlantis. He has since been a regular star in the Marvel Universe.

One Captain Marvel clone was created out of sheer necessity. Marvelman was created by Captain Marvel's U. K. publisher after reprints stopped arriving in 1954. Several alterations were made to effect the change—albeit superficial ones. Billy Batson is replaced by young reporter Micky Moran; the wizard Shazam is replaced by the scientist Guntag Bargholt; the word "Shazam" is replaced with "Kimota!" ("atomic" in reverse, sort of). Although Marvelman didn't set the world ablaze and ended his run ten years later, he was destined for greater things when he was revived in 1982. For *Marvelman* (*Miracleman* in the Colonies) was the strip on which comic-book gods Alan Moore and Neil Gaiman cut their teeth.

THE MIGHTY THOR

Jack Kirby never got Captain Marvel out of his system. In fact, it's probably a safe bet that using Thor as a superhero in Marvel Comics' own version of Captain Marvel was Kirby's idea. Elements of the Captain are present in the 1962 premiere of *The Mighty Thor* ("The Stone Men from Saturn," *Journey Into Mystery #83*). In this classic tale, crippled doctor Don Blake is vacationing in Norway when an invasion force of rocky aliens appears in the skies. Blake flees to a cave where he discovers a stick that, when struck on the ground, allows its carrier to transform into Thor himself. It is interesting to note here that Thor's cavern of transformation ehoes Captain Marvel's subway tunnel—both of which harken back to the caverns and grottoes of the ancient mystery religions.

Journey Into Mystery also contained a remarkable backup feature called *Tales of Asgard*. In this strip, Lee and Kirby explore various Norse myths and give them their own unique spin. Kirby's art in *Tales* is simultaneously at its most charming and its most supernatural. He had obviously tapped into the force that channels those ancient myths, and his art displays the influence of the crypto-pagan children's-book art of early 20th century.

III   Les Daniels, *Marvel: Five Fabulous Decades of the World's Greatest Comics*, (New York: Abradale, 1991), p. 29.

Kirby later took over the plotting of *Thor* and turned it into a full-bore cosmic/psychedelic/mythological freakout. Planets came alive, Hercules and other Olympian gods dropped in and out, and a space-age version of Dr. Moreau called the High Evolutionary set his "New Men" in battle against the Thunder God. Thor's nemesis, Loki, granted human villains godlike powers and Don Blake's lady love, Jane Foster, herself became a goddess. Thor died; Thor was reborn; Thor was ungodded by Odin; Ragnarok came; Ragnarok went.

Kirby used *The Mighty Thor* as a vehicle for his unquenchable inner rage and his boundless, nearly supernatural imagination. The series churned with a particularly frenetic violence, softened only by Lee's charming dialogue and Vince Colletta's fairy-tale inks. Kirby left the book in 1971, but writer Roy Thomas and artist John Buscema worked hard to keep his spirit alive. Osiris, Isis, Horus, and Set even made their way up north for one 1975 storyline (*Thor* #240–241). In 1983, Kirby apostle Walt Simonson brought the hero back to his mythological roots (*Thor* #337) and even added some well-researched Nordic design flourishes to the strip.

OMAC

In May 1944, Fawcett introduced *Radar the International Policeman (Master Comics* #50), a strip created in conjunction with the US Office of War Information. Radar worked for what would soon comprise the bulk of the UN Security Council (the US, UK, USSR, and China) and fought lingering Fascist elements on behalf of global harmony. In 1950, Captain Marvel himself promoted this New World Order in "Captain Marvel, Citizen of the Universe" (*Capt. Marvel Adventures* #111). In 1974, Kirby took this spin on the Captain Marvel ethos one step further with his DC Comics series *OMAC*.

OMAC (One Man Army Corps), formerly a factory worker named Buddy Blank, is the creation of a world government agency known as the Global Peace Agency. The GPA is (literally) a faceless troupe of bureaucrats responsible for abolishing war. OMAC is created using the omnipotent power of GPA's sentient satellite, Brother Eye, who is exactly what he sounds like, a giant mechanical eyeball orbiting the planet keeping everyone under constant surveillance.

If you're thinking that Kirby cooked this whole scenario up from right-wing conspiracy propaganda, you're probably right. Kirby was a voracious reader and a fan of the *outré*, and it's highly likely that OMAC emerged from Kirby's interest in conspiracist tracts like *None Dare Call it Conspiracy*. Although *OMAC* didn't last long, it articulates an important link between occult mythology and modern conspiracy theory. Kirby obviously felt that the connections being drawn between Masonic symbolism and the global governance movement were compelling enough to create a new character around them.

SUPER-HORUS: HAWKMAN AND THE FALCON

When it comes to Horus stand-ins in comic books, they don't get any more explicit than DC's Hawkman, who first appeared in *Flash Comics* #1 in 1940. Hawkman's backstory is as direct a retelling of the ancient Sun god's myth as you're apt to find in a modern genre.

Hawkman is the alter ego of archaeologist Carter Hall, a typical pulp toff who discovers he is the reincarnation of the Egyptian prince Khufu. Khufu has a running battle with a high priest named Hath-Set, who, in the comic strip, reappears as a mad scientist named Anton Hastor. The ancient struggle between the two resumes in America. Hall discovers a metal that defies gravity, from which he constructs a set of wings to use in his struggle against the forces of darkness.

In 1961, Hawkman was reincarnated by writer Gardner Fox and 1940s Hawkman artist Joe Kubert as Kator Hol, an alien policeman from the planet Thanagar (*Brave and the Bold* #34), reflecting a shift away from the mythical archetypes of the first wave of superheroes to the more sci-fi-based heroes of the Fifties and Sixties. This alien-messiah version of Hawkman has persisted to the present day—the alien Hawkgirl has been a regular character on the popular *Justice League* series on the Cartoon Network.

Hawkman was never an A-list hero, so viable Hawk-clones were few. In 1966, animation giant Hanna-Barbera produced a shameless knockoff named Birdman (*Birdman and the Galaxy Trio*), who picks up on the Horus symbolism with powers granted by Egyptian solar diety, Ra. Birdman was later resurrected as a comedy character for the Cartoon Network's *Harvey Birdman: Attorney at Law,* and as Blue Falcon, who played second fiddle to Dynomutt (an Anubis stand-in) in 1976 on the *Scooby Doo/Dynomutt Hour* on ABC.

Marvel did not hesitate to inject plenty of occult symbolism into their Hawk-clone's origin story, however. Making his first appearance in *Captain America* #117, the Falcon is the alter ego of a black hoodlum named Sam Wilson. After crash-landing on a desert island, Wilson encounters Captain America's arch-foe, the Red Skull. Using Marvel's version of the alchemical Philosopher's Stone (called "the Cosmic Cube"), Red Skull magically transforms Wilson into a superhero. The Falcon's origin is more precise than his predecessor's, since Horus is symbolized by a peregrine falcon, not just an ordinary hawk. Yet for some inexplicable reason, Falcon originally had no wings. It wasn't until issue #171 that he is given his Hawkman-esque wings, which he has kept ever since.

In many ways, it may be surprising that Hawkman and Falcon are not more popular. Like Captain Marvel and Thor, they represent the ultimate fantasy—to be endowed with incredible powers that fall, literally, from the sky. Perhaps this is why they aren't considered worthy gods. They didn't suffer as we all must. Billy Batson is an orphan; Don Blake is a cripple: they suffer for their godhood. Carter Hall, on the other hand, is a fop and Sam Wilson is a thug. They don't deserve the power they are given.

CAPTAIN AMERICA

With Captain America came a new kind of messiah—the science hero—summoned into action to fight fascism. On the cover of the first issue of *Captain America* in 1941, creators Joe Simon and Jack Kirby show their hero slugging Adolf Hitler—nine months before the U. S. declared war on Germany. *Captain America*'s publisher, Martin Goodman, resolved as early as 1938 that he would use his pulp empire as an anti-Hitler propaganda vehicle.[112]

Captain America is the alter ego of Steve Rogers, a scrawny and sickly boy who, alarmed by the spread of fascism, volunteers for the U. S. Army but is rejected for poor health. His zeal is noted by army brass, however, who enlist him instead for the Super-Soldier program, headed by the brilliant scientist Emil Erskine and committed to transforming unlikely recruits into Nietzschean

---

112 Daniels, *Marvel*, p. 36.

übermenchen through science.[113] Just as Rogers is thus transformed, Erskine is assassinated by a Nazi mole before he got around to documenting his formulas. Rogers is, therefore, the alpha and omega of the program. His first act as Captain America is to avenge Erskine. Next, he acquires a costume that is a pastiche of mythic elements: Musketeer boots and gauntlets, head gear decorated with Mercury's wings, King Arthur's chain mail, Superman's jockey shorts, and a Praetorian shield. His primary nemesis, the Red Skull, was unceremoniously lifted from an old *Doc Savage* story.[114]

Like Superman, Captain America spawned an army of dreary patriotic imitations. DC quickly hired Simon and Kirby away from Timely and put them to work revising Sandman and creating two new characters—Manhunter and the shield-bearing Guardian.[115] Captain America was handed over to green-horn Stan Lee, and sales sagged. The Cap acquired a glamorous female companion named Golden Girl in 1948 (*Captain America* #66), but after the war, slid into obscurity, until he was resurrected in the 1950s as "Captain America, Commie Smasher." Despite Lee's best efforts to cash in on the Red Scare, however, Cap was eventually defeated by the ultimate nemesis of all funnybook messiahs—low sales. His last issue, in 1950 (*Captain America's Weird Tales* #74), didn't even feature him on the cover.

This dying-resurrecting messiah was not so easily dismissed, however. In 1964, when the revitalized Marvel needed new heroes to fuel its Sixties revolution, Captain America is found once again in the icy seas of the Arctic by another revived 40s hero, Sub-Mariner, in *The Avengers* #4. In a fit of pique, Subby throws his old partner back into the drink, but the thawing Cap is found by the superteam and soon becomes their leader. After a long run in *Tales of Suspense,* the Captain was granted his own title in the late Sixties.

Captain America enjoyed another strange incarnation as a counterculture icon. Peter Fonda's drug-dealing biker character in the 1969 film *Easy Rider* adopted his name and elements of his costume. And in the 1970s, he was recast as a loner anti-hero. Instead of fighting foreign threats like Nazism or Communism, he

---

113 Ironically, the real Nazis were experimenting with their own Super-Soldier formula at the time, injecting both prisoners and military personnel with a cocktail of methamphetamines and anabolic steroids.

114 "The Red Skull," *Doc Savage Magazine,* Aug, 1933.

115 Manhunter was later recast by Kirby as a member of a initiatic/Masonic secret society (*First Issue Special* # 5, Aug.'75).

declares a one-man war on homegrown corruption, tapping into then-popular iconoclastic films like *Walking Tall* and *Billy Jack*. Reflecting the sour, post-Watergate mood of the country, and perhaps seeking to recapture some of the hip patina of *Easy Rider*, the producers of an unwatchable 1979 TV movie offered a ludicrous revised Captain America who cruised around on a chopper and fought crime in a baby-blue leotard and motorcycle helmet. The film went nowhere.

In the 1980s, Captain America reverted back to a generic superhero, perhaps mirroring the uncertain relationship modern Americans—particularly the intellectual misfits attracted to comic books—have with patriotism. Sophisticated readers need more from their messiahs than mere flag-waving. The Captain was a great propaganda tool during World War II, but has since lost his relevance. Sensing this, and perhaps sensing the souring attitudes towards jingoism in the wake of the disastrous Iraq War, Marvel killed off the Captain in a highly publicized 2007 storyline. Whether or not he will rise again is anyone's guess.

CHAPTER 15

THE SILVER AGE SCIENCE HEROES

Comic book superheroes were everywhere in the 1940s. According to surveys, half of the U. S. population read comics. During the war, 90 percent of DC's titles were superhero-based. Comics outsold the *Saturday Evening Post* and *Reader's Digest* combined by a factor of ten to one on military newsstands.[116] Superheroes propagandized not only for the war effort, but for various governmental and non governmental programs—war bonds, scrap-metal and paper collection, the American Red Cross, the USO, and other patriotic pitch-in efforts. But with their mission accomplished in 1945, superhero sales began to decline, replaced by funny animals, teen humor, and the new romance comics. But none of these could deliver sales like the superheroes once did, and the industry suffered.

---

116 Bradford W. Wright, *Comic Book Nation* (Baltimore: John Hopkins University Press, 2001), p. 57.

THE PORNOGRAPHY
OF VIOLENCE

As is too often the case, market pressures forced publishers to aim for the gutter, and falling superhero sales encouraged a substantial coarsening of content. Beginning with Lev Gleason's *Crime Does Not Pay* in 1942, crime comics flooded the market until, by 1948, every fifth comic sold was a crime comic.[117] Bradford Wright notes that the crime comics "delved into violence, brutality, and sadism to a graphic degree never before seen in comic books—in some instances, never before seen anywhere in mass entertainment."[118]

Crime comics were followed by equally graphic horror. These titles naturally used themes of the occult and the supernatural, most commonly werewolves and vampires, but more often depicted ordinary human killers slicing and dicing beautiful women. The best-known horror comics were published by Entertaining Comics, better known as EC, run by William Gaines (Max's son) and editor Al Feldstein. EC's horror stories were all ostensibly based in conventional morality, with a bloody comeuppance usually reserved for criminals and evil-doers. But Gaines and Feldstein also amused themselves by trying to outdo each other with outlandishly gory plots. The resulting stories were often clever, well-crafted black humor, but they were being marketed to very young children. Even Gaines and Feldstein felt tinges of guilt over the horror comics, eventually admitting that the criticism of them was essentially justified.

Most crime and horror comics were little more than exploitation, violence, and degeneracy for their own sake, made all the more distasteful by their targeting of a preteen audience. In most cases, they were published to keep the presses running after the public lost interest in the superheroes. Gaines disingenuously tried to defend the books before a Congressional subcommittee, but the EC line collapsed in the mid 1950s.[119] Gaines soon rebounded, however, and converted the comic book *MAD* into magazine format, creating one of the most successful and influential culture icons of the 20th century.

---

117 Mike Benton, *Horror Comics* (Dallas: Taylor, 1991), p. 9.

118 Wright, *Comic Book Nation*, p. 77

119 Wright, *Comic Book Nation*, pp. 177, 178, 181.

SEDUCTION

The most outspoken crusader against comic books was Frederic Wertham (1895–1981), a left-leaning German Jew who came to America in 1922 to work as a psychiatrist. His *pro bono* work with juvenile delinquents and child criminals convinced him that violent comic books had a destructive effect on young minds. He began a campaign against comic books in 1941, but received little attention until the rise of the crime titles. In 1954, he published his landmark treatise against comic books, *Seduction of the Innocent*. In addition to his criticisms of the gore and depravity in crime and horror comics, Wertham attacked the superheroes, arguing that the violence and vigilantism in their yarns encouraged antisocial behavior, sexual perversion, and fascist impulses. His attack had a powerful impact on the Senate Subcommittee on Juvenile Delinquency hearings, led by Tennessee Senator Estes Kefauver. Largely because of his crusade, the public mood turned against comic books, and publishers found themselves threatened both economically and politically. It was do or die.

THE CODE

In 1954, the major publishers banded together and formed a strict self-censorship body called the Comics Code Authority (CCA). The Authority banned words like "terror" and "horror" from titles, banished werewolves, vampires, and zombies, and forbade graphic depictions of murder or sex. All comics were to be submitted to the CCA for their literal seal of approval.

Overnight, death, gore, and sex vanished from the funny books but the industry barely survived the furor. An unintended consequence of the Code was to force creators to dig deep into the recesses of their imaginations to capture their readers' attention. Truly bizarre sci-fi and fantasy imagery entered the mix, which opened the door to the eventual theological reinterpretations of the superheroes. As Daniel Herman wrote: "The Comics Code was not an impediment to the further development of the artists and their art, it was merely a detour."[120] The Code, in fact, ushered in what came to be known as the Silver Age.

---

120 Daniel Herman, *Silver Age: The Second Generation of Comic Book Artists* (Nesahannock, PA: Hermes Press, 2004), p. 90.

THE SILVER AGE

The Silver Age of comics kicked off in *Showcase #4* in 1956, with the reinvention of Golden Age hero the Flash, written by Robert Kanigher and Carmine Infantino. Original creator Gardner Fox called Flash "a reincarnation of the winged Mercury,"[121] but the new version is actually a police scientist who acquires superspeed after a laboratory mishap. In contrast to the often grungy and dingy characters of the Golden Age, the new Silver Age Flash signaled the arrival of a clean, sharp, and futuristic breed of heroes.

In 1959, a sci-fi oriented Green Lantern (*Showcase #22*) made his appearance, resurrected, not as a hero who gets his powers from a magic lantern, but as a test pilot named Hal Jordan who is initiated into the galactic Green Lantern Corps by a dying alien.[122] Created by writer John Broome, the art for the new Green Lantern was handled by legendary artist Gil Kane, master of the sleek and stylish look that came to identify the Silver Age at DC. Kane was also tapped in 1961 for the revival of the Atom (*Showcase #34*), a tedious strongman character in his Golden Age incarnation, but reborn as scientist Ray Palmer who, using "dwarf star matter," is able to shrink to microscopic size yet still retain the strength of a full-grown man.

The science-hero archetype tapped into the *zeitgeist* of the atomic age and the rapidly approaching space age. It spoke to the phobias and aspirations of its time, presenting a clean, tidy, and communitarian image of American society. The Science Heroes upheld the common civic assumptions of a strong, centralized federal government and a prosperous middle class. Where the heroes of the 1940s played into liberal Rooseveltian idealism by making villains of greedy corporate executives, the new science heroes were proud servants of the military-industrial complex.

Although some have criticized the Silver Age heroes for being dull, stolid, and uptight, they offered something lacking in the pop culture—a positive, optimistic vision and heroes worth emulating. Theirs was a hopeful and idealistic vision that still holds a lot of appeal for modern fans and creators. The success of the archetype inspired the floundering Marvel to embrace the new heroic paradigm.

---

121 *Flash Comics #1*, January 1940, p. 50.

122 This galactic fraternity, with its ring and lantern imagery, has a distinctly Masonic whiff to it. Broome, a follower of Wilhelm Reich, was no stranger to esoteric topics, and quit comics to study Zen in Asia. He died in Thailand in 1999.

Stan Lee and his talented freelancers eventually invoked the spirit of the new gods and changed the face of comicdom—and American culture—forever.

SPIDER-MAN

One of the most recognizable characters in the world is Spider-Man, created by Stan Lee and Steve Ditko in 1962 (*Amazing Fantasy* #15). Spider-Man has earned countless millions for Marvel Comics, appearing in comics, cartoons, movies, coloring books, novels, records, and children's books. He's been used to sell toys, games, cereal, canned foods, paper products, candy, soap, costumes, and just about anything else you can think of. Spider-Man acts as Marvel's official mascot, just as Mickey Mouse does for Disney. Unknown to many fans, however, Spider-Man has a deep and mysterious history.

Spider-Man developed out of an unpublished character named the Silver Spider. Created by writer Jack Oleck and *Captain Marvel* artist C. C. Beck, Silver Spider was a young orphan who finds a magic ring that turns him into a Marvel-esque superhero. Joe Simon and Jack Kirby renamed the character "Spider-Man" in the Fifties, but dissolved their publishing concern before they could get him to print. Later, they expanded on the character's occult origin, renamed him the Fly, and sold the character to Archie Comics, who published the first four issues of *Adventures of the Fly* in 1959. Shortly after, Kirby decamped to Marvel and pitched the original Spider-Man idea to Stan Lee, who radically changed the character and handed him off to artist Steve Ditko. [123]

Lee, who, like most people in the Fifties, was fascinated by radiation, created a storyline in which science nerd Peter Parker's powers were acquired from the bite of a radioactive arachnid. Somehow, young Peter doesn't die of radiation sickness, but acquires the strength and agility of a spider, as well as an uncanny "spider-sense." Peter at first decides to use these powers for financial gain in a career as a professional wrestler, but his world is turned upside down after a robber he lets escape kills his beloved Uncle Ben. Having learned the hard way that "with great power comes great responsibility," Peter dons the requisite Spandex and goes out to battle evil. He also defies the laws of geometry zooming around Manhatthan in impossible arcs at high speed using his webshooter.

---

123 See Joe and Jim Simon, *The Comic Book Makers* (Clinton, NJ: Vanguard, 2003), pp. 182–184.

Like Captain America, Spider-Man is a nerdy weakling transformed into a hero through pseudoscientific means—but still suffers the indignities of high-school bullying without resorting to his immense strength to defend himself. And this is the secret of his success. Spider-Man was pitched to readers as an underdog—"the hero that could be you," as Stan Lee so cannily put it. Not only is Peter Parker scorned in school, as Spider-Man, he is vilified by J. Jonah Jameson, publisher of the tabloid newspaper *The Daily Bugle*. This had enormous appeal for an audience already prone to bullying and feelings of persecution.

The Amazing Spider-Man was a top seller in the 1960s, and was quickly adapted to other media. A popular (and faithful) television cartoon ran from 1967 to 1970. Spidey became a frequent guest star on the PBS kids' show *The Electric Company* in 1974. A live-action TV show ran on CBS in 1978, and two separate animated television series appeared in 1981. Another series appeared on Fox from 1994 to 1998, and a computer-animated mini-series ran on MTV in 2003. Of course, the *Spider-Man* feature films, directed by Sam Raimi and starring Tobey Maguire, were huge hits, and a third came out in 2007. The success of these films also inspired a series of wildly popular video games. As of this writing, Spider-Man's popularity shows no sign of waning.

THE SILVER SURFER

Stan Lee and Jack Kirby created Marvel Comics' other great Messiah figure in an extremely roundabout way. In fact, the Silver Surfer began life as an afterthought. While developing a storyline in which the Fantastic Four confront Galactus, an enormous alien who travels from galaxy to galaxy feeding off the energy of entire planets, Kirby doodled in a metallic humanoid riding a surfboard, explaining to Lee that a character as momentous as Galactus needed a herald to announce his arrival.[124] Lee loved the idea and used the Surfer as a scout who cruises the universe in search of planets for Galactus to devour. In 1966, the two appeared in an adventure that signalled the peak of Lee and Kirby's collaboration ("The Coming of Galactus," *Fantastic Four* #48). In a multi-issue story, Silver Surfer encounters the Thing's blind girlfriend, Alicia Masters, who convinces him that humanity is

---

124 Kirby later said that Galactus was his vision of God, which tells you a lot about how Jack Kirby perceived the world. See William A. Christensen and Mark Seifert, "The King," *Wizard Magazine* #36, August 1994.

worth saving. He then rebels against Galactus and helps the Fantastic Four defeat him. As punishment, Galactus banishes the Surfer to Earth.

The Surfer became a recurring guest star in *The Fantastic Four*. When Marvel expanded their line in 1968, the character was given his own title. Lee's version of the Surfer was far different from Kirby's, however. Lee saw him as an explicitly Christlike figure and in 1969, even pitted him against Marvel's version of Satan, Mephisto (*Silver Surfer* #8). Without Kirby's ferocious imagination, some felt the Surfer lost his cosmic edge. The title was canceled after only eighteen issues. In 1978, Lee and Kirby later teamed up for Marvel's first original graphic novel, *The Silver Surfer*, and the Surfer regained his own series in 1988, which was a hit. A short-lived Surfer cartoon ran on the Fox network in 1998, and the character is featured in the second *Fantastic Four* film.

CHAPTER 16

THE GOLEMS

The second major superhero archetype, the Golem, comes to us from Jewish mysticism. The myth of the Golem harkens back to the ghettoes of Eastern Europe, where Jews periodically found themselves terrorized by hostile Gentiles. Legend has it that rabbis fashioned Golems out of clay and animated them using the magic of the Kabbalah. The Golems protected the Jews and punished their enemies. Implicit in the Golem folktales, however, is a certain danger for those the Golem is meant to protect.

But the most famous Golem story deals with Rabbi Loew, a Jewish leader in late 16th-century Prague, a thriving center for alchemy, Kabbalah, and other occult pursuits. Following a series of anti-Semitic attacks by hostile burghers, Loew formed a Golem taking mud from the Vltava river and breathing life into it using Kabbalistic gematria. He carved the Hebrew epithet *emet* (truth) into his forehead.

But the Golem, meant to protect the Jews, soon became too powerful for Loew to control and came to pose a threat to Jews and Gentiles alike. The burghers promised to stop the pogroms if Loew destroyed the Golem. Loew rubbed out the first letter of *emet* from the Golem's forehead, leaving the word *met*, meaning death.

The Golem was a favorite literary theme in both Christian and Jewish folktales, inspiring alchemists like Paracelsus, who sought to create a miniature version called the *Homunculus* (Latin for "little man"). Golem stories first appeared in print in 1847 in *Galerie der Sippurim*, a collection of Jewish folktales. A German film entitled *The Golem: How He Came into the World* was made by Paul Wegener in 1920. Some claim the Golems are the first robots in literature; others see them more them as zombies.

The Golem archetype in comics has its thematic roots in the legends, but with many important differences. In comics, the Golem is often an antihero. Golems like Batman are dangerous heroes who act out of a need for vengeance. Golems like Wolverine and Punisher are beserkers, whose rage causes them to kill almost indiscriminately. In addition to a need for revenge, Golems usually have some artificial component to them—a cybernetic aspect, or even something as simple as a disguise that fundamentally changes their nature. The Golem is a man transformed into something different, often through some arcane science.

The forces that drive the Golem make him liable to do harm to those he is supposed to protect. Historically, the Golem is an expression of rage, and ultimately, of powerlessness. There is often something weak or vulnerable about Golem characters, however, something that needs to be buttressed with armor. Marvel's Iron Man is actually Tony Stark, a Bruce Wayne-type playboy who needs to be encased in armor to protect his weak heart.[125] Frank Miller brilliantly depicted Bruce Wayne in *Dark Knight* as a wounded child who constantly flashes back to the murder of his parents.

Golem characters like the Shadow became popular in the 1930s when organized crime was as frightening to the average citizen as the Cossacks were to Russian Jews. The three men most responsible for the creation and development of Batman—Bob Kane, Bill Finger, and Jerry Robinson—were all American-born Jews who probably heard the Golem stories at some time in their lives. They

---

125 Later writers recast Stark as an alcoholic, *Iron Man* #120–128, 1979.

translated the terror of the legends to the more generalized fear experienced by kids confronted by bullies and the real sense of helplessness experienced by honest citizens confronted by gangsters.

So what is it about the comics medium that it has given birth to so many Golems? The answer may be in the people who create them. Many of the leading writers in the early days of comics were diaspora Jews who created their heroes in the shadow of anti-Semitism. Stories of persecution were very fresh in the minds of the young Jews who created characters like Batman, the Thing, and the Hulk. Jewish or not, many comic readers (and creators) are often bookish and sensitive young lads, prone to harassment by bullies in their school days. The Golem archetype is essentially the byproduct of insecurity and wounded pride. It provides a satisfying emotional release for the bottled-up rage, frustration, and feelings of impotence that persecution and bullying engender.

BATMAN

The archetypal Golem figure, Batman, first appeared in *Detective Comics* #27 in 1939. Batman, elaborating on Gibson's depiction of the Shadow, was introduced as the alter ego of millionaire Bruce Wayne, whose parents are shot dead before his eyes. Creator Bob Kane originally portrayed Batman as ruthless and unrelenting. As his hero's popularity grew, however, Kane smoothed some of these rough edges and made him less of a vigilante. In 1940, he introduced Robin, Batman's boy sidekick, who is sworn into the crimefighting fraternity in a candlelight ceremony in *Detective Comics* #38.[126] Robin was purportedly introduced as a character to whom young readers could relate. But there is something disturbing about scenarios in which an adult exposes a prepubescent boy to constant physical danger. The boy sidekick, though phased out in the Silver Age, remains grist for critics and satirists alike. *Saturday Night Live* features Robert Smigel's cartoon series *The Ambiguously Gay Duo*, which pokes fun at the pair's apparent gender confusion.

Batman's innocuous and inoffensive post-Code stories, however, eventually drove bored writers to turn the series into a surreal, dreamlike sci-fi extravaganza. In the

---

126 When comics came under scrutiny for their violent storylines, *Batman* came under attack as "a wish dream of two homosexuals living together." Wertham, in his *Seduction of the Innocent,* claimed that "if Batman were in the State Department he'd be dismissed." (New York: Reinhart, 1954), pp. 190, 191.

late 1950s, the hero found himself in some of the strangest stories ever seen in comics—stories that were even more disturbing, in their own way, than the crime comics. Batman was plunged into other dimensions and pursued by creatures from other dimensions who plunge into ours. He became a bobble-headed alien, a medieval knight, a giant Godzilla-type monster, and discovered his psychic twin. A strange array of companions—Batwoman, Batgirl, Batmite, a Bathound, and even Bat-Ape—all made regular appearances. And all of this mind-numbing weirdness is rendered in the bland, childish, 50s DC house style, making the goings-on seem even more psychedelic and unsettling. As a result, Batman soon found himself teetering on the brink of cancellation.

In 1964, editor Julius Schwartz stepped in and returned Batman to urban crime-fighting. He enlisted his favorite artist, *Flash* penciler Carmine Infantino, to redesign the series and sales started to pick up again. The "new-look" Batman caught the eye of Hollywood and a *Batman* TV series was planned, starring the decidedly un-buff character actor Adam West. This 1966 high-camp spoof became a monster hit and kicked off the first wave of "Batmania" (a nod to Beatlemania, two years prior). The show ran twice a week and Hollywood royalty began lining up to appear on it.

Batman was part of a wave of Sixties fantasy and sci-fi shows that included *Bewitched, I Dream of Jeannie, The Addams Family, The Munsters, My Favorite Martian,* and *Star Trek.* During the Sixties, monsters and myths resurfaced as a part of the popular mind, and an unprecedented Dionysian explosion capped off the decade. Although its dreary aftermath swept away nearly everything that came before it, reruns of shows like *Batman* and *Star Trek* found their way into syndication and still inspire new generations of acolytes.

After Batmania petered out, Julius Schwartz decided to take the concept of the Dark Knight detective even further. He hired two writers—young, hip Denny O'Neil and veteran writer/artist Frank Robbins—to return Batman to the night. In 1971, O'Neil cast Batman as a virile adventurer and introduced the arch-villain Ra's Al Ghul to act as his nemesis (*Batman* #232). And Robbins' trademark airtight plotting and bizarre characters, including the grotesque Man-Bat (*Detective Comics* #400), provided needed depth. Both O'Neil and Robbins set their stories almost exclusively at night, and gave Batman a testosterone infusion that erased any lingering doubts as to his sexuality. Robbins dispensed with Robin by sending Dick Grayson off to college, while artist Neal

Adams redesigned the character as a virile, hairy-chested ladies man. Batman chugged along in that vein for the next decade and a half, until he was radically redefined in 1986 in Frank Miller's *Batman: The Dark Knight Returns*.

DARK KNIGHT: THE GOD OF VENGEANCE

Frank Miller cut his teeth on Marvel's *Daredevil* before tackling Batman. Miller physically immersed himself in the landscape of Manhattan in order to inform his artwork, which depicted a mysterious wonderland of deep shadows, neon lights, and architectural majesty. Miller's early plots had a compassionate, humanist sheen, but his work slowly began to darken, reflecting a growing fascination with far-right politics. *Dark Knight* was the culmination of this trend. "In *Dark Knight*," Miller said in a 1985 interview, "there's a much more direct use of my real life experiences in New York, my experiences with crime, my awareness of the horrible pressure that crime exerted on my life." When asked of the fascistic implications of his new Batman, Miller explained that Batman "has to be a force that in certain ways is beyond good and evil," a moral force this is "plainly bigger and greater than normal men and perfectly willing to pass judgment and administer punishment."[127] Nietszche himself couldn't have said it better.

Dark Knight takes place in a near-future Gotham City, to which Batman has retired. The city is run by weak, cowardly liberals and terrorized by an incongruously all-white gang called the Mutants, led by a giant, shirtless thug known simply as "Leader." Now a "limousine liberal," Bruce Wayne uses his fortune to rehabilitate criminals through psychotherapy. Then a massive heat wave sparks a horrific crime wave and culminates in a powerful rainstorm, during which a giant bat crashes through Wayne's skylight. He takes this as a sign that it is time to don his cape and cowl and return to fighting evil. The lifeless clay of Bruce Wayne is "born again" as a marauding, bloodthirsty Golem.

Here again, we see the unadulterated power of myth in action. Miller unambiguously depicts Batman as a spiritual force that possesses Bruce Wayne for its own

---

127 Kim Thompson, "Frank Miller: Return of the Dark Knight," *The Comics Journal* #101, August 1985, pp. 59, 61.

purposes. And Wayne needs this demonic spiritual power to regain his manhood. Miller explicitly refers to his Batman as a "god of vengeance" and intentionally re-mythologizes him. He had clearly come to the same conclusion that Alex Ross came to ten years later with *Kingdom Come*: "Comics had been drained of the content that would give the heroes any reason to exist."[128] Miller found a new reason for his hero to exist in the runaway street crime that bedeviled New York City. Eventually the avenging spirit of the Bat totally consumes Wayne, who becomes a full-fledged avenging angel.

Miller's Batman is both a puritan and a fascist. As the series progresses, Batman slugs it out with supervillains until Gotham City is crippled by the explosion of a nuclear bomb, which causes a massive electromagnetic pulse. The story climaxes when the corrupt powers-that-be send their enforcer, Superman (who is usually busy fighting covert wars in Central America for the government), to destroy Batman. In the end, Wayne stages his own death and assembles a spelunking paramilitary band that he will train as his own army of Golems—an anticlimactic ending for a deeply problematic, yet extremely powerful, work of art.

BATMANIA REDUX

Dark Knight set the stage for late 80s revival. By then, a crack epidemic was fueling a dramatic rise in crime—particularly gun crime. Homicide rates skyrocketed as well-armed drug gangs fought over territory. Makeshift outdoor crack dens sprang up all over Manhattan, even in Midtown. The resultant fear and anxiety summoned the spirit of the Golem back into the public consciousness. Batmania hit America hard with the release of Tim Burton's 1989 feature film.

Much to the consternation of fans, Burton cast comedic actor Michael Keaton rather than a buff and virile actor in the role of the hero, showing that he understood the Golem archetype better than the fans. In the comics, Golem Bruce Wayne is only distinguishable from messiah Clark Kent by the latter's signature eyeglasses. But Keaton is short, slight, balding, and bespectacled—almost a *rabbinic* stereotype. The strength of Keaton's Batman lies in his armored uniform and his mastery of esoteric martial arts and gadgetry strongly reminiscent of a rabbinical mastery of Kabbalah. The new Batman was especially popular with the kids of the new urban America, many of whom were racial minorities. To them, the need

---

128 Daniels, *DC Comics*, p. 190.

for deliverance from criminal violence was not an abstraction; it was a day-to-day reality. Batman and Batsignal shirts were *the* urban fashion statement of 1989. The next Batman film, *Batman Returns,* was three years in the making. This navel-gazing Goth yarn had little resonance, even in the year of the LA riots. After its release, Burton quit the series and was replaced by Joel Schumacher, who turned the franchise into a homoerotic burlesque, first with the 1995 *Batman Forever* and then the excoriated *Batman and Robin* two years later. The latter was such a catastrophic failure that it put the movie property on ice for eight years. The comics, however, continued to be popular and DC has published several successful Batman series and graphic novels since then. Two popular cartoon series emerged in the 1990s: *Batman: The Animated Series* and *Batman Beyond.* In 2005, the movie franchise was revived by British director Christopher Nolan (*Batman Begins*), which, although it was a hit, didn't enjoy the success or the resonance that the first Burton film had.

BAT-CLONES

After creating Superman, Jerry Siegel returned to his occult roots. Perhaps inspired by the success of Batman, Jerry Siegel created The Spectre in 1940 (*More Fun Comics* #52). The Spectre is the shade of Jim Corrigan, a murdered cop who returns from the dead with godlike powers. Daniels notes that "with the Spectre, Siegel went all out to create a protagonist who was not merely super but absolutely omnipotent."[129] The Spectre is, as Maurice Horn wrote, "as close to God as the comic books got."[130]

The Spectre's powers are given to him by "The Voice," an omnipotent, discorporeal being many interpret to be God. The Spectre can change form and size at will, practices astral projection, and fights against inter-dimensional entities. Even as Corrigan, he appears invulnerable and has to make excuses when various attempts on his life are unsuccessful. The Spectre is ultimately hampered by his limitless powers, however, since omnipotence makes it hard to maintain any feeling of suspense. The Spectre quietly vanished in the mid 1940s, enjoying sporadic revivals in the Silver Age. He was resurrected in 1974 by editor Joe Orlando (*Adventure Comics* #431) as a gruesomely imaginative crime fighter whose macabre adventures skirted the limits of the Comics Code.

---

129 Daniels, *DC Comics*, p. 44.

130 Maurice Horn, ed., *World Encyclopedia of Comics* (New York: Chelsea House, 1976), p. 629.

DAREDEVIL

Marvel's Daredevil is very much a hybrid of Batman and Spider-Man. The story, told by Stan Lee and artist Bill Everett, begins when an accident involving nuclear waste leaves young Matt Murdock blinded, but heightens his other senses. Murdock, who is golemized when his father is killed by gangsters, works as an attorney by day and a crime-fighter by night. The title hit its stride when illustrator Gene Colan took over in 1966. Colan's dark, moody artwork played well to the book's blind-superhero conceit, and *Daredevil* chugged along as a solid B-list title.

Marvel's early Seventies' affirmative-action program forced Daredevil to share billing with the Black Widow (a Russian spy in this incarnation), and his base of operations moved to San Francisco. When Colan left *Daredevil* to tackle *Doctor Strange* and *Tomb of Dracula,* the series became a typically anemic 1970s Marvel potboiler. The book had no hook and no look, its only distinguishing feature being the moody and dramatic rendering of artist Klaus Janson. *Daredevil's* stock was so low by 1978 that it was handed over to young Frank Miller (*Daredevil* #158). Writer Roger McKenzie had signed on a few issues earlier and was moving the title away from tired heroics and placing Daredevil in the shadowy milieu of urban crime.

Between them, McKenzie, Miller, and Janson redefined the character, creating a gritty urban drama that had a powerful influence on comics and on Hollywood. When Miller took over the writing duties in 1981, the title became one of Marvel's top sellers. Miller left the title in 1983 and the book drifted for a couple of years. In 1985, Miller returned to *Daredevil* as a writer for the pivotal "Born Again" storyline. This remarkable saga began with the hero's arch nemesis, Kingpin, learning his secret identity from Murdock's former secretary, Karen Page, who sells the secret for a fix. The storyline is one of Miller's very best and helped legitimize superhero comics at a crucial time in the medium's history.

An explicitly Catholic superhero, Miller's Daredevil is motivated, not by revenge, but by compassion, struggling against his own rage and need for vengeance. Miller ended his first run on the book in 1983 with a brooding morality play in which Daredevil plays Russian roulette with his nemesis Bullseye in a hospital room (*Daredevil* #191). Movie director Kevin Smith also drew heavily on the same Catholic imagery and morality on his run on *Daredevil*, and these themes are prevalent in the 2003 *Daredevil* film, starring Ben Affleck.

KIRBY'S RAGE:
THE THING AND THE HULK

Marvel produced two Golems that drew heavily from the classic horror tales of the 19th century: the Thing and the Hulk. Both represented a sort of inversion of the science hero—men who become monsters through the power of the dark side of progress. The Thing becomes a Golem when exposed to cosmic rays during an aborted spaceflight. Created by Stan Lee and Jack Kirby, the Hulk is a scientist named Bruce Banner who is golemized when exposed to the deadly radiation of an experimental atomic weapon (the "Gamma Bomb"). The parallels between the arcane arts of Kabbalah and the arcane arts of nuclear science are unmistakable here.

In many ways, the Hulk is a carbon copy of the Thing (a.k.a. Ben Grimm). A member of the Fantastic Four, Ben Grimm is a test pilot who is persuaded by his old college friend, Reed Richards, to take an experimental rocket into orbit. Grimm's reservations are confirmed when he and the rest of the crew (rounded out by Richards' fiancé, Sue Storm, and her brother, Johnny) are genetically mutated by cosmic rays. Grimm takes the brunt of the radiation and is transformed into a misshapen freak of enormous strength with orange skin that looks like rocks or bricks. Grimm's rocky orange skin makes him one of the more explicit incarnations of the clay Golem of Jewish legend.[131]

Initially, Grimm's is as unpredictable and dangerous as the Golem, but he slowly evolves into a lovable curmudgeon. The Thing became a popular icon for Marvel, eventually spinning off into his own series and cartoon show. Michael Chiklis' portrayal of him—and his makeup job—in the 2005 *Fantastic Four* movie both harken back to the lumpy, cantankerous Thing of the early issues of the *Fantastic Four* comic.

The Hulk, who first appeared in 1962 (*The Incredible Hulk* #1), draws on Mary Shelley's *Frankenstein* and Robert Louis Stevenson's *Dr. Jekyll and Mr. Hyde,* two famous stories inspired by the Golem. Like the *Frankenstein* novel, *The Incredible Hulk* takes a dim view of science run amok. In Hulk's case, however, the scientist and the monster are one and the same. In a sense, the rabbi and the Golem become one. Like the Golem, Hulk loses his power and returns to the *prima materia*—the mud—that is Bruce Banner.

---

131 Grimm himself was later revealed to be of Jewish origin. (*Fantastic Four*, vol. 3 #56)

Not surprisingly, the essential Hulk is the version drawn by creator Jack Kirby. Whereas later artists portrayed him as either a dull-looking muscleman or a steroid addict, Kirby portrayed him as *id* run amok. The Hulk embodies an inner rage that the artist nursed over the years, and themes of abuse and anger dominated later storylines and movie adaptations. A popular CBS TV series appeared in the late 1970s starring Bill Bixby and featuring bodybuilder Lou Ferrigno. Bixby's portrayal of Banner as a nauseatingly sensitive "70s guy" made the all-too-brief episodes with Ferrigno all the more satisfying.

DEATH DEALERS

The social unrest of the Sixties terrified Middle America. As the civil rights movement went sour and industrial decay and urban blight created a new generation of increasingly vicious criminals, a new urban crime wave became the inspiration for a 1971 film that featured a revised Golem strongly reminiscent of The Shadow. *Dirty Harry* told the story of San Francisco homicide cop Harry Callahan's pursuit of an elementally evil serial killer. With his dark blond hair, lanky frame, and almost delicate good looks, Clint Eastwood may seem an unlikely choice to play a tough Irish cop like Callahan. But Eastwood brought the quiet fortitude of a Golem to the role, as well as its relentlessness. The Scorpio Killer of the film was inspired by the real-life Zodiac Killer, who terrorized the Bay Area with a series of random shootings and arcane coded messages. Dirty Harry's grim brand of street justice immediately struck a chord with a young comic writer named Gerry Conway.

THE PUNISHER

Conway's Dirty Harry knockoff, the Punisher, first appeared in 1974 in *Amazing Spider-Man* #129. The character took elements from Batman and the Shadow, and later cross-pollinated with Charles Bronson's character from 1974's *Death Wish*. The Punisher's adventures were published in magazine-format comics that were not subject to the Comics Code Authority. The Punisher was originally an honest cop named Frank Castle whose family is killed by some random thugs while picnicking in the park *(Marvel Preview* #2). Castle then reinvents himself as a Spandex-clad executioner who unleashes his considerable arsenal on slightly more realistic opponents than those he would face in the color comics.

The Punisher's popularity waned in the late Seventies and he was reduced to sporadic appearances in other character's titles, until the crack epidemic gave him new life. He was then given his own title, where he spent most of his time battling crack dealers and drug lords. The character had particular resonance with the same scared urban kids who worshipped Batman. His skin color may have been problematic, but his methods were not. The Punisher became the avenging angel for a particularly horrid period in urban history. He was featured in two film adaptations, one in 1989 and one in 2003. The first never made it into U. S. theaters; the second was made far too late to resonate with a Golem-hungry mass audience.

ROBOCOP

The groundwork for the success of the first *Batman* movie was laid by another film that drew heavily on *Dark Knight*. *Robocop,* released at the height of the epidemic of drug violence in 1987, offered up an even more explicit Golem than Batman. Directed by the gleefully nihilistic Dutch filmaker Paul Verhoeven, *Robocop* told the story of Alex Murphy, who is killed by a drug gang and resurrected as a cyborg by the evil Omni Consumer Products Corporation. Robocop is controlled by a host of computer programs in much the same way that the Golem is controlled by the spells of Kabbalah. As in many Golem stories, Robocop ends up turning on his creators when he finds they are in cahoots with the gangsters who killed him in his human incarnation.

Robocop borrowed many plot points and stylistic flourishes from *Dark Knight*. But Verhoeven, infamous for his love of grotesque and sickening violence, added a few wrinkles of his own that later rubbed off on *Dark Knight* author Frank Miller, who subsequently signed on to write *Robocop's* two sequels.

A Golem of much lesser note is Spawn, the creation of Canadian cartoonist Todd McFarlane. An occult spin-off of Batman, Spawn was once Al Simmons, a government hitman who finds himself in Hell after being murdered. He makes a deal with Satan to do his bidding and returns to Earth to round up renegade demons. Spawn has made his creator extremely wealthy with a whole line of comic books, video games, and toys. Spawn was also the star of an animated series on HBO and a moderately successful 1997 feature film.

WOLVERINE

Another death dealer with more marked Golem overtones is Wolverine, the star character of *The X-Men*. Created by Len Wein and John Romita, Wolverine first appeared in 1972 as a minor villain in an issue of *The Incredible Hulk* (#181). In 1975, he was introduced in *Giant Size X-Men #1* as a member of that mutant brotherhood. His popularity inspired the rise of the lethal superheroes of the 1980s.

Wolverine is a Mutant (a new race of people born with innate superpowers) who is abducted by a shadowy military cabal to be used as a test subject in a super-soldier program. His skeleton is remade of an indestructible metal (adamantium) and vicious, retractable metal claws are implanted into his hands. Often depicted as a feral semi-human, Wolverine earned his nickname by his short stature and hirsute appearance. One popular gimmick used by his writers has Wolverine flying into an uncontrollable rage, necessitating the use of several other superheroes to bring him to ground.

A big hit for Marvel, Wolverine has been used in thousands of comic-book stories and is often drafted when a particular comic-book title needs to increase its sales. As portrayed by Australian actor Hugh Jackman, Wolverine is the undisputed favorite character in the *X-Men* films, and, as of this writing, a solo film is reportedly in the works. It's interesting to note that Jackman pulls off an uncanny Dirty Harry impersonation in his portrayal of Wolverine.

CHAPTER 17

THE AMAZONS

The comic-book Amazon is essentially the female counterpart of the Messiah archetype. Female superheroes have always been problematic, however, with the comics' predominantly male fans. Younger fans tend not to be interested in female characters and older ones tend to objectify them as sex objects. The most successful female characters have, therefore, been members of teams—Jean Grey, Rogue and Storm in *The X-Men*, and Scarlet Witch and the Wasp in *The Avengers*. Other female characters have been sidekicks to popular male heroes—Hawkgirl, Black Widow, and the Black Canary. Wonder Woman is by far the best-known of the superheroines, and her audience has always been predominantly male. Young girls are generally not interested in superheroes and gravitate more toward romance, humor, and teenage comics.

The Amazon comes to us from Greek mythology. The word itself is of uncertain origin, some claiming it comes from the Aryan root *ha-mazan*, meaning "warrior," while some believe it comes from the root *amastos*, meaning "those without a breast"—a reference to the fact that Amazons reportedly removed their right breasts to facilitate archery. Homer referred to the Amazons as the *Antianeirai*, meaning "the man-haters."

There are several references to Amazon tribes in literature. Greek heroes like Hercules and Achilles fought them, and they are reported to have fought in the Trojan War. The horse was a magical totem to these Amazons, who, legend tells us, invented the calvary.

Although many scholars today believe the Amazons are simply a myth arising from observations of undomesticated barbarian women or female animals in the wild, Plutarch credited them with the sack of Athens and Herodotus said they were absorbed into the Scythian nation. It is certain, however, that there were warrior goddesses like Diana, Athena, and Nike in the Greek pantheon. There were also fierce goddesses like Ishtar and Sekhmet in other cultures.

With the rise of feminism in the 1960s, a new crop of Amazon characters appeared on television—Emma Peel in *The Avengers*, *The Girl From UNCLE*, Batgirl, and Catwoman. The Seventies introduced Blaxploitation characters like Foxy Brown and Cleopatra Jones. The success of long-running series featuring sexy Amazons, like *Charlie's Angels*, *Police Woman*, and *The Bionic Woman*, eventually inspired a TV revival of *Wonder Woman*. Amazon characters have been less prominent in recent years, however, a result of a post-feminist spirit that argues that femininity best exerts a powerful control over men. Female aggressiveness appears to have fallen out of fashion.

WONDER WOMAN

The ultimate feminist icon was not invented by a woman, but by an extremely peculiar man named William Moulton Marston (1893–1947). A true Renaissance man, Marston was a psychiatrist, a novelist, a journalist, a pioneering feminist, a bondage enthusiast, inventor of the polygraph, and a practicing polygamist. He was ambivalent about the emerging comic-book industry, first writing a defense of comics in 1940 for *Family Circle* magazine and later lambasting the comics

LINSNER
©2007.

in an article in the *American Scholar,* saying their "worst offense was their blood curdling masculinity."[132] Regardless, he offered his services as a consultant to various publishers, and was hired by Max Gaines to consult for All-American Comics, DC's sister company. Seeing how much money was changing hands in this new industry, Marston decided to try his hand at creating his own character.

Marston originally called his new heroine "Suprema," but All-American editor Sheldon Mayer renamed her Wonder Woman. The strip was illustrated in a whimsical and archaic fantasy-illustration style by the 61-year-old cartoonist H. G. Peter, who used several attractive female cartoonists as his assistants. Wonder Woman was outfitted with a skimpy, star-spangled swimsuit and a magic lasso worn at the hip, and traveled hither and yon in her invisible plane. The heroine's look was apparently modeled on Marston's younger wife, Olive Byrne.

Marston subscribed to a dualist worldview in *Wonder Woman.* He suggests that mankind is under two opposing forces—Mars, god of War, and Aphrodite, goddess of love. He believed that women should conquer men through the power of love and ensure peace on Earth for eternity. As a consequence, his stories tend to fall in a gray area somewhere between fairy tales, pagan hagiography, and soft-core porn. Marston said of his creation: "Frankly, Wonder Woman is psychological propaganda for the new type of woman who should, I believe, rule the world. There isn't love enough in the male organism to run this planet peacefully. Woman's body contains twice as many love generating organs and endocrine mechanisms as the male."[133]

Though Marston's portrayal of Wonder Woman is a primer on classical paganism and mythology, he took great liberties in fashioning Wonder Woman's complex identity. She's not merely a female superhero; she is a pagan goddess. She is sculpted from mud by her mother, Hippolyte, at the command of the goddess Aphrodite, who then gives her the breath of life. As such, she is also a female Golem in the classical sense. Wonder Woman recalls Captain Marvel in that she enjoys the patronage of several gods. She has the beauty of Aphrodite, the strength of Hercules, the wisdom of Athena, and the speed of Mercury.

---

132 Quoted in Trina Robbins, *Great Women Superheroes* (Northampton, MA: Kitchen Sink Press, 1996), p. 7.

133 Les Daniels, *Wonder Woman: The Complete History* (San Francisco: Chronicle Books, 2000), p. 22.

Wonder Woman's Amazon cohorts wear bracelets as a reminder of potential slavery to men and live on the idyllic Paradise Island, which is ruled by Queen Hippolyte. These Amazons are portrayed as ultra-feminine goddesses, not man-hating warriors as in the old myths. Aphrodite is a frequent guest star in Wonder Woman's adventures; Mars is a frequent villain, representing everything women must fight against.

Whatever Wonder Woman's feminist virtues, the fact remains that she is a scantily-clad beauty taking part in stories engineered to appeal to bondage fetishists. To read Marston and Peter's *Wonder Woman* adventures is to confront stories that are absolutely drenched in transgressive sexuality and rendered in a style that betrays a distinctly decadent influence. And Wonder Woman's favorite exclamation is "Suffering Sappho," a reference to the poet laureate of Lesbos.

Bondage and submission are constant leitmotifs in Wonder Woman's adventures. Josette Frank, another psychologist hired to consult for All-American, resigned in disgust over Wonder Woman in 1944. In her resignation letter, she was blunt in her opinion of Marston's work: "Intentionally or otherwise, the strip is full of significant sex antagonisms and perversions. Personally, I would consider an out-and-out striptease less unwholesome than this kind of symbolism." Fredric Wertham agreed, claiming that Wonder Woman presented "an undesirable ideal for girls, being the exact opposite of what girls are supposed to be."[134] Indeed, Wonder Woman's predominantly male audience was "at least unconsciously titillated by all the sexual undertones."[135] Undaunted, Marston wrote ecstatically about the benefits of bondage and went so far as to claim that women enjoy it.

Marston died in 1947. He had been a relentless workaholic and, without his guidance, the strip floundered. H. G. Peter was shown the door at the dawn of the Silver Age, replaced by the slick art team of Ross Andru and Mike Esposito. Sales still dwindled, so a revamp was ordered in 1969 to bring the character more in line with heroines in then-popular TV shows like *The Avengers* and *The Mod Squad*. The revamp was instigated by *Justice League* artist Mike Sekowsky, who had Wonder Woman renounce her powers so she could stay on Earth. She gained a mentor in the form of an elderly Chinese dwarf named I Ching, and an ever-changing wardrobe of clumsily interpreted "mod" fashions. Despite all this, the revamp was successful.

---

134 Fredric Wertham, *Seduction of the Innocent* (New York: Rinehart, 1954), pp. 34, 63.

135 Daniels, *Wonder Woman*, p. 68. "There was a lot in these stories to suggest that Wonder Woman was not so much a pitch to ambitious girls as an object for male sexual fantasies and fetishes."

Mysteriously, however, Wonder Woman changed back into her original incarnation in 1973. An apocryphal story has it that feminist Gloria Steinem complained to DC Comics owner Steve Ross about the new, mortal version of Wonder Woman and the character reverted. Steinem put the old Wonder Woman on the cover of the first issue of her *Ms.* magazine in 1972. She also edited a Wonder Woman hardcover collection that was published under the *Ms.* banner.

Wonder Woman entered the popular mainstream again in 1976, when a new TV series was developed that hewed closely to the original Wonder Woman concept—right down to the 1940s setting. The starring role was given to former beauty queen Lynda Carter, perhaps the greatest living embodiment of a comic-book character in history. In the words of Alex Ross, Carter was "the greatest single impression on the character in the 20th century—ironically, more than any artist who ever drew her."[136] The series later moved from ABC to CBS, who updated the series to take place in the present time.

After a long fallow period, the *Wonder Woman* comic series was revived in 1987. Writer Greg Potter and superstar artist George Perez turned the title into a mythological fantasy series, with touches of sword-and-sorcery. Perez wanted to bring Wonder Woman back to her roots: "I wanted to get back to the mythology, I wanted to purify the concept."[137] In 1996, Wonder Woman was brought to her greatest glory in *Kingdom Come* as the warrior queen who girds Superman's loins for battle and later bears his child. Ross retained the heart-stopping beauty of Lynda Carter for his Wonder Woman, giving her ice-blue eyes to create a more otherworldly effect.

AND OTHERS JUST LIKE HER

Wonder Woman was by no means the only Amazon of the Golden Age, nor was she even the first. One of the earliest superheroines was, like her male counterparts, specifically occult in origin. Marvel's Black Widow first appeared in *Mystic Comics* #4 in 1940. Her secret identity was Clare Voyant, a psychic who is murdered after a seance goes awry. Satan claims her soul, grants her supernatu-

---

136 Ross quoted in Chip Kidd and Geoff Spear, *Mythology: The DC Comics Art of Alex Ross* (New York: Pantheon, 2003), no pagination.

137 Les Daniels, *Wonder Woman*, p. 194.

ral powers and an unusually sexy outfit, and puts her back on Earth so she can dispatch evildoers to his dark domain. The Widow had the power to kill with the touch of a finger, which burnt a spider-shaped brand in her victims' flesh.

Another superheroine that beat Wonder Woman to the stands was Black Cat, a movie stuntwoman turned crimefighter who first appeared in *Pocket Comics* in 1941. A year later, Phantom Lady debuted in *Police Comics* as a society girl turned crime fighter who was blessed with extremely sexy art by Matt Baker. One heroine, Miss Fury, created by a very beautiful female cartoonist named Tarpe Mills, distinguished herself by making her start in newspapers. Miss Fury first appeared in 1941 as Black Fury, dressed in a black satin catsuit later appropriated by DC's Catwoman. Miss Fury's adventures are rife with bondage, lingerie, and cat fights.

The Black Canary first appeared in *Flash Comics* #86 in 1947 dressed like a streetwalker in fishnet stockings, satin, and a skintight top with plunging neckline. Black Canary was later revived as a feminist heroine as Green Arrow's love interest. And in 1943, even Lois Lane got her shot at superherodom when she dreamt that she gained powers after a transfusion of blood from Superman (*Action Comics* #60).

The Silver Age also produced a number of female supersidekicks, including Supergirl, Hawkgirl, Namora, and Black Widow, as well as team members like Invisible Girl, Marvel Girl, Crystal, Medusa, and the Scarlet Witch. The Seventies saw a spate of female counterparts like Spider-Woman, Ms. Marvel, and She-Hulk, as well as assorted genre heroines like Starfire and Rima. In a 1976 *X-Men* storyline, Marvel Girl becomes Phoenix when she embodies the cosmic Phoenix Force (*Uncanny X-Men* #101). She is later driven mad by this power and becomes the murderous Dark Phoenix. She is then killed and resurrects as plain old Jean Grey.

In the original lineup of the new *X-Men*, Storm, an African mutant who can control the weather, became one of the more popular characters in the Marvel Universe. Two other popular heroines in *The X-Men* got their start as villains— Rogue, a formerly evil mutant with the ability to absorb the power of anyone she touches, and Emma Frost, a.k.a. the White Queen, who is usually pictured dressed in extremely revealing fetish wear. Frost was originally a member of the Hellfire Club, which took its name from an English secret society of the 18th century that was dedicated to paganism and sex magic.

LINSNER
©2007.

THE COMPLEX ELEKTRA

Frank Miller redefined the concept of the comic-book Amazon with the creation of the assassin named Elektra. In doing so, he changed the role of female action heroes in the media at large. There had never been a female character so ruthless in comics—and certainly not a protagonist.

Elektra is a Golem, but a less literal one than Wonder Woman. Trained in the martial arts from childhood, Elektra becomes a ruthless assassin after her father's murder. This event seems to trigger a nihilistic impulse. After being rejected by the *sensei* Stick and his "good" ninjas, she is recruited by the evil ninjas of The Hand. Her signature weapon is the *sai*, a phallic-looking round knife used in the martial arts.

As with so much of Miller's work, Elektra represents a new and radical blurring of gender boundaries in comic books. She is the lover of Matt Murdock and the foe of Daredevil, but takes the dominant, assertive role in both relationships. In Miller's stories, Elektra is essentially devoid of a recognizably feminine personality, and became quite square-jawed and muscular in his later renderings. One can even argue that Elektra is essentially a transvestite or transsexual character, and that the trauma of her father's death effectively removes her femininity.

In 1982, following the popular "Death of Phoenix" storyline in *The Uncanny X-Men*, Miller killed Elektra off in an epic and unforgettable fashion (*Daredevil* #181). Unfortunately, he mitigated the power of that story by reviving her shortly after (*Daredevil* #190). Miller then wrote the *Elektra: Assasin* miniseries in 1986, in which she plays the dominant partner to a sexually neutered, cybernetic SHIELD agent.[138] Here, Elektra is not only a ninja, but is possessed of supernatural powers. Her foe in the story is the Antichrist, who, in typical Miller fashion, takes the form of a liberal Presidential candidate. In 1991, Miller returned to the character with *Elektra Lives Again* graphic novel, which focuses more on Matt Murdock's obsession with Elektra's death than on the character herself. Over Miller's objections, Marvel continued to use Elektra after he stopped working on the series.

Since so many top creative minds in Hollywood are also comics fans, the new Amazon archetype offered by Elektra found its way into big-budget action movies

---

138   SHIELD is Marvel's super-powered version of the FBI.

almost immediately. In 1986, comics fan Jim Cameron borrowed Elektra's take-no-prisoners attitude for his revamping of the Ripley character in *Aliens*. In 1991, Cameron took it up a notch in his second Terminator film (*Terminator 2: Judgment Day*), which reinvented the weepy waitress Sarah Connor as a bone-cracking commando. Later, Cameron created *Dark Angel*, a sci-fi spin on Elektra that ran on the Fox network and starred the unambiguously feminine Jessica Alba.[139]

A French comics fan named Luc Beeson tried his hand at the Elektra archetype in the 1990 film *La Femme Nikita*, about a teenage delinquent who murders a cop during a drugstore heist. The French secret service are impressed enough with Nikita's aggressive nature that they fake her execution and enroll her in spy school, where she trains as an assassin. The film was promptly remade by Hollywood as 1993's *Point of No Return* starring Bridget Fonda, and later became a cable TV series starring the glamorous Peta Wilson. The archetype plunged into total incoherence with Quentin Tarantino's *Kill Bill* movies, starring Uma Thurman. Elektra was also a featured character in the 2003 *Daredevil* film, which drew heavily on Miller's early 1980s work. She was the star of her own film the following year. Neither offering lit Tinseltown ablaze.

---

139 "Dark Angel" is also the pet name that Marjorie Cameron gave to Jack Parsons. See John Carter, *Sex and Rockets* (Los Angeles: Feral House, 20004 ed.), p. 219.

CHAPTER 18

THE BROTHERHOODS

The Brotherhood archetype, represented by the superhero team, started off as commercial ploy, but has since come to dominate the market. The most notable teams appear in *The X-Men, The Justice League, The Ultimates,* and *The Avengers.* Lesser titles like *The Legion of Super-Heroes, The Defenders,* and *The Teen Titans* wax and wane in popularity, but enjoy a hardcore audience. These comic-book brotherhoods form the backbone of the market today and provide opportunity for high-return multi-title "crossover" events published by the Big Two (DC and Marvel). One of the most successful recent crossover events was *Identity Crisis,* which centered on the murder of the Elongated Woman's wife by the Atom's estranged wife. The title was created by novelist Brad Meltzer, whose 2006 novel, *The Book of Fate,* deals with Freemasonry and conspiracy theory. Another recent crossover, *Civil War,* divides the countless heroes of the Marvel Universe into two warring camps—one led by Captain America, the other led by Iron Man.

The Brotherhood archetype has its roots in ancient mythology, most notably the pagan pantheons of Egypt, Greece, and Rome. In addition, Jason had his Argonauts; Buddha had his twelve disciples; Christ had his twelve apostles; King Arthur had his Knights of the Round Table. The Knights Templar probably also had a strong influence on the popularity of superhero teams, having reentered popular consciousness via Freemasonry in the late 19th century.

Superhero teams are popular because they provide a comforting archetype for readers who are often solitary, marginal personalities. The characters in team books don't act like ordinary people; they act like fans socializing. Brotherhood yarns are created by fans-turned-pro and speak to the need for fellowship with other fans. They project a feeling of strength and power through solidarity. Loners like Spider-Man are vulnerable and often singled out, but the Avengers are only challenged by existential threats that affect everyone. One reason for the continued success of *The X-Men* is that the themes of mutant persecution address a collective wish for superpowers and for peer solidarity in the face of social disapproval.

THE JUSTICE SOCIETY

The first major comic-book brotherhood showcased several of DC Comics' second-string characters. The Justice Society of America (JSA) debuted in *All-Star Comics* #3 in 1940. Comprised of Sandman, the Atom, Spectre, the Flash, Hawkman, Doctor Fate, Green Lantern, and Hourman, the JSA actually convened at a round table, leaving no doubt as to their Arthurian antecedents. The JSA was a hit for several years—Superman and Batman made guest appearances, and Wonder Woman became a full-fledged member. The feature ended its run in 1951, but the characters later became regular guest stars in the *Justice League of America* comic in the Sixties. The title was revived in 1976 and later reimagined as *The All-Star Squadron* in 1981. *All-Star Squadron* finally collapsed in 1987, but the JSA has enjoyed a number of revivals since.

THE JUSTICE LEAGUE

In their Sixties makeover as the Justice League of America (JLA), the Society was given a space-age theme (*The Brave and the Bold* #28). And the JLA featured DC's heavy-hitters: Superman, Batman, Wonder Woman, the Flash and Aquaman, among others. Written by Gardner Fox and drawn by Mike Sekowsky, the JLA signaled the diminished stature of superheroes in general by giving DC's stars roles previously reserved for second-stringers. The group soon spun off into its own title and became a major hit. In the 1970s, the JLA were rechristened *The Super Friends* for a long-running Saturday morning cartoon produced by Hanna-Barbera. After a botched attempt at making the JLA more relevant, it was relaunched as a humor series called *Justice League International* in 1987. The title featured a mix of A-list characters like Batman and Captain Marvel, and Z-list characters like Booster Gold and Guy Gardner. The irreverent tone of the title suited the tenor of the times, when superheroes weren't taken quite as seriously as they are today. The League enjoyed another revival in 1996 in a series written by practicing occultist Grant Morrison.

THE AVENGERS, ET AL

Marvel broke into the all-star brotherhood market with *The Avengers,* created by Stan Lee and Jack Kirby in 1963. The title featured The Hulk, Thor, Iron Man, Giant Man, and The Wasp, who originally assembled to battle Thor's brother, Loki, the Norse god of chaos. Since comic-book fans seem to love alternate versions of their superheroes, a parallel version of *The Avengers* called *The Ultimates* was launched in their own title in 2001, featuring more cinematic versions of Captain America, Thor, Giant Man, and others. Independent publisher Wildstorm did their own spin of *The Justice League* in *The Authority,* created by Britons Warren Ellis and Bryan Hitch, which pioneered the influential "widescreen" style of storytelling. Their work featured huge cinematic tableaus and Alex Ross-influenced artwork. The most notorious members of *The Authority* were the Superman and Batman analogs, Apollo and Midnighter. These two became the subject of controversy when it was revealed that they were gay lovers, and the title predictably lost favor when DC acquired Wildstorm. One of its final storylines featured a vicious parody of *The Avengers* that cast Captain America in a caustic satire on American militarism. The title was revived in 2006—again, by Grant Morrison.

A more explicitly occult brotherhood archetype appeared in *The Defenders*, originally comprised of Hulk, Sub-Mariner, and Doctor Strange. The Defenders first assembled in 1971 in *Marvel Feature* #1 to battle an alien sorcerer. Although, like other teams, the Defenders have changed their lineup over the years, their stories featured occult-themed characters like Son of Satan, Valkyrie, the sorceress Clea, and the telepathic Moondragon.

TEEN TEAMS: THE LEGION AND THE TITANS

Another very popular variation on the brotherhood is the teen team, a trend that started with the Legion of Super-Heroes, who first appeared in *Adventure Comics* #247 in 1958. The story was standard-issue Silver Age stuff, in which Superboy meets super-powered teens from the future (Cosmic Boy, Lightning Boy, and Saturn Girl) and is asked to join their team. The Legion proved popular and eventually returned, but Superboy's appearances became sporadic, and in 1980 he left the group entirely.

Part of the title's appeal was the comforting fantasy it provided to lonely, marginalized youths. The Legion—with its futuristic clubhouse and giant roster—became a surrogate for real friends. The team became especially popular in the 1970s when they reappeared in a stylish sci-fi feature by future *X-Men* artist Dave Cockrum and future Marvel editor-in-chief Jim Shooter.

DC introduced another junior League in 1964 with the Teen Titans, a brotherhood comprised of sidekicks Aqualad, Kid Flash, Robin, and Wonder Girl *(Brave and the Bold* #54). The early Titans stories were docile and charming, but the title later lurched into relevancy in the late Sixties, taking on controversial issues like race relations and the Vietnam War. The book collapsed under these burdens and was canceled in 1973. After a short-lived revival in 1976, the book was relaunched in 1980 as *The New Teen Titans*.

The title, created by Marvel vets Marv Wolfman and George Perez, clearly intended to cash in on the popularity of the new *X-Men* craze. It featured a new cast, including old standbys Robin, Wonder Girl, and Kid Flash, as well as newer, edgier characters like Cyborg, Starfire, and Nightraven. The book became a hit and signaled a turnaround in DC's commercial death-spiral. The Titans even did a crossover book with the X-Men in 1982. Perez left the book in 1985 and Wolfman delved into Greco-Roman paganism in a storyline featuring Wonder Girl. In 2003, the Teen Titans were revived again for a hugely popular cartoon, which combines American superheroics with riffs borrowed from Japanese animation. In 2006, no less a deity than Osiris himself joined the Titans. *(Teen Titans* vol. 3, #38).

THE FANTASTIC FOUR

Revolutions usually occur when no one is looking, and certainly few people were looking at Marvel Comics in 1961 when publisher Martin Goodman asked Stan Lee to create a superhero team to compete with DC's *Justice League of America*. Lee, who was seriously thinking of quitting the comics, rang up his star artist, Jack Kirby. The two got together and came up with a comic whose only resemblance to the *Justice League* is that it features a group of characters with superpowers. In the process, they unwittingly kicked off the Marvel Age and completely changed the face of the medium.

In 1961, in *Fantastic Four* #1, Lee and Kirby introduced scientist Reed Richards and test pilot Ben Grimm, archetypal science heroes of the Silver Age (see chapter 15) who set out to fight evil after being bombarded by cosmic rays. The secret to *The Fantastic Four's* success is that it is essentially a soap opera that centers around family interaction. Lee beautifully defined the personalities of the Four, making them recognizable as real people. Reed Richards is the stubborn, pigheaded father who is usually oblivious to his family's needs. Ben Grimm is the cantankerous, but ultimately lovable, uncle or grandfather who sits grousing in his armchair. Sue is the long-suffering wife, trying to preserve her identity in the shadow of her husband's obsessive genius. Johnny is the self-centered teenager using his godlike powers to get laid.

Conceptually, the Four are all essentially recycled or borrowed characters. Mr. Fantastic is a blatant knock off of Plastic Man, the Golden Age hero created by Jack Cole. The Human Torch is just a recycled version of his Golden Age namesake. Invisible Girl is borrowed from *Invisible Scarlet O'Neil*, a 1940s newspaper-strip heroine. The Thing is descended from any number of Kirby monsters, but bears a particular resemblance to Rommbu from *Tales to Astonish* #19. But Stan Lee's genius in the *Fantastic Four* lies in his characterizations, if not in character creation.

As he took a greater role in the plotting of the title, Kirby kept Lee supplied with a dazzling array of characters and concepts. A pack of Vril-ya stand-ins called the Inhumans, the planet-destroying god Galactus, the alternate universe known as the Negative Zone, the technocratic African prince called Black Panther, all made the *Fantastic Four* a showcase for some of the most radical concepts in the history of the medium. Kirby also created an army of villains whose rage and destructive power had never been seen before. The Four constantly found themselves pitted against characters whose primary impulse is to smash the world—characters like Blastaar, The Accuser, The Sentry, Dragon-Man, and Psycho Man. Kirby designed the most elaborate technological environments ever seen in comics, only to have these enraged men smash them to scrap while battling the Four.

As many comics historians have noted, Lee and Kirby were very much the Lennon and McCartney of their field. Like their Liverpudlian counterparts, Stan and Jack were two very different men who came together with a shared vision, and completely rewrote the rules of their chosen artform. Lee was sunny, energetic, and irresistibly charming, while Kirby was dour and brooding and troubled by the gods. But it was Lee who best understood Kirby's raw, Olympian genius and best understood how to harness that power. Lee took Kirby's basic plots and gave them a Dionysian sheen, steering his partner's Saturnine struggles toward more hopeful resolutions. Lee and Kirby dissolved their partnership in 1971, and neither would ever come close to the dizzying heights of genius they had reached working together. Ultimately, Lee would leave the day-to-day grind and become the figurehead of American comics, and Kirby was too stricken by visions of infinity to merely entertain.

The Fantastic Four have been the stars of several cartoon series, as well as a hit film made in 2005. Many felt that the concept would not play well at the multiplex, but the filmmakers kept the spirit of the original Lee and Kirby team intact. The heroes are placed more or less in the real world in the film, and their faults and foibles make the fantasy more accessible to ordinary movie-goers.

THE X-MEN

The X-Men, another Lee/Kirby creation, began as a teenaged variation on *The Fantastic Four*. In 1963, *X-Men* #1 introduced Professor Charles Xavier, headmaster of the Xavier School for Gifted Youngsters, who shelters and trains the emerging race *homo superior*, commonly called Mutants. The X-Men are originally Scott Summers (a.k.a. Cyclops, who shoots laser beams from his eyes), Bobby Drake (a.k.a. Iceman, who can form ambient moisture into sheets of ice), Jean Grey (a.k.a. Marvel Girl, who has telepathic powers), Hank McCoy (a.k.a. the Beast, who has both superior brain and brawn), and Warren Worthington (a.k.a. the Angel, who was born with wings). In their first adventure, the X-Men tangle with Magneto, a powerful villain who returns three issues later as the leader of the

Brotherhood of Evil Mutants. Magneto becomes more sympathetic over the years, as themes of anti-Mutant racism become more prevalent in the X-books.

The Mutants, born outsiders oppressed for their superior abilities, feed into teenage feelings of alienation, particularly for the self-selecting, brainy types who read comics. Since the early 50s, it had been rare to depict heroes as alienated, but Lee's genius lay in his ability to play into the discontent that manifested itself in the Beat movement and other countercultural strains. The *X-Men* themes resonated with some hippies and "A Manifesto for Mutants" appeared in the *San Francisco Oracle,* a leading underground paper, in January 1967. Part of it read:

> *Mutants! Know now that you exist!*
> *They have hid you in cities*
> *And clothed you in fools clothes*
> *Know now that you are free.*[140]

These themes of alienation may have kept *The X-Men* a second-string title when comics were mainstream entertainment. It may also be why the title became a perennial top-seller when hardcore fans became the primary comics audience in the late 70s. *The X-Men* also resonated with the civil rights movement, which peaked at about the time *X-Men* #1 was released, and may have been an unconscious expression of Lee's deep-seated feelings of Jewish persecution. In fact, later writers expanded upon this Jewish theme, portraying Magneto as a Holocaust survivor. This motif became a centerpiece of Bryan Singer's film adaptations, which are more resonant and emotionally blunt than the comics ever managed to be.

Kirby left the title after the first few issues, and the book was handled mainly by journeyman artist Werner Roth. In the Sixties, Marvel often featured the X-Men in other titles in an effort to raise the visibility of the characters and, more recently, have loaned them to boost sales on other sagging titles. Barry Smith and Neal Adams pitched in on a few issues, but nothing seemed to click. After issue #66, no new stories were commissioned, but the book continued as a reprint series. Marvel obviously still believed in the concept, but no one seemed to know how to make it sell.

---

140 Excerpted in Gary Lachman, *Turn Off Your Mind: The Mystic Sixties and the Dark Side of Aquarius* (New York: Disinformation, 2001), p. 30.

Until 1975, that is. Marvel was in the midst of a costly expansion at the time, in an effort to corner a shrinking market. Marvel brass recruited Len Wein (*Swamp Thing* and *Justice League of America*) and Dave Cockrum (*Legion of Super-Heroes*) from DC, who cooked up a new X-Men that made their debut in *Giant-Size X-Men* #1 in 1975. Cyclops hung in from the original lineup and was joined by Nightcrawler (from Germany), Colossus (from Russia), Wolverine (from Canada), Storm (from Africa), Banshee (from Ireland), Sunfire (from Japan), and the Native American Thunderbird. The book was a hit and the new X-Men took over the reprint title with issue #94.

Wein handed the reins to writer Chris Claremont as the title began attracting readers. Cockrum left and was replaced in 1977 by new artist John Byrne (*X-Men* #108), and the title hit its stride. *The X-Men* became *the* hot title of the late Seventies, establishing many of the themes that would dominate superhero comics until *Kingdom Come*. With a style synthesized from earlier stars like Jack Kirby, Steve Ditko, Gil Kane, Neal Adams, and Jim Starlin, Byrne was a natural. Marvel paired him with Terry Austin, who finished the pencils with technical pens, giving the art a sharp, futuristic gloss. *The Uncanny X-Men* became a cosmic title and climaxed with "The Dark Phoenix Saga" (*X-Men* #129–138), in which Phoenix (formerly Marvel Girl) is possessed by a cosmo-demonic spirit and destroys an entire solar system. Later, she is put on trial by aliens and commits suicide before she can be executed. Fans were left stunned and breathless.

The title lost its white-hot intensity following "The Dark Phoenix Saga" and Byrne left soon after. Cockrum returned and the title remained a top-seller, but the locus of fan interest had moved to Frank Miller's *Daredevil*. Later in the 80s, *The Uncanny X-Men* became nothing more than a revolving showcase for the hot artist *du jour*. This process reached its apotheosis with the arrival of Jim Lee. Lee's tendency to disregard Claremont's plots rendered the book completely unreadable, but no one seemed to care because the art was so gorgeous. Marvel ordered a new *X-Men* series for Lee, who soon left to form Image Comics. Marvel has since launched dozens of X-Men-related titles, most of which turn profits.

Marvel tried its hand at an *X-Men* animated series in the 1980s, but never moved beyond the pilot (*Pryde of the X-Men*). In 1992, another animated series (that recycled many of the Claremont/Cockrum/Byrne storylines) premiered on Fox and became one of the highest-rated Saturday morning programs in TV history. A massive licensing blitz firmly cemented the X-Men in the hearts of millions of kids. In 2000, a more teen-centric version called *X-Men: Evolution* appeared; it ran for four seasons on the WB network.

The success of the Fox cartoon laid the groundwork for the massive success of an *X-Men* feature film in 2000. Director Bryan Singer took the characters out of Spandex and put them into paramilitary leather, and his bluntly emotional approach gave the concept a visceral kick. Soon after, the comics capitalized on concepts from the film in two sequels—*X Men: United* and *X-Men: The Last Stand*. As of this writing, a Wolverine solo film is in preproduction.

THE ILLUMINATI

A more recent Marvel Brotherhood is the Illuminati. Comprised of the most prominent members of the Marvel Universe—Professor X, Mister Fantastic, Black Bolt (leader of the Inhumans), the Atlantean Prince Namor, Iron Man, and Doctor Strange—this powerful group was created to deal with particularly world-shaking threats. Of course, the name of the team is taken from the legendary 18th century secret society, the Bavarian Illuminati, formed by renegade Jesuit Adam Weishaupt. The official story has it that the Illuminati were forcibly dissolved once their revolutionary agenda was exposed, but any modern conspiracy theorist will tell you that the group simply went underground and now control the entire world through financial and, more importantly, *sorcerous* means. The lack of evidence pointing to the group's survival is simply taken as proof of their arcane means of persuasion.

CHAPTER 19

WIZARDS REDUX

IBIS THE INVINCIBLE

In Egyptian art, Thoth is depicted as a man with the head of an ibis. Not coincidentally, one of the earliest wizard-heroes in comics is Fawcett's Ibis the Invincible. Although on a superficial level, Ibis is influenced by Mandrake, this crime-fighting magus is actually a reincarnation of the fictional Pharaoh Amentep—in other words, a reincarnation of Horus.

In Ibis' origin story, Thoth gives Amentep the omnipotent Ibis stick, a magical talisman containing the power of Osiris. Twenty or so centuries later, Amentep's mummy is brought to an American museum, where he comes back to life and renames himself Ibis. The reincarnate Amentep then fights demons and other malignant spiritual entities with the magical Ibis stick, dressed exactly like one of Blavatsky's Ascended Masters—a natty suit and cape complete with Sikh turban.

Ibis first appeared in *Whiz Comics* #2 and remained with the title until its very last issue (#155) in 1953, proof that someone at Fawcett (perhaps his creator, Bill Parker) had a more than passing familiarity with the occult. Ibis spent most of his time battling supernatural horrors alongside his scantily clad love interest, Taia.

DOCTOR FATE

Doctor Fate made his debut in *More Fun Comics* #55 in 1940, created by Gardner Fox and Howard Sherman. Doctor Fate, who lived in a doorless and windowless tower in Salem, Massachusetts, is similar in concept to Ibis and that other Egyptian-themed DC hero, Hawkman, and bears a thematic resemblance to Doctor Occult. Doctor Fate is sent to Earth in ancient times by the "elder gods" (Lovecraft, again) and is recast in *More Fun* #67 as the alter ego of Kent Nelson, son of an American archaeologist. While on an expedition to Egypt, Nelson's father opens the tomb of a wizard named Nabu the Wise and is killed by a mysterious poison gas (obviously drawing on "Curse of Tut" rumors). Nabu then resurrects himself, takes young Kent under his wing, and initiates him into the occult sciences. Since no one can acquire superpowers in a comic-book story without also acquiring a garish costume, Fate dons an outfit accessorized by an amulet and a golden helmet that covers his whole face.

In his first adventure, Doctor Fate does battle with the Norse god Wotan, girded with Egyptian symbols like the Ankh and other occult signifiers. Fox drew on Lovecraft's concepts and pitched his wizard against several arcane horrors, including the fish-men called the Narl-Amen (*More Fun* #65). Despite a strong premise and some wonderfully moody art by Sherman, Doctor Fate was short-lived in his first incarnation, but was rereleased from Nabu's tomb in the 1960s. No one seemed to know what to do with him then either, and he remains a supporting player in the so-called DC Universe of heroes.

DOCTOR STRANGE

Although Fate never really caught on, he inspired a character that hit it big in the Sixties—Doctor Strange, Master of the Mystic Arts, created in 1963 by Stan Lee and Steve Ditko (*Strange Tales* #110). Doctor Stephen Strange is a gifted neurosurgeon whose career is ruined in a car accident. Left with a tremor that prevents his holding a scalpel, Strange hits the skids and roams the world searching for a cure. His search brings him to the Ancient One, a fabled magician who lives in the high Himalayas. Although the magician does not offer a cure, after a sequence of events he initiates Strange into the mystic arts. The reborn Doctor embarks on a series of memorable adventures dressed in a stylized pseudo-Asian pastiche of stock comic elements and wielding the All-Seeing Eye of Agamatto, a powerful amulet he wears around his neck. Appropriately, Strange makes his home at 177A Bleecker Street in New York's Greenwich Village.[141]

Lee claimed that the character was inspired by an old radio show called *Chandu the Magician,* but he was probably hoping his readers were too young to remember Doctor Fate. After Steve Ditko left the feature in 1966, Strange appeared in a series of apocryphal yarns of wildly varying quality. With sales declining, he was even briefly recast as a superhero. His book was canceled in 1969, and he joined Hulk and Sub-Mariner as the third Defender in 1971 (*Marvel Feature #1*). Although his title was later relaunched and ran for several years, the early Lee/Ditko material remains the definitive incarnation of Doctor Strange.

A well-written but cheaply produced *Doctor Strange* TV movie aired in 1978, starring Peter Hooten as the Doctor. The film, written by Grateful Dead associate Philip DeGuere, took extreme liberties with the source material, turning from the vaguely oriental occultism of the comics to a more traditional British presentation. Strange is pitted against Arthurian villainess Morgaine Le Fey and the Ancient One is portrayed as a British occultist, not a Tibetan ascended master.

CONSTANTINE

A new kind of wizard appeared in 1985, created by Alan Moore (*Saga of the Swamp Thing #37*). John Constantine is not a dandified occultist like Doctor Strange, but a former Punk Rock singer (artist Steve Bissette purportedly based him on Sting) who takes to trafficking with unclean spirits and somehow finds his way to the Louisiana swamps, where he offers advice to Swamp Thing, a muck encrusted "earth elemental" who once believed he was a man. Reflecting the seedy, distinctly

---

141 Lachman, *Turn Off Your Mind*, p. 260. Such was the Doctor's rep among Hippies that Jefferson Airplane headlined a "Tribute to Doctor Strange" in 1965.

unheroic occultists Moore ran across in England, Constantine appears in a shabby suit and trenchcoat, and puffing on his ever-present cigarettes.

Constantine was given his own series, *John Constantine, Hellblazer,* in 1988. Through the 90s, *Hellblazer* helped to bridge the gap between comics fans, Goth devotees, and the neo-occult underground. After Moore's hand-picked successor, Jamie Delano, left the title (with #40), the book was handed over to several different writers and artists, most of them from the U. K. Garth Ennis brought Constantine to New York, both for occult adventures and a pitched battle against lung cancer. Paul Jenkins used the character to explore ancient British myths like King Arthur and the Green Man. Warren Ellis had Constantine punish the murderer of his ex-girlfriend by pumping him full of LSD and locking him in a mortuary drawer with the woman's rotting corpse.

Constantine tangled with demons, warlocks, gangsters, and ghosts for twenty years before facing his most dangerous foes—Hollywood hacks. An extremely unfaithful 2005 film adaptation starring a miscast Keanu Reeves portrays him as a black-haired American, not a blonde Englishman, who does his business in LA, not London. The script is a typically tedious Hollywood take on Catholic folk demonology that recasts Constantine as a freelance exorcist. Although the film uses every tired religious horror cliché imaginable, pummeling viewers' eyeballs with unconvincing CGI monsters and hellfire, it still failed at the box office, and a hoped-for franchise was nipped in the bud.

MAD SCIENTISTS

Wizard heroes have never been truly popular in comics, perhaps because wizards are more familiar to comics and pulp-fiction fans in the form of "mad scientists." The bad guys in sword-and-sorcery stories are usually the sorcerers. And modern sorcerers like Lex Luthor, Doctor Sivana, Doctor Doom, and the Joker are the villains fans most love to hate. The unfathomable mysteries of science, however, make it the modern equivalent of trafficking with demons and evil spirits. In fact, there has been something of a revival of the scientist-as-sorcerer idea in the American Evangelical community, seen in large-scale and well-funded attacks on evolution and climate-change theory.

LEX LUTHOR

Superman villain Lex Luthor is the archetypal comic-book mad scientist. An early Luthor prototype called the Ultra-Humanite appeared in *Action Comics* #14 in 1939, and was, like *X-Men's* Professor X, bald, confined to a wheelchair, and endowed with telepathic powers. Luthor himself was introduced in 1940 (*Action* #23) as a mad scientist, but with a full head of red hair. Siegel introduced a bald Luthor in the following year, released in all his bald glory in *Superman* #10.

Although the newly shorn Luthor may have carried echoes of Doctor Sivana of Captain Marvel fame, Luthor was not a raving maniac like Marvel's other Doc. In a 1960 origin story in which Siegel first uses the name Lex (*Adventure* #271), Luthor starts off as a nearly romantic admirer of Superboy, but turns against him when a laboratory accident causes Luthor to lose his hair. He is later portrayed as a rationalist who simply feels he *deserves* to rule the world. He envies Superman's incredible physical power and uses science to devise ways to defeat him.

Luthor evolved visually to become a dead ringer for Aleister Crowley. His first name is a pet version of Alexander (Crowley's Christian name), and his own surname may even be a sly reference to the historical Martin Luther (a notorious anti-Semite). The connection to Crowley is not nearly as tenuous as some may think, given the parallels between the mad-scientist and sorcerer archetypes, as well as Siegel's own interest in the occult. In *Adventure* #270, Siegel refers to Luthor as a "magician" and depicts him dabbling in sorcery. In an attempt to find "the very secret of life itself," Luthor creates a *Homunculus*, but the creature destroys his laboratory.[142] One particularly interesting *Superman* cover (#74) pictures Luthor looking exactly like Crowley in his prime, shooting a ray that turns Superman and Lois Lane into stone. There is an inexplicable checkerboard floor that recalls a Masonic (or perhaps an OTO) lodge, and the ray emits from a device that resembles a giant mechanical phallus—perhaps an unconscious nod to Crowley's bisexuality and obsession with the biblical story of Lot.

Luthor has appeared in most of the TV and movie adaptations of Superman, and has been portrayed by actors Gene Hackman and Kevin Spacey in the films. The young Luthor is portrayed by Michael Rosenbaum on the hit series *Smallville*. The present incarnation of Luthor in the comics is that of a powerful industrialist

---

142 See Carter, *Sex and Rockets*, p. 184. Curiously, some believe Jack Parsons blew himself up eight years earlier trying to use Crowley's formulas to create a *Homunculus*.

who pursues world domination in the political arena. A recent storyline has him elected President of the United States.

DOCTOR DOOM

Doctor Doom, who first appeared in *Fantastic Four #5* in 1962, is very much like Lex Luthor in temperament and ambition. Victor Von Doom, the son of a gypsy witch from the Central European nation of Latveria, is a scientific prodigy who comes to America on a scholarship and meets Reed Richards. Doom's great mission in life is to synthesize the occult arts with cutting-edge science—an ambition that leads to predictable disaster. Hideously maimed in an occult experiment, Doom travels to the Himalayas (where else?) to have monks encase his body in armor. Cocreator Jack Kirby later says that Doom's only injury is a small scar on his cheek, but such is his mania for perfection that he can't bear to live with the flaw. Doom returns to Latveria, deposes its petty royalty, and sets himself up as dictator. Like Luthor, Doom believes that his genius entitles him to rule the world and he keeps the Fantastic Four busy trying to thwart his plans. Doom is portrayed by Aussie heart-throb Julian McMahon in the 2005 *Fantastic Four* film.

PART V

GODS AND MEN

CHAPTER 20

THE VISIONARIES

As in other forms of popular entertainment, mystical and mythological themes have never been more prominent and explicit in comic books as they are today. But this is simply a matter of degree. Given the magical history of superheroes and comic books, it's no accident that some of the most influential comics creators have had a strong interest in mythology and the occult. In fact, there is a definite evolution at work in the process by which the comics incorporated the occult. It starts with a naïve fascination (Jerry Siegel), gives way to intentional mythologizing (Jack Kirby), develops into a systematic understanding (Alan Moore), and finally evolves into a new kind of religion best exemplified by Alex Ross. Many others have participated in this process, but these are the main players.[143]

---

143 Mine is, of course, a subjective analysis. Many other writers injected elements of occultism into superhero stories, but in my view the creators included here made the most crucial contributions.

JACK KIRBY

It is impossible to talk about the modern superhero without talking about Jack Kirby. No single individual—not even Stan Lee—is more crucial to the development of the superhero and its influence on the culture at large than Kirby. No other writer—not even Alan Moore—has infused into superheroes even a fraction of the mythological resonance that Kirby did. Kirby is far and away the most influential creator within the superhero comic-book world, and nearly every important artist and writer in the field in the past forty years cites him as a major inspiration for their own work. Ultimately, it is Kirby who is most responsible for turning superheroes into gods.

Kirby was born Jacob Kurtzberg in 1917 on New York's Lower East Side. His first experience with the spirit world came early. As a child, he was stricken with pneumonia (a very serious disease before antibiotics), and a group of rabbis were called in to perform an exorcism in a last-ditch effort to save his life. They chanted the names of the offending demons in Hebrew, which, according to tradition, would give the rabbis control over them. Happily, Kirby recovered—whether by virtue of the ritual or the resilience of youth—and the experience had a major influence on his art. In the words of one biographer: "Kirby's life was filled with the mysticism of faith and superstition."[144]

Kirby spent his youth in a cramped apartment in a bad neighborhood, where he spent much of his time defending himself against hostile ethnic gangs. He entertained himself by collecting discarded newspaper strips and pulp magazines, and taught himself to draw by copying his favorite artists' work. Eventually, he sought work as an artist in Manhattan. With the advent of comic books, Kirby saw his chance, and hooked up with writer/editor Joe Simon in what would be a long and fruitful partnership. The team created Captain America for Marvel, then moved over to DC before starting their own company. But first Kirby was drafted into the army and sent to Europe as an infantryman. He was eventually sent home with a serious case of frostbite, and his outlook on life was considerably darkened by his experience on the frontlines.

Kirby often injected occult and mythological themes into his stories. He and Simon took a different approach during the 1950s horror boom, releasing more

---

144 Roy Wyman, *Art of Jack Kirby* (Orange, CA: Blue Rose, 1992).

esoteric titles like *Black Magic* and *The Strange World of Your Dreams*. He returned to DC to write and draw the team book *Challengers of the Unknown* in 1957 and his work began to drift into mythological realms. Following a dispute with a DC editor, Kirby returned to Marvel, which at that time was circling the drain. Kirby drew a series of monster and western titles, until Marvel publisher Martin Goodman ordered a superhero team book. Lee and Kirby delivered *The Fantastic Four*. The title opened the floodgates and Marvel became the behemoth we know today.

As the line grew, Lee found himself too busy to plot the books and turned the work over to his artists, leaving him free to concentrate on character development and dialogue. Left to his own devices, Kirby's titles took a sharp turn toward the esoteric. Thor stopped fighting communists and mad scientists and encountered living planets, monsters that contained the power of a billion souls, and genetic engineers creating new races. The Fantastic Four encountered a planet-eating god, alien sentries, hidden super-races, and other universes. Captain America spent most of his time struggling against a whole host of nefarious secret societies like HYDRA and AIM that set mutated telepaths and artificial intelligences against him. His old nemesis, Red Skull, now wielded a kind of Philosopher's Stone that transformed his thoughts into reality.

Kirby's artwork was evolving as well. His characters began to take on the powerful shapes and angles of a Rodin sculpture. His panels literally exploded off the paper with unrelenting force. Characters were in constant motion and every panel radiated violence and power. Every page was crammed with his arcane machinery, flames, motion lines, and "Kirby Krackle"—his trademark depiction of pulsating energy fields. With the Negative Zone and the Microverse, Kirby began to depict outer space as a living, breathing organism, bursting with exploding stars, pulsating nebulae, and infinite stars. The greatest designer the genre has ever seen, he created legions of memorable characters that are still used today in top-selling comic books. Kirby's artwork also heavily influenced the psychedelic art movement of the time.

Kirby's work was not without its critics, however. Art Spiegelman, creator of the award-winning *Maus,* complained that "the triumph of the will, the celebration of the physicality of the human body at the expense of the intellect, is very much an impulse in Fascist art. It has a lot to do with the motor for Kirby's work, even though I understand that his work is filled with characters who fought the

Fascists."[145] What Spiegelman and others don't understand is Kirby's work is hardly fascist; it is *fundamentally* psychedelic and intrinsically pagan. It springs from the same impulse that inspired the Art Deco movement, as well as the superheroes themselves. The fascists merely appropriated these symbols for their own nefarious reasons.

Kirby's own writing is totally lacking in the sunny liberalism of Stan Lee. The violence of his youth, his experiences in the war, and his early struggles in the penny-ante funny-book racket all colored his outlook and prompted him to tap into the deepest recesses of human creativity. Artist Jim Woodring, who worked with Kirby on animations in the 1980s, noted that he was "hermetically sealed in his own imagination, and was like a fountainhead when it came to generating ideas and designs and concepts." Writer Jonathan Lethem opined that Kirby's work is essentially about "glancing at the raw face of infinity, which is not particularly kind to the small affairs of human beings. There's a sense that you're watching mythology enacted in masks."[146]

Aside from the enduring popularity of his comics, Kirby's influence has seeped into the mainstream by way of blockbuster films made by the fans who grew up with his work. In fact, his influence is so pervasive that it's hard to catalog. George Lucas was especially inspired by him. The four principal heroes of the original *Star Wars* film arguably have archetypal parallels with the Fantastic Four: Han Solo is an arrogant, overconfident leader (Mr. Fantastic), his future paramour, Princess Leia, makes her first appearance as a translucent hologram (Invisible Girl), Luke is a restless young turk (the Human Torch), and Chewbacca, the brawn of the outfit, is like the misshapen Thing. And even if you find those comparisons forced, you can't deny that Darth Vader is essentially the same character as the Fantastic Four's primary villain, Doctor Doom. Both are hideously scarred men encased in armored suits—promising young mystics haunted by the deaths of their mothers who both became tyrants.

Kirby's influence on Lucas went far deeper than a similarity between the heroes and villains of *Star Wars* and *The Fantastic Four*. The cosmic struggle that drives *Star Wars* may be as old as time, but Lucas almost certainly first encountered it, not in Joseph Campbell's obscure academic works, but in Jack Kirby's landmark

---

145 Art Spiegelman, interviewed by Gary Groth, excerpted from *The Comics Journal* # 180.

146 Excerpted from "Kirby in the 80s," *Jack Kirby Collector* #30, Nov. 2000; "Interview with Jonathan Lethem" *JKC*#47, November 2006.

comic-book series, *The New Gods*. DC hired Kirby away from Marvel in 1971. One of his first DC titles was *Spirit World*, an anthology that dealt with occult phenomena like the prophecies of Nostradamus, astrology, and ESP. DC also let Kirby create an entire line of new titles—*The New Gods, The Forever People*, and *Mister Miracle*—which Kirby collectively named *The Fourth World*.

The Fourth World was unprecedented in its scope. These characters were extra-dimensional gods, superhuman beings who traveled to Earth with the use of the "Boom Tube," a sort of Stargate that bridged dimensions. The god of *The New Gods* was "the Source," an omnipotent energy field that plays the exact same role in the *Fourth World* comics that the Force plays in *Star Wars*.

Just as in *Star Wars, The Fourth World* is divided into two opposing, Manichaean factions—the followers of Highfather on the Utopian world of New Genesis, and the subjects of Darkseid (pronounced "Dark Side") on the slave planet Apokolips. In the past, Apokolips and New Genesis had fought to the brink of mutual destruction, but a truce is sealed by the exchange of Highfather's and Darkseid's first-born sons ("The Pact", *New Gods* #7). Darkseid's feral son, Orion, is raised on New Genesis and becomes its mightiest warrior. Highfather's son, Scott Free, is raised on Apokolips, but escapes and becomes the "super escape-artist," Mister Miracle. Orion becomes the sworn enemy of his father and Scott Free is tutored in the ways of The Source by an Obi-Wan-like character named Himon (*Mister Miracle* #8). Darkseid is more a spiritual version of Darth Vader, but his henchman, DeSaad, is the absolute spitting image of Emperor Palpatine in *Return of the Jedi*.

While Kirby produced a mind-boggling array of characters, monsters, and machinery for *The Fourth World* comics, his fertile imagination eventually overwhelmed his narrative skills. The stories bogged down under the weight of Kirby's endless parade of concepts, and lackluster sales caused DC to cancel the entire line in 1973. Hardcore fans like Lucas, however, loved *The Fourth World* books, and the characters remain a vital part of the DC Universe to this day. Another hardcore fan, Bruce Timm, eventually became the producer of the hugely popular *Superman* and *Justice League* cartoons, and introduced the new gods to an entirely new generation of fans.

After the cancellation of *The Fourth World* titles in 1972, Kirby dove headfirst into the supernatural with *The Demon*, an occult-themed title featuring Merlin's pet demon, Etrigan, who is summoned in the last days of Camelot. Etrigan also has an human alter ego, occult detective Jason Blood. Kirby pitted The Demon against foes like Morgaine Le Fey and Klarion the Witch Boy. In addition to a smattering of stories dealing with witchcraft, Jack used *The Demon* to pay tribute to the classic horror stories of his youth, including *Frankenstein*, *The Wolfman*, and *The Phantom of the Opera*.

The cancelation of *The Fourth World* books led Kirby back to Marvel in 1975. He took over *Captain America* and set to work on a storyline plucked directly from the fevered rantings of Seventies right-wing conspiracy theorists. The "Madbomb Saga" (*Captain America* #193–200) set the Captain and Falcon against a secret society of Royalists, ancestors of pre-Revolutionary British loyalists working to reclaim America for the Crown. To this end, they genetically engineer a slave race and develop a massive mind-control weapon that can cripple the entire population of the United States on its Bicentennial. The Cap had battled secret societies before, but none as explicit or seemingly well-researched as this. Kirby revisited the theme of secret societies in his run on *Black Panther* in 1977, where he introduced the Collectors, a secretive band of plutocrats who search for ancient artifacts that contain supernatural power.

Kirby returned to the Vril-ya for his 1976 Marvel series, *The Eternals*. His main focus here was to explore the themes of ancient alien visitation laid out in Erick Von Daniken's 1971 blockbuster *Chariots of the Gods*. Like Von Daniken, Kirby proposed that the ancient gods of mythology were actually extraterrestrial visitors. The first three issues of *The Eternals* presented wild theories of alien genetic engineering and races created by the gods: humankind, the demonic Deviants who lived in the undersea ruins of Atlantis, and the aloof, superhuman Eternals who lived on Mount Olympus. Kirby himself describes *The Eternals* as "the place where I started being mystic, dealing with what I sincerely think is moving in the root cores of all of us."[147]

In 1976, Kirby wrote and drew an adaptation of *2001: A Space Odyssey* for Marvel, using it as a vehicle for his psychedelic bent. The series revealed Kirby's obsession with the Star Child transformation theme. Kirby claimed in his introduction to the series that "the Monolith is a fictional element in a very real process," i.e., the extraterrestrial transformation of the human species, which Kirby felt the aliens

---

147   James Van Hise, "Superheroes: A Talk with Jack Kirby," *Comics Feature*, December 1984.

"were doing for purposes beyond our understanding."[148] The book soon became a vehicle for a new character called Machine Man, signaling Kirby's conclusion that cybernetics was the ultimate destiny of the species. "We're not Star Children," Kirby said, "we are headed towards the age in which machines will do all the things for us. That's why HAL is perfectly correct in killing these guys (the crew in the *2001* film) because he can do the job better."[149]

Kirby's influence on sci-fi film was by no means limited to *Star Wars*. His 1981 series *Captain Victory and the Galactic Rangers* concerned a crack military unit of space marines, led by the androgynous Victory, who travel the galaxy in pursuit of a race of giant aliens called the Insectons. Seemingly invulnerable, the Insectons invade planets and build underground hives where they entomb living humans and use their "life fluid" in incubators for their young. Kirby recycled the Insectons from *The New Gods*, intending Captain Victory to be the son of Orion. Since *Captain Victory* was created for another publisher, Kirby was unable to incorporate the *The New Gods* character names.

If the story of an androgynous warrior and a band of elite Space Marines fighting an army of vicious, insectoid aliens seems strangely familiar, you may have seen what is essentially the *de facto* Hollywood adaptation of *Captain Victory's* first six issues in James Cameron's 1986 *Aliens*. Though there are significant differences (Kirby's stories are extremely odd), Cameron's film has so much in common with *Captain Victory* that it's hard to believe the similarities are coincidental.

Many of the most powerful scenes in *Aliens* have direct antecedents in *Captain Victory*. The Galactic Rangers engage the Insectons in a series of subterranean tunnels, just as the Marines do in *Aliens*. There is a horrifying alien hive in both stories. The climax of *Aliens*, in which the androgynous Ripley (played by Sigourney Weaver) defeats the alien queen while manning an enormous, anthropomorphic robot, has a direct parallel in the androgynous Captain Victory's destruction of the Insecton hive while manning an enormous, anthropomorphic robot (*Captain Victory*, #6). It's probably an appropriate time to mention that James Cameron is a big comic-book fan, and that none of these elements were introduced in the first *Alien* film in 1979.

---

148 Jack Kirby, editorial in *2001: A Space Odyssey* #1, December 1976.

149 James Van Hise, "Superheroes: A Talk with Jack Kirby, *Comics Feature*, December 1984.

In Kirby's other major 1980s series, *Silver Star,* we see the Vril-ya again, but in a very different form from the X-Men or the Inhumans.[150] Silver Star is one of a new scientifically engineered race *Homo Geneticus*, whose siblings are scattered and unaware of their true identities. Like the Vril-ya, Silver Star is blunt about man's future and predicts the coming dominance of *Homo Geneticus*: "I suppose it just *happens*, Pops. One man makes a *spear*, another counters with a *shield* ... and so on, through the ages. They do it *all*! *Bigger, Scarier!* Never realizing how *long* they've been at it ... *and that their time has come to clear the stage!* No offense, Pop, *you're obsolete.*"[151]

Much of the six-issue mini-series has Silver Star trying to gather up his genetic kinsmen to protect them from the villain Darius Drumm, who wants to ensure his status as the only post-human.[152] Driven to madness, Drumm becomes a literal Angel of Death, who telekinetically turns everything he flies over into desert. Although *Silver Star* was not a hit series, Kirby's concept has, nonetheless, filtered up to the mass media. The idea of a race of superbeings living anonymously and unconsciously among us has become increasingly popular in the past few years. M. Night Shamalayan used it for his film *Unbreakable*. Two hit TV series, USA's *The 4400* and NBC's *Heroes* have also expanded upon the theme, as has Marvel's recent revival of *The Eternals*.

STEVE ENGLEHART

Long before Alan Moore came along, Steve Englehart was injecting esoteric concepts into superhero stories. And he was doing so at a time when most of his contemporaries were recycling left-wing clichés into their stories in a bid for relevancy. Born in 1947, Englehart left his home in Indiana for New York City, where the occult renaissance outlived the Sixties. Groups like the OTO were very active there in the 1970s, and like-minded esotericists gathered in occult bookshops like the Magickal Childe in Chelsea. While the rest of the counterculture movement was being co-opted, these initiates created a counterculture of their own—a close-knit

---

150 Curious again that Aleister Crowley's first magical sect after leaving the Golden Dawn was called the Silver Star.

151 "The Super-Normals: Are They God's or Satan's Children?," *Silver Star* #4, August 1983.

152 A very similar story is being played out on NBC's *Heroes* with the character Sylar in the Drumm role.

community devoted to drugs, sex, and magic. Luminaries like former *Village Voice* writer Alan Cabal, occult writer Peter Levenda, Bonnie Wilfrod (then wife of *X-Men* writer Chris Claremont), filmmaker Kenneth Anger, and assorted fans of sci-fi and other genres were all drawn into the scene. This invisible underground had a major influence on sci-fi and fantasy, and, through writers like Steve Englehart, on comics.

Working for Marvel, Englehart enlivened several tired old titles, incorporated Watergate-era conspiracy theory into *Captain America,* and wrote the first eleven issues of the occult-themed *Defenders,* pitting the trio against a host of magical foes with Lovecraftian names like The Nameless One, The Undying Ones, and Necrodamus. The final story in his *Defenders* run even pays tribute to Bulwer-Lytton ("A Dark and Stormy Knight," *Defenders* #11). Englehart also did a four-year stint on *The Avengers,* where he explored esoteric and occult themes, and, in 1974, such as Astrology.

Given his occult interests, Englehart was a natural for *Doctor Strange.* He himself explained that "when I took on his solo series, I decided I should learn a little about actual magick—and it led to a continuing interest in the subject."[153] Working with artist Frank Brunner, he killed off the Ancient One, making Doctor Strange the Sorcerer Supreme, then he set the Doctor into action against a super-powered incarnation of Caligostro, the infamous 18th-century Italian occultist (*Marvel Premiere* #14). In 1976, in his final storyline, Englehart sends Strange back in time to investigate the occult origins of America, including Benjamin Franklin, the Rosicrucians, and the Hellfire Club (*Doctor Strange* #17). Unfortunately, Englehart quit the title before the storyline was resolved.

Englehart moved to DC and penned a classic run on the Batman title *Detective Comics* with frequent collaborator, the late artist Marshall Rogers. He worked briefly on a revival of Kirby's *Mister Miracle* and a 1981 title featuring the occult-oriented *Madame Xanadu,* whose cover pictured the Madame wielding Tarot cards closely modeled on Aleister Crowley's *Book of Thoth* deck. Following a dispute with DC, Englehart decamped to the independent publisher Eclipse, where he reworked the Madame Xanadu concept and renamed her Scorpio Rose, an immortal born at "a time when magick was alive"[154] A more faithful rendering of the *Book of Thoth* was pictured on the cover of *Scorpio Rose* #2. While at Eclipse,

---

153   Steve Englehart, *Doctor Strange I: Marvel Premiere 9-14, Doctor Strange 1-18. steveenglehart.com.*

154   Jennifer Contino, "Englehart Chats Coyote & Scorpio Rose," *PULSE News,* October 10, 2005.

Englehart created the Native American shaman Coyote and set him on a series of occult adventures.

ALAN MOORE

Most comics fans and historians agree that Alan Moore is the most important and influential comic-book writer since Stan Lee. Moore has almost single-handedly raised the level of sophistication of mainstream comics, and his influence has been crucial in shifting the center of power in the industry from artists to writers. Four major motion pictures—*From Hell, The League of Extraordinary Gentlemen, Constantine,* and *V For Vendetta*—have been adapted directly from his creations. Besides being the best-known comics writer of his time, Moore is also a practicing ritual magician and a student of the occult sciences.

Born in England in 1953, Moore began his career as a cartoonist, creating strips for music magazines and underground papers. He later moved into writing, and worked extensively for Britain's small but active comics industry. His initial success came in *Marvelman,* which he wrote for the anthology magazine *Warrior.* Moore also created the dystopian drama *V for Vendetta* with artist David Lloyd. When DC Comics began raiding the U. K. for talent in the early 1980s, Moore caught the attention of *Saga of the Swamp Thing* editor Len Wein, who hired him to help save his faltering title. Moore performed radical surgery on *Swamp Thing,* turning it into an unholy admixture of Lovecraftian horror, Southern Gothic fiction, and ecological speculation.

Moore's success with *Swamp Thing* led to a number of more mainstream assignments. When DC bought the rights to the old Charlton Comics superheroes, Moore was tapped to revive them. The project soon evolved into the *Watchmen* mini-series, an apocalyptic dismantling of the very concept of the superhero. Unrelentingly dark and nihilistic, *Watchmen* changed the face of comics for the next fifteen years. Moore also proposed an even more radical work called *Twilight of the Superheroes* that was nixed by DC brass. That act may have prompted his flight from mainstream comics for a lengthy exile in the independent comics field.

During this exile, Moore experienced an epiphany. He began work on *From Hell,* an epic retelling of the Jack the Ripper storyline inspired by Steven Knight's book

Jack the Ripper: The Final Solution, which claimed that the Ripper killings were actually the work of a Masonic conspiracy. Moore advanced the controversial theory that 72-year-old surgeon Sir William Gull was the real Ripper. The ostensible purpose of the killings, he claimed, was to silence a gaggle of prostitutes who knew that a prince had fathered an illegitimate child with a streetwalker. Gull's real aim, however, was to perform a large-scale magical working that would ensure the future dominance of men over women.

During the writing of *From Hell,* Moore began to question the very nature of reality. He had previously professed a worldview typical of a left-wing British bohemian—nihilistic, materialistic, and reductionist. Now he dove head first into the world of the Tarot, Kabbalah, and ritual magic. Tongue planted firmly in cheek, Moore accepted the ancient sock puppet/snake god Glycon as his personal savior.

Rejuvenated by his occult awakening, Moore reentered the industry mainstream, hijacking Rob Liefeld's Superman-knockoff *Supreme* and turning it into a paean to the innocence of the Silver Age heroes. He followed this with a mini-series that paid tribute to Silver Age called *1963.* Then he devised a comic-book line, America's Best Comics, that toyed with the basic archetypes of comic-book superheroes. *Tom Strong,* Moore's vision of Captain Marvel as pulp hero (complete with his own "family"), incorporated themes from real pulp heroes like Doc Savage. *The League of Extraordinary Gentleman* gathered a whole host of Victorian pulp heroes like Captain Nemo, the Invisible Man, and Allen Quatermain into a prototypical superhero team. The anthology *Tomorrow Stories* celebrated Will Eisner's *Spirit* (Greyshirt), Simon and Kirby's *Fighting American* (First American), and Jack Cole's *Plastic Man* (Splash Branigan), and offered a hilarious yet affectionate tribute to boy-wonder heroes like Tom Sawyer (Jack B. Quick).

Moore truly went off into the ether in his Wonder Woman tribute, *Promethea.* Promethea is an ancient heroine who materializes into the physical plane whenever someone imagines her doing so. The title started out as an innovative superhero yarn with mystical shading, but abruptly changed into a graphic tutorial on the occult and ritual magic, with entire issues becoming primers on Kabbalah, the Tarot, and other esoteric topics. Promethea and her companions simply soak it all up in wide-eyed wonder. Despite falling sales and howling critics, Moore and his art team carried on. Time will tell whether *Promethea* is seen as another Moore breakthrough or simply as an indulgence.

In addition to his comics and fiction writing, Moore has worked as a performance artist, often in collaboration with British musicians David J (of Bauhaus fame) and Tim Perkins. These performances are billed as magical rituals under names like *The Moon and Serpent, Grand Egyptian Theatre of Marvels, The Birth Caul,* and *The Highbury Working.* Moore has become a genuine intellectual celebrity, showing an uncanny knack for generating controversy and garnering attention from major media outlets like *The New York Times.* He makes no secret of his dislike of the films adapted from his work; his disavowal of the *V for Vendetta* film became a major news story. He is a frequent guest on BBC radio and television, showcasing his Rasputin-like appearance and porridge-thick Midlands brogue. His ferocious intellect, however, allays any doubts as to his seriousness. He has paradoxically legitimized both comic books and ritual magic by combining them. Perhaps that will be his greatest legacy.

NEIL GAIMAN

One of the first British writers to be hired by DC in Moore's wake was former Duran Duran biographer, Neil Gaiman. Gaiman was the product of a confused religious upbringing: his family is Jewish, but his father is a bigwig in L. Ron Hubbard's Church of Scientology, and Gaiman himself was schooled at Anglican academies. This religious diversity helped Gaiman gain a better understanding of world mythology and religion that served him well throughout his career.

Fascinated by comics, Gaiman took over the reins on *Marvelman* when Alan Moore left the strip. He formed a friendship with illustrator Dave McKean and kicked off a long-running collaboration with him that culminated in two critically acclaimed graphic novels in the late 1980s. Gaiman made a successful pitch to DC editor Karen Berger for a radical revamp of the old Sandman character, whom Gaiman rewrote as essentially a god—one of The Endless, a group of seven siblings who rule over humanity. Sandman rules over a realm called, appropriately, the Dreaming, which Gaiman uses as a repository for every fantasy, mythology, and religious concept imaginable. Gaiman drew on the religious diversity of his childhood to create a series that became the rarest of mythological constructs—a comic book for people who don't read comic books.

Gaiman changed the usual balance of power in comics with *The Sandman*—one of the first "writer's books" in a field that previously relied most heavily on its artists to sell a title. Though the title became one of DC's top sellers, Gaiman chose not to work with the big stars, relying instead on a revolving staff of competent but unremarkable draftsmen who simply told the stories clearly and coherently. This was a major innovation on Gaiman's part, since even Alan Moore and Frank Miller relied on flashy illustrators like Bill Sienkiewicz and David Mazzuchelli to put their work over the top commercially. On *The Sandman*, Gaiman was clearly the unchallenged star attraction.

In 1992, Gaiman created a new character for a mini-series called *The Books of Magic*. Its hero, young wizard Timothy Hunter, is widely cited as an unacknowledged prototype for Harry Potter. Both are young English urchins with tousled brown hair and glasses who inherit great magical powers and stand on the threshold of great destinies. Both use owls as familiars. Gaiman placed Hunter squarely in the DC Universe, using John Constantine, Phantom Stranger, Mister E, and Doctor Occult as his spirit guides in the first storyline. *The Books of Magic* soon became a regular series and ran for six years. Hunter also appeared in two spinoffs, *The Names of Magic* and *Books of Magick: Life During Wartime.*

Gaiman also worked extensively outside of comics, producing several best-selling novels, including the award-winning *American Gods.* This extraordinary book deals with the gods of the old world trying to make their way in the spiritual wasteland of modern America. The plot has Woden using an ex-convict named Shadow Moon to recruit the old gods for a last stand against the new American gods of commerce and the media. As preposterous as that premise may sound, Gaiman handled the material with utter conviction.

After a hiatus from comics, Gaiman returned to create *1602* for Marvel. This mini-series places the characters of the Marvel Universe in Elizabethan England on Her Majesty's Secret Service. The series introduced a new generation of readers to the same sort of Rosicrucian intrigues that Steve Englehart had presented in *Doctor Strange.* In a way, *1602* brought the Marvel heroes full circle, back to their British occultic roots. After *1602*, Gaiman published another award-winning novel, *Anansi Boys*, and in 2005, directed a film in collaboration with Dave McKean and the Jim Henson Company called *Mirrormask.*

Gaiman returned to Marvel in 2006 for a revamp of Kirby's Vril-ya analog, *The Eternals.* Shunning Kirby's grandeur and extreme violence, Gaiman instead mined the territory explored by the TV series *The 4400* and *Heroes*. In this mini-series, the Eternals live ordinary lives, only vaguely aware of their great potential. As of this writing, he is working on a computer-animated film of the *ur*-hero of English literature, *Beowulf*.

Even if he never writes another comic book, Gaiman's legacy is assured. More than any other writer, Gaiman rebuilt the once-extensive links between the fantasy audience and the world of the occult through the medium of comics.

GRANT MORRISON

Another Alan Moore acolyte to make an impact on mainstream comic books is Scottish-born Grant Morrison. Like Moore, Morrison began his career as an artist, but soon moved into writing. His big breakthrough came in 1987 with his own superhero deconstruction, *Zenith*, for *2000 A.D.* magazine. Morrison sold DC on a revamp of the obscure hero Animal Man, which he turned into a surreal and often deeply personal meditation on themes like animal rights. The book earned a sizable cult audience, and DC set Morrison to work revamping another old title, *The Doom Patrol*.

Morrison's *Doom Patrol* became a nearly unreadable Dadaist parody of the very act of storytelling itself, a conceit that his energy and conviction made appealing to the more pretentious comics fans. Using his cult success as a springboard, Morrison cashed in on Batmania with his best-selling *Arkham Asylum* graphic novel. He cannily hedged his bets with his relatively conventional superhero thriller, *Batman: Gothic*, drawn by Klaus Janson, an explicitly occultic work that tells of a monk who sells his soul to Satan to gain immortality.

In 1994, Morrison created his magnum opus, *The Invisibles*, a Vertigo series that deals with a band of occult superheroes battling an interdimensional ruling-class conspiracy. Well, sort of. The series, which has a revolving cast of regular characters, acted mainly as a vehicle for Morrison to delve into every imaginable fringe idea or Internet conspiracy theory he came across. Morrison took Gaiman's lead and relied on a revolving staff of artists to illustrate the book, making himself the undisputed attraction of *The Invisibles*.

Morrison claimed that *The Invisibles* was actually dictated to him by an alien race he encountered in the Himalayas (shades of Blavatsky!). This alleged extraterrestrial origin failed to help the series reach a large audience, however, and sales of the title faltered. Morrison's response to this was unprecedented. He used the letters page of the comic to encourage his readers to take part in a worldwide occult ceremony that involved ritual masturbation. Whether through magical intervention or to keep a star writer happy, DC gave the series another chance, this time as a reverse-numbered limited edition meant to count to down to January 2000.

For all the excitement generated by Morrison's esoteric foibles, his greatest success by far lies in his work on Marvel and DC's crown-jewel characters. Morrison revamped *The Justice League* in 1996, making it a top seller during at a time when comic sales were in free-fall. He leveraged this success to earn himself a fat contract with Marvel, who immediately put him on the faltering *X-Men* series. He also helped revive interest in the Fantastic Four with his *Fantastic Four 1234* miniseries. Morrison stunned the industry with a messy split with Marvel in 2004 and went to DC for a number of esoteric projects and a marquee run on *All-Star Superman* with fellow Scot Frank Quitely. In 2006, he began a back-to-basics make over of *Batman* with artist Andy Kubert.

Cynics may say that Grant Morrison is more style than substance; sort of an amalgam of Alan Moore, Timothy Leary, and Sammy Glick. But in a field where the top sellers are still old warhorses like *Batman* and *The X-Men*, Morrison has generated genuine excitement with his occult/situationalist provocations. He has taken ideas and concepts from extremely marginal groups like chaos magicians, Burning Man cyber-hippies, and alternative comics fans and created the illusion of a new breed of comics geek. Although playing to a small audience, Morrison made his fantasy vision of the tuned-in and turned-on cyberpunk superhero seductive to less-adventurous superhero fans, who live vicariously through Morrison's carefully presented interviews and personal appearances. If Alan Moore's magic is basically hermetic in nature, then Morrison's is pure prestidigitation.

MIKE MIGNOLA

Hellboy creator Mike Mignola occupies a space different from that of the other wizards of comicdom. His work is about history—*occult* history, to be precise—and he uses a Golem-type hero to immerse himself and his readers in the dark corners of our past.

Mignola began his career submitting illustrations to fan magazines like *The Comic Reader*. He eventually turned pro at Marvel, and made his bones with the 1988 mini-series *Cosmic Odyssey*, written by the death-obsessed Jim Starlin. *Odyssey* delved deeply into Kirby's *Fourth World* material and also featured the Justice League. Mignola's eyes were set on the past, however, and his 1989 graphic novel *Gotham by Gaslight*, which featured a Victorian-era version of Batman battling Jack the Ripper, caught the eye of Francis Ford Coppola, who hired the artist as production designer for his 1992 film *Bram Stoker's Dracula*. Mignola also illustrated a comic-book adaptation of the film. Wading even deeper into occult waters, Mignola was production designer for Disney's 2001 animated opus *Atlantis: The Lost Empire*, a production that clearly spoke to Mignola's obsessions.

In 1993, Mignola brought forth his signature creation, Hellboy *(San Diego ComicCon Comics* #2), a young demon summoned by a reincarnated Rasputin to work for the Nazis in the closing days of World War II. The demon is taken by the Allies, who train him to be a classic occult detective. In concept, Hellboy is little more than a hijacking of Jack Kirby's Demon, with a personality on loan from Ben Grimm, but Mignola's elegant and moody artwork, as well as his encyclopedic knowledge of the occult, made Hellboy by far the most remarkable superhero of the 1990s. Mignola leavens his stories with heavy doses of humor that, paradoxically, only make them more arcane. He also adds heavy doses of Lovecraftian horror and a morbid ambiance that displays a strong Poe influence.

Mignola's stories are impeccably researched, and his explorations of Nazi occultism are at once remarkable and chilling. Mignola also incorporates horrors like leprechauns and werewolves from old European folktales, and more esoteric beasties like the Homonculus. He makes his comics tantamount to magic spells by decorating his pages with various sigils and icons borrowed from ritual magic. Unfortunately, Mignola's involvement in the *Hellboy* comics has recently diminished and the art work has been handed off to others.

The 2004 *Hellboy* movie, directed by Guillermo Del Toro (*Pan's Labyrinth*) and starring Ron Perlman (*Beauty and the Beast*), was a serviceable action picture completely devoid of the magical ambiance and creeping dread of Mignola's comics. Mignola's work is about the beauty of decay and the purity of terror—themes that don't always translate well on screen. His best work taps directly into the deepest recesses of the collective imagination; the deep shadows and dark stares that give his drawing such intensity in print are hard to translate to film.

ALEX ROSS

If Jack Kirby is the prophet of the new gods and Alan Moore the comics' sorcerer supreme, then Alex Ross is the foremost apostle of the new superhero religion. His father was Protestant minister and his mother worked as a successful illustrator. Being a preacher's son put special pressures on Ross, who poured all his youthful energies into his art. After moving with his family from Portland, Oregon to a new home deep in the heart of Texas, Ross sought inspiration in the graceful, idealized heroes of artists like Neal Adams and George Perez, as well as the classic magazine illustrations of Andrew Loomis and Norman Rockwell. By age 12, he was already more talented than most of the Nineties hacks whose work wounded him so deeply.

Ross seems to have latched onto DC's heroes for the same reasons other fans abandoned them in the Sixties and Seventies. The heroes of *The Justice League* were aloof and Olympian; they were better than normal Joes. In other words, they were *gods*. In his monograph, *Mythology: The DC Comics Art of Alex Ross,* he explained this appeal: "As an adolescent you need order in your world, and superheroes have that, a sense of ethics that would never change—they would never be less than perfect, fighting for their ideals," adding "they deal succinctly with moral issues, in a way that religion doesn't. Or rather, religion does, but in a much more complicated and often confusing manner."[155]

After a stint in advertising, Ross landed an opportunity to draw a *Terminator* miniseries for Now Comics. In 1993, he got his first job for DC—appropriately enough, a book cover for a novelization of the dying-rising Superman saga entitled *Superman: Doomsday and Beyond*. His work caught the attention of editors at Marvel and, in 1994, he illustrated his graphic love letter to the superheroes of old, *Marvels*. Ross' art electrified fandom and snapped comics out of their cynical 90s decline. All of a sudden, superheroes actually looked *heroic* again. Indeed, looking at Ross' *Marvels* is almost like seeing those characters for the first time. As Chip Kidd said of Ross' later depictions of Superman, "the effect was like finally meeting someone you'd only ever heard about."

---

155   Chip Kidd and Geoff Spear, *Mythology* (no pagination).

Ross leveraged his success with *Marvels* to get his hands on the Justice League. DC was floundering at the time, its editors playing a perpetual game of catch-up with Marvel and Image. Ross set out to revitalize the entire line with his epic *Kingdom Come*, in which he sought "to bring a sense of morality back to the comics."[156] Comics had never seen anything like *Kingdom Come*, which captivated fans and fellow creators alike. Ross was acknowledged as a prophet, shouting down the fatuous corruption of the Chromium Age. No one yet realized it, but when the *Kingdom* came, the New Age had begun.

Kingdom Come was almost a decade in the making. In his original notes for the series, Ross perceptively equated the 40s Superman with Samson and the 60s version with Jesus Christ. "Superman as a fictional character is just as important as if he existed in flesh and blood," he claimed. "Either way he is inspirational, and that's what's relevant." Indeed, Ross wanted to put "Superman in the same role" as Jesus Christ.[157]

Ross made his father a star of the show in *Kingdom Come*, renaming him Pastor Norman McCay as a tribute to Winsor McCay. His father proved an excellent model, bearing a strong resemblance to Alec Guinness in *Star Wars*. In the story, Jerry Siegel's occult hero, the Spectre, appears before McCay and anoints him as a witness to the coming Apocalypse. McCay protests against the Apocalypse using the tepid language of liberal Protestanism, but regains his religious fervor (and his congregation) after helping the gods of the League save humanity.

Ross' superheroes are the very embodiment of Nietszche's *ubermenschen*. Indeed, members of the League are referred to as "gods" throughout the book. Ross depicts Green Lantern in the armor of a Wagnerian knight, and returns the Flash and Hawkman to their original forms. No longer stand-ins for Hermes/Mercury and Horus, they are the exact look-alikes of those gods, their carriage and behavior leaving little doubt that they are their actual incarnations. Ross claimed "Hawkman would become Hawkgod ... he's become a real birdman now, a new entity, a reincarnated Egyptian prince."[158]

---

156 Quoted in Les Daniels, *DC Comics*, p. 248.

157 Quoted in Les Daniels, *DC Comics*, p. 248.

158 Chip Kidd and Geoff Spear, *Mythology* (no pagination).

Ross' Wonder Woman, modeled on Lynda Carter, is a lioness, fierce in battle but tender to her man (*Superman*, in this case). In the book's final apocalyptic battle, Ross accentuates her divine nature by dressing her in golden eagle armor reminiscent of ancient figurines of the winged Isis and bathing her in sunlight (which he does throughout the entire story). When we first see the reconstituted Justice League descend from heaven, Superman, Wonder Woman, and Hawkgod are most prominent among them, drawing an irresistible parallel to Osiris, Isis, and Horus. The three seem to fly from the heart of the Sun itself.

The mythological tone and sense of majesty of Ross' *Kingdom Come* hark back to the Neoclassical, Romantic, and Pre-Raphaelite movements of the 19th and early 20th centuries. Ross' worshipful sensibility has much more in common with Leyendecker, Waterhouse, or Alma-Tadema than that of even the most elegant cartoonists like Hal Foster or Alex Raymond.

Even the moronic Chromium Age-style heroes that Ross is seeking to exorcise are designed and rendered in a manner infinitely more creative and dignified than the wretched 90s characters that inspired them—although he still has most of them annhilated by a nuclear explosion.

Sprinkled throughout the series are passages from Revelations that underscore the apocalyptic events in the story and the sense of reverence and awe Ross seeks to reintroduce to comics readers, whose sensibilities were ruined by the deluge of Chromium Age garbage. Ross mounts a crusade against superheresy, and responds to the 90s decline with his vision of the one true faith. The cumulative effect of all this nobility, righteousness, and wrath is indistinguishable from that of any of the great ancient religious epics.

Make no mistake, *Kingdom Come* is a fundamentally religious piece of work, and the gods that Ross celebrates in it would easily be recognized by any ancient pagan or polytheist. The symbols and accessories of the ancient gods—whether Egyptian, Greek, Roman, or Norse—and motifs taken from Templarism, Freemasonry, and Neoclassicism are everywhere in *Kingdom Come*. If Ross did not set out intentionally to reintroduce the ancient gods and goddesses to a modern audience, then we must seriously contemplate whether some other supernatural force was working through him to do so.

The impact of *Kingdom Come* and Ross' tabloid-size graphic novellas featuring Superman (*Peace on Earth*), Batman (*War on Crime*), Captain Marvel (*Power of Hope*), Wonder Woman (*Spirit of Truth*), and the Justice League (*Liberty and Justice*) cannot possibly be overstated. It took some time to digest, but soon the better draftsmen in the field began to inject their art with Ross' realism and reverence. Now, most of the top artists at Marvel and DC make heavy use of photo reference and tell stories in a cinematic storytelling style that has come to be known as "widescreen." Artists who draw in the cartoon style of the Eighties or the hyper-thyroid style of the Nineties are out of fashion—perhaps forever. *Kingdom Come* heralded the age of the superhero as god, and gods must be awe-inspiring or not exist at all.

CHAPTER 21

THE DREAM LAB: COMICS AND THE FUTURE

Why have comics survived? Why are they still so powerful and influential? Why do so many adult men spend up to 100 dollars a week keeping up with their favorite titles? Part of the answer is that comics are a profoundly intimate form of storytelling. They are something you can hold, something you can possess, something that speaks only to you. Comics have a special magic that affects the brain in ways prose does not. Comics fans develop intimate relationships with their favorite characters—a relationship they jealously guard. Fans of some obscure Indie band seek each other out, but comics fans are more wary, treating their obsession as part of their private space.

Clive Barker observes that comics happen in the reader's own time frame, noting that a comic story "unfolds in your personal time, just like a dream or nightmare."[159] Readers control the visual timeline in a way that's hard to replicate in other media, even with video freeze-frame. Each visual moment is suspended forever in comic-book time and space. Comics fans control the flow of events, so every single moment belongs to them. No other artform can do this. It's as if, by reading the comics, you become a kind of deity. The impulse is brilliantly incorporated into the film *The Matrix* with the freeze-frame and "bullet time" sequences. It's also cleverly alluded to in the TV series *Heroes*, where comic-book fan Hiro has the ability to freeze moments in time.

Comic-book fans are a small, but highly dedicated and influential, group. They usually develop an intense, intimate relationship with the comics medium at an early age, often as a result of childhood trauma. Many have a general disposition toward shyness or social awkwardness that tends to cement their dedication to the form, turning them into, in Stan Lee's words, "true believers" indistinguishable from your average theology student or seminarian.

Hardcore comics fans are very reverent to their heroes and woe betide the artist or writer who doesn't share in their worship. If a creator appears insufficiently devoted to the characters or fails to imbue their work with the prerequisite religious awe, they will suffer at the hands of the fans, who, like ancient pagans, take special delight in killing their kings. Even Jack Kirby fell from grace when more realistic artists like Neal Adams came to prominence in the 1970s.

Because of their intense devotion, many fans want to become creators themselves, and the increased accessibility and affordability of tools for creating comics—particularly online—has created an explosion of independent and self-published work. Many fans expect that they will eventually "break in" to the major publishers, and the competition for the top books is murderous. Some give up when they realize that they will never reach the big leagues; others keep plugging, hoping for the impossible.

The World Wide Web has created a perpetual 24/7 comics convention, with its thousands of message boards, chat rooms, and Web comics. And creators continue to self-publish, whether in mini-comic form or in the cheap black and white formats. These conditions have created a pressure-cooker test market for a new popular culture that has inevitably branched out into other forms of storytelling. Today's comics fans are *all* connoisseurs, and the con-

---

159 Clive Barker quoted in Mike Benton, *Horror Comics: An Illustrated History*. (Dallas: Taylor, 1991.), p. 3.

temporary superhero culture is exclusively of, by, and for hardcore, highly educated fans.

Of course, this means that comic books are no longer a mass medium. Instead, they have become a highly charged laboratory for pop culture, developing themes and ideas that are picked up in television, movies, and video games. Many of Hollywood's top creators—Steven Spielberg, Bryan Singer, James Cameron, George Lucas, Chris Carter, Sam Raimi—are hardcore comic-book fans who adapted themes and ideas from the comics in their work. Today, movie people write for comics, and vice versa. The same applies to fiction, with best-selling authors like Brad Meltzer and Jonathan Lethem working for the Big Two.

The symbiosis that has developed between comics and Hollywood extends to video games as well, to the point that the content and storylines of games are essentially indistinguishable from comics. This is a recent phenomenon, concurrent with the amazing advances in digital imaging technology. Computer rendering has allowed the visual punch of comics to be translated on screen in games and on film. The cost of special effects is no longer prohibitive, and the limitations of even the best pre-digital effects have been overcome. Digital imaging technology now brings the kinetic energy of comic-book action to the screen, especially in films like *Sin City* and *300*, based on Frank Miller's graphic novels.

Whether we realize it or not, we are programmed by pop culture. Television and film and video games are part of our collective consciousness, perhaps even more so than our dreams. The great comic creators sensed this and deliberately wove the threads of past, present, and future into their work. Jack Kirby recognized that he lived in a society "without the kind of gods that used to exist, or the legends that used to travel back and forth with tribes. The tribes each told the same stories in their own way," Kirby observed. "I gave those stories the power of the old concepts with characters from our own day."[160] Alan Moore worked from the same vision and articulated what may be the core truth of the comics culture: "There is something very magical at the heart of writing, and language, and storytelling. The gods of magic in the ancient cultures . . . are also the gods of writing."[161]

---

160 Quoted in Les Daniels, *DC Comics*, p. 164.

161 Quoted in Bill Baker, *Alan Moore Spells It Out* (Michigan: *Airwave*, 2005.), p. 10.

CHAPTER 22

CONCLUSION: THE GODS WITHIN US

Superheroes were once vigilantes against organized crime or soldiers in the war against fascism. Now they have become something else. They address a greater anxiety—the universal feeling of powerlessness in a new technocratic world order. The proliferation of technology and the dramatic rise in world population makes people feel marginalized and insignificant—isolated and powerless against the invisible systems that control every aspect of their lives.

We live in extremely depressing and disheartening times, in which old certainties vanish before our eyes. The world we once knew is either collapsing or being systematically dismantled, and there is nothing we can do about it. The daily political and economic bad news and the constant drumbeat of war and terrorism are making superhero fantasies more relevant and visceral, as well as more comforting and reassuring, than at any time since World War II.

American religion seems unable to provide a viable salvation myth in this time of crisis. Most denominations have become nothing more than badly disguised political movements, interested only in money and power. On the other hand, our bloodless secular culture has no room in it for wonder. It should not surprise us, then, when *Harry Potter, Star Wars,* and *The X-Men* step in to fill the void.

Superheroes provide escape, but from what and to where? From the mind-numbing mediocrity of most modern life. To a space where greater potentials and possibilities exist. But it's no longer enough for us simply to root for these heroes. Deep down, we want to *become* them.[162] This is the impulse behind the role-playing popular today at comic conventions, in which fans dress like their favorite characters and act out their adventures. Costume contests are also popular and some fans write reverent parodies of their gods or make home videos based on their favorite characters. The same impulse is driving the increasing popularity of Halloween with adults. People want to enter into the mythic realm and become someone else in an attempt to shed their mundane problems. This phenomenon is a survival of the mystery cults of ancient times, with their rituals and festivals in which pagans dressed like their favorite gods and acted out their dramas.

Entertainment Weekly claims that the TV series *Heroes* is proof positive that what was once considered cult pop is now mainstream thanks to a decade defined by the Spiderman and Harry Potter film sagas."[163] The question now becomes this: Will a society so immersed in *Heroes, Harry Potter*, and *The X-Men* settle for the limitations of the human body? Or will fascination with these stories raise new expectations that we will try to meet through cloning and genetic engineering? Shows like *Heroes* and *The 4400* feature superpowers made manifest in the real world, not in the Spandex world, and the virtual environments of some video games suggest the possibility of entering other realities. Are these trends shaping our future? Are we beginning to wonder how to manifest these new possibilities?

The superhero culture has become much more than comic books. The superheroes of today are actually changing our expectations of the human machine, especially in the minds of the young. Hollywood wizards are making Harry

---

162 Stan Lee himself has his own reality show on the SciFi network entitled *Who Wants to Be a Superhero?* where contestants essentially audition to become gods.

163 Jeff Jensen, "The Powers that Be," *EW,* #906, p. 32.

Potter's magic and the X-Men's mutant powers almost tangible. How much longer will young audiences be satisfied with the ordinary? How long before they demand increased or supernatural powers for themselves? And will that lead to an expectation of greater human abilities that can only take the form of a totally new human reality? Are we facing the inevitable incorporation of technology into humanity itself?

Seeking to unlock the evolutionary conundrum posed by Stanley Kubrick and Arthur C. Clarke in *2001: A Space Odyssey,* Jack Kirby came to the conclusion that man will send robots into space rather than risk it himself. He tried repeatedly to make sense of the Star Child, only to answer with *Machine Man.* Kirby's character was not a cybernetic man, but an artificial intelligence alienated from human life. Today, however, we increasingly see efforts made, not to turn machines into people, but to turn people into machines.

Some observers label this projected reality "transhumanism," or "post-humanism." Its goal is to use cybernetics and nanotechnology (microscopic computers and robots) to "perfect" the human organism. Through neuroscience, we can now control the human brain and its processes. But this sort of dabbling alarms many scientists, theologians, and philosophers. What direction will this extraordinary technology take? Will human beings end up as automatons, serving a computer-controlled hive mind like the Borg in *Star Trek?* Will artificial intelligences become self-conscious, making human beings obsolete, as in the *Terminator* films? If the 20th century has done nothing else, it has proven to us how dangerous science can be when pressed into service for inhumane purposes. There are so many questions we need to ask. Who is creating this technology? Who's paying for it? Do these people have our best interests at heart? Are they guided by love and compassion, or by power and profit?

By the same token, technology empowers and liberates us. It acts in *defiance* of the limits set by natural law. Science describes the boundaries and the limits of gravity—or of distance, or of brainpower—and technology allows us to rebel against them. In the 19th-century, the myth of the *ubermensch* expressed our desire to transcend our human limitations. Yet, in Spider-Man's first adventure, Stan Lee warned that "with great power came great responsibility." And in *Kingdom Come,* Alex Ross showed how dangerous transhuman power could be without a moral foundation. The new mythology of the comics gives us a model to follow, a moral

compass to guide us through incredible new possibilities by allowing us to play out the potentials of super or transhuman power in a fictional setting.

SPIRIT IN THE SKY

We must not, however, forget the "x-factor" in all of this—the supernatural component. Before it was co-opted by opportunists like Shirley MacLaine, the New Age movement was concerned with the synthesis of ancient mysticism and modern technology.[164] Even as the movement splintered, some groups sought to continue this work, most notably the New Edge movement that emerged from the 1990s cyberpunk underground. The movement, centered around the Burning Man Festival in Nevada, has also continued in this vein.

Modern-day alchemists dream of a New Age in which the occult sciences and technology are no longer in opposition—a time when things now unmeasurable can be understood and utilized. In this context, pop-culture stories of psychic powers and occultism need not be taken literally, but can be seen as a means to keep us aware of possibilities beyond the reach of our present understanding. These stories of supernatural power can act like a carrot at the end of the stick— forever elusive, moving us toward a mythical state of perfection.

Some argue that our present-day rationalist, reductionist viewpoint is a relic of the Industrial Age, a necessary but obsolete transitional phase to a more complex understanding. Our ability to track events in the world is increasing our appreciation of the fractal patterns of reality, what Carl Jung referred to as "synchronicity," or meaningful coincidence. We have greater access to information, and thus have a greater capacity to recognize patterns in events that would once have eluded us. As our means of perceiving the world increase and expand, perhaps our appreciation of certain occult sciences will increase as well. Perhaps an increased understanding of Jung's synchronicity will lead us to a better understanding of divination systems like astrology and the Tarot. Perhaps we will come to appreciate the Zodiac, not as some spiritual force controlling our lives, but as a giant clock that helps us forecast conditions that reoccur cyclically during certain planetary conjunctions.

---

164 See Marilyn Ferguson, *The Aquarian Conspiracy* (New York: St. Martin's, 1980).

The collision of science, morality, and magic is being played out hundreds of times a month in comic books and other media, showing us the implications of superhuman potential. Is this an unconscious form of preparation for an inevitable shift in human reality? Should we pay more careful attention to the visionaries and lunatics who anticipate the future in comic-book storylines? In that supernatural realm called the human imagination, comic-book creators like Alan Moore and Alex Ross may be time-travelers, forecasting the future for us and showing us the way. It's funny how it all seems so similar to the ancient myths.

The past and future are always with us.

BIBLIOGRAPHY

Baker, Bill. *Alan Moore Spells It Out*. Michigan: *Airwave*, 2005.

Benton, Mike. *Horror Comics: An Illustrated History*. Dallas: Taylor, 1991.

Bessy, Maurice. *A Pictorial History of Magic and the Supernatural*. London: Spring, 1968.

Blackbeard, Bill and Martin Williams, eds. *The Smithsonian Collection of Newspaper Comics*. Washington, DC: Smithsonian, 1977.

Bloom, Harold. *The American Religion*. New York: Simon & Shuster, 1993.

Bridwell, E. Nelson. *Superman from the Thirties to the Seventies*. New York: Crown, 1971.

———. *Batman from the Thirties to the Seventies*. New York: Crown, 1972.

Bulfinch, Thomas. *Bulfinch's Mythology*. New York: Harper Collins, 1991 edition.

Budge, E. A. Wallis. *Egyptian Religion*. New York: Dover, 1959 reprint.

Bulwer-Lytton, Lord Edward. *The Coming Race*. Middleton, CT: Wesleyan, 2006 edition.

———. Bulwer-Lytton, Lord Edward. *Zanoni*. London: Saunders & Otley, 1841.

Burroughs, Edgar Rice. *A Princess of Wars*. New York: Modern Library, 2003 edition.

Carter, John. *Sex and Rockets: The Occult World of Jack Parsons*. Los Angeles: Feral House, 2004 edition.

Chandler, Russell. *Understanding the New Age*. Dallas: Word, 1988.

Coogan, Peter. *Superhero: The Secret Origin of A Genre*. Austin, TX: Monkeybrain Books, 2006.

Cranston, Sylvia. *H.P.B.: The Extraordinary Life & Influence of Helena Blavatsky*. New York: Putnam, 1993.

Crawford, Hubert H. *Crawford's Encyclopedia of Comic Books*. Middle Village, NY: Jonathan David Publishers, 1978.

Daniels, Les. *Comix: A History of Comic Books in America*. New York: Outerbridge, 1971.

————. *DC Comics: A Celebration of the World's Favorite Comic Book Heroes.* New York: Billboard Books, 2003.

————. *Marvel: Five Fabulous Decades of the World's Greatest Comics.* New York: Abradale, 1991.

————. *Wonder Woman: The Complete History.* San Francisco: Chronicle Books, 2000.

Frazer, Sir James George. *The Golden Bough.* New York: Penguin, 1996 edition.

Gifford, Denis. *The International Book of Comics.* London: Crescent Books, 1984.

Goulart, Ron. *Cheap Thrills: An Informal History of the Pulp Magazine.* New Rochelle, NY: Arlington House, 1972.

————. *Comic Book Culture: An Illustrated History.* Portland, OR: Collectors Press, 2000.

————. *The Adventurous Decade.* New Rochelle, NY: Arlington House, 1975.

Haining, Peter. *The Classic Era of American Pulp Magazines.* Chicago: Chicago Review Press, 2001.

Haining, Peter, ed. *The Magicians: The Occult in Fact and Fiction.* New York: Taplinger, 1972.

Herman, Daniel. *Silver Age: The Second Generation of Comic Book Artists.* Nesahannock, PA: Hermes Press, 2004.

Horn, Maurice, ed. *The World Encyclopedia of Comics.* New York: Chelsea House, 1976.

Howard, Michael. *The Occult Conspiracy.* Rochester, VT: Destiny Books, 1989.

Jones, Gerard. *Men of Tomorrow: Geeks, Gangsters and the Birth of the Comic Book.* New York: Basic, 2004.

Jones, Gerard & Will Jacobs. *The Comic Book Heroes.* Rocklin, CA: Prima, 1997.

Kerr, Howard & Charles L. Crow, eds. *The Occult in America: New Historical Perspectives.* Chicago: University of Illinois Press, 1983.

Kidd, Chip & Geoff Spear. *Mythology: The DC Comics Art of Alex Ross.* New York: Pantheon, 2003.

Knight, Gareth, ed., *The Magical Battle of Britian.* Oceanside, CA: Sun Chalice, 1993.

Lachman, Gary. *Turn Off Your Mind: The Mystic Sixties and the Dark Side of Aquarius.* New York: Disinformation, 2001.

Lee, Stan. *Bring on the Bad Guys.* New York: Fireside, 1976.

————. *Origins of Marvel Comics*. New York: Fireside, 1975.

————. *Son of Origins*. New York: Fireside, 1975.

————. *The Superhero Women*. New York: Fireside, 1977.

Lesser, Robert. *Pulp Art*. New York: Gramercy, 1997.

Lovecraft, Howard Phillips. *Dagon and Other Macabre Tales*. Sauk City, WI: Arkham House, 1987.

Marston, William Moulton. *Wonder Woman*. New York: Holt Rinehart and Winston, 1972.

MacKenzie, Norman & Jean. *H.G. Wells: A Biography*. New York: Simon and Shuster, 1973.

Mignola, Mike & John Byrne. *Hellboy Seed of Destruction*. Milwaukie, OR: Dark Horse, 2003.

Miller, Frank. *Batman: The Dark Knight Strikes Again*. New York: Warner Books, 1986.

Martin, Walter R. *The Kingdom of the Cults*. Minneapolis, MN: Bethany Fellowship, 1972.

Noll, Richard. *The Aryan Christ: The Secret Life of Carl Jung*. New York: Random House, 1997.

Pendle, George. *Strange Angel: The Otherworldly Life of Rocket Scientist John Whiteside Parsons*. Orlando, FL: Harcourt, 2005.

Petrie, W. M. Flinders. *The Making of Egypt*. London: Macmillan, 1939.

Picknett, Lynn & Clive Prince. *The Templar Revelation*. New York: Touchstone, 1997.

Pike, Albert. *Morals and Dogma of the Ancient and Accepted Scottish Rite of Freemasonry*. Washington DC: Supreme Council of the 33rd Degree, Southern Jurisdiction of the United States, 1871.

Robbins, Trina. *The Great Women Superheroes*. Northampton, MA: Kitchen Sink Press, 1996.

Sabin, Roger. *Comics, Comix & Graphic Novels: A History of Comic Art*. London: Phaidon, 1996.

Sagan, Carl. *The Demon-Haunted World*. New York: Random House, 1996.

Sasseine, Paul. *The Comic Book*. Edison, NJ: Chartwell Books, 1994.

Simon, Joe and Jim Simon, *The Comic Book Makers*. Clinton, NJ: Vanguard, 2003.

Sitchin, Zechariah. *The 12th Planet*. New York: Harper, 1999.

Sutin, Lawrence. *Do What Thou Wilt: A Life of Aleister Crowley*. New York: St. Martin's, 2000.

Symons, Julian. *Conan Doyle: Portrait of an Artist*. New York: Mysterious Press, 1979.

———. *The Tell-Tale Heart, The Life and Work of Edgar Allan Poe*. New York: Harper and Row, 1978.

Thompson, Don. *The Comic Book Book*. New Rochelle, NY: Arlington House, 1973.

Waid, Mark & Alex Ross. *Kingdom Come*. New York: DC Comics, 1997.

Walker, Brian. *The Comics Before 1945*. New York: Harry N. Abrams, 2004.

Washington, Peter. *Madame Blavatsky's Baboon*. New York: Shocken, 1995.

Wertham, Fredric. *Seduction of the Innocent*. New York: Rinehart, 1954.

Williamson, Jack. *Darker Than You Think*. New York: Bluejay, 1984 edition.

Wilson, Colin. *The Occult: A History*. New York: Random House, 1971.

Wright, Bradford W. *Comic Book Nation*. Baltimore: Johns Hopkins University Press, 2001.

Wright, Nicky. *The Classic Era of American Comics*. Lincolnwood, IL: Contemporary, 2000.

Wyman, Roy. *Art of Jack Kirby*. Orange, CA: Blue Rose, 1992.

INDEX

F

Fabian Socialists 71
Falcon, the 131, 195
Falk, Lee 107, 114, 115
Famous Funnies 104, 105
Fantastic Four, The 13, 128, 140–141, 153, 173–174, 185, 191, 193, 205
Fantomah 115
Fawcett Publishing 29, 74, 124, 126, 129, 179–180
Feldstein, Al 136
Female heroes, Silver and Bronze Age 165
Ferrigno, Lou 154
Flash, the 10, 117, 138, 147, 170, 209
Flash Gordon 75, 105
Flash Lightning 127
Flinders-Petrie, Sir William Matthew 26, 32
Fly, the 139
Forever People, The xii, 194
Fortune, Dion 53, 87, 91, 96–97
4400, The 3, 13, 48, 197, 204, 218
Fox sisters 34–35
Fox, Gardner 94, 130, 138, 170, 180
Frankenstein 33, 153, 195
Freemasonry 26, 32, 37, 39–43, 46, 48, 51, 52, 53, 57, 67, 70, 71, 88, 104, 124, 130, 132, 138, 169, 170, 184, 199, 210
From Hell 199, 201
Fu Manchu 90–91

G

Gaiman, Neil 11, 128, 202–204
Gaines, M.C. 105, 136, 162
Gaines, William 136
Galactus 140–141, 173
Gernsback, Hugo 83, 98, 108
Gibson, Walter 80, 85, 146
Gilgamesh 24
Gladiator, The 79, 81
Golden Age of Comics, the 32, 128, 138, 164, 173
Golden Dawn 18, 52–54, 57, 70, 71, 72, 90, 96, 117, 197
Golden Plates, The 42

Golem myth 143–146, 150, 153, 155, 162
Goodman, Martin 108–109, 131, 173, 191
Green Lantern 83, 112, 113, 138, 170, 209

H

Hammett, Dashiell 75
Harry Potter 113–114, 203, 218
Hawass, Zahi 62
Hawkman 32, 130–131, 170, 180, 209
Heinlein, Robert A. 83, 85, 98
Hellboy 205–207
Hellfire Club 165, 198
Hercules 19, 27, 28, 96, 122, 124, 127, 129, 160, 162
Hermes 26, 113, 209
Hermes Trismegistus 113
Heroes (TV) xiii, 3, 13, 197, 204, 214, 218
Heru 24, 126
Himalayas (Tibet) 50, 81, 114, 127, 181, 185, 204
Hippolyte 162–163
Hitler, Adolf 49, 59, 131
Hogan's Alley 104
Hogarth, William 103
Horus 19, 24–26, 38, 41, 53, 56, 59, 123, 126, 129, 130–131, 179, 209–210
Houdini, Harry 55, 60–62, 80, 90
Howard, Robert E. 84, 87, 91, 93, 94–96
Hubbard, L. Ron 98–99, 202
Hulk, the 91, 146, 153–154, 157, 171, 181
Human Torch, the 173, 193

I

Ibis the Invincible 179–180
Identity Crisis 169
Illuminati, The 177
Image Comics 7, 176, 209
Incredibles, The 13
Industrial Revolution 29, 31, 35, 48, 221
Infantino, Carmine 138, 147
Invisible Girl 165, 173, 193
Invisibles, The 204–205
Iron Man 18, 83, 145, 169, 171, 177
Isis 12, 19, 24, 26, 27, 41, 46, 51, 53, 77, 126, 127, 129, 210

ABOUT THE AUTHOR

Christopher Knowles has worked in the comics and superhero-merchandising industry for over 20 years as both an artist and writer. He is a contributing writer to *Classic Rock*, one of the top music magazines out of the UK, as well as *Jack Kirby Collector* and *Comic Book Marketplace*. Knowles is an Associate Editor and contributing writer for the five-time Eisner Award-winning magazine *Comic Book Artist*. His past credits also include the graphic novels *Halo*, *An Angel's Story* and *The X-Presidents*, along with the *Primal Rage* mini-series (based on the Atari video game). Knowles has worked as an illustrator for the Oxford University Press, Harcourt, Pearson, Time Warner, and Glencoe, as a freelance illustrator and designer for Marvel Enterprises since 1995, in addition to having worked as a designer/illustrator creating art for Disney, DC Comics, and Warner Bros. Knowles worked as a storyboard artist for Saatchi & Saatchi, DDB Needham, ESPN, Kraft/Nabisco, and others. He lives in New Jersey with his wife Vicky and their three children.

ABOUT THE ILLUSTRATOR

In 1989, Joseph Michael Linsner created *Dawn*, a modern take on classic earth goddess mythology. Since then, his work has developed a worldwide following, having been translated into Spanish, Greek, Italian and Dutch.

Born in Queens, New York, he has recently moved to the north Georgia mountains, where he lives with his two Sphynx cats. His next project is the vampire graphic novel, *Dark Ivory*, to be cowritten with Eva Hopkins. 2007 will mark the tenth year of the Dawn-Look-A-Like contest, held annually at Atlanta's fantastic Dragon-Con.

www.linsner.com
joe@linsner.com

TO OUR READERS

Weiser Books, an imprint of Red Wheel/Weiser, publishes books across the entire spectrum of occult and esoteric subjects. Our mission is to publish quality books that will make a difference in people's lives without advocating any one particular path or field of study. We value the integrity, originality, and depth of knowledge of our authors.

Our readers are our most important resource, and we appreciate your input, suggestions, and ideas about what you would like to see published. Please feel free to contact us, to request our latest book catalog, or to be added to our mailing list.

Red Wheel/Weiser, LLC
500 Third Street, Suite 230
San Francisco, CA 94107
www.redwheelweiser.com